LARISA SEKLITOVA
AND
LUDMILA STRELNIKOVA

UNORDINARY LIFE
OF
HEAVENLY TEACHERS

Channelings with Higher Cosmic Mind

Order this book online at www.trafford.com
or email orders@trafford.com

Most Trafford titles are also available at major online book retailers.

«UNORDINARY LIFE OF HEAVENLY TEACHERS»
Channelings with Higher Cosmic Mind.
"Beyond the Bounds of Unknown" series.

Translator: Nadezhda Tchoporova

The book reveals the following secrets: how Heavenly Teachers control people, how they
participate in child's birth, how the energy is transmitted between the Teacher and the pupil. For
the first time the reader is told about spiritualization energy, about spiritual Universes and their
transformations, about the secrets of the Moon and hologram-based architecture of worlds. It
also tells the reader about computer secrets and about wherefrom computer virus appears.

The writers appreciate material assistance of all the readers in translation of this book.

Printed in the United States of America.

ISBN: 978-1-4269-7099-3 (sc)
ISBN: 978-1-4269-7100-6 (e)

Trafford rev. 06/01/2011

North America & international
toll-free: 1 888 232 4444 (USA & Canada)
phone: 250 383 6864 ♦ fax: 812 355 4082

Have the courage to admit the truth.
Have the wisdom to understand it.

(a maxim of wise men)

«««<>»» INTRODUCTION «««<>»»»

The given book continues the series of books called «Beyond the Bounds of Unknown», which is the result of our years-long channelings with Higher Creator. The last channelings cover the period from 1998 to 2000.

The goal of God is to provide new concepts of the objective reality of macrocosm and to forge new mindset of mankind through contacts with people and based on His revelations.

The visual environment surrounding us proves to be much more rich and complex than the human perception is able to embrace. The man does not see the deeds of God performed above the earthly plane in just the same way as a mole does not see what is done by the man above the ground.

Therefore the given book is an attempt of the Creator to enlighten people and disclose the truth for them. But after that everything depends on the man himself: those who wish to see the light will see it and those who prefer to be under restful misapprehension will keep on their way of improvement until their souls attain the evolutionary maturity.

Our books will help the reader to find answers to many vital questions and explanations of enigmas, to understand *raison d'etre* and to gain an insight into the global changes which are currently under way on Earth. Old mysteries will vanish, the new ones will arise.

Chapter 1
ORDINARY LIFE OF HEAVENLY TEACHERS

Introduction

For a long time people have heard about Heavenly Teachers, mysterious celestial beings, who rule over earthly life from their empyreal heights but nobody has ever known exactly – whether they really exist; and if they do, what they look like and how we can feel or see them. Where does the knowledge about Heavenly Teachers come from? Perhaps, is the information about them just a creation of deformed imagination or exuberant dreams of people?

However, for many centuries people have been recording the facts of appearance of gleaming Angels or just eidolons (forms of fine plane), who communed with the elects or send messages warning them against dangers.

Some Heavenly Teachers had the capacity of partial materialization. They descended to the nether physical layers of the Earth and acquired the shapes, which the people took for Angels, the more so, as those objects did not use legs in their movements: they simply flew in the air. But in those times people thought that being airborne, one could move only with the help of wings. That is why in their mind's eyes they added wings to the images they saw. Therefore many spiritually mature people saw their Heavenly Teachers as certain gleaming forms.

There were recorded also a lot of cases when people heard the Teachers or received some new information from them. People of quick observation basing just on mere facts of available circumstances were capable to understand the influence of invisible mystical forces on their fates. Sometimes they noticed that, for no explicable reasons, their wishes came true, or, on the contrary, some invisible hand began to preclude them from realization of forethought plans and to break down everything around.

Nowadays people have become even more sharp-eyed and sensitive. They "see and hear" a lot with their hearts and ask themselves a tormenting question – where does this odd feeling, that they are watched or their thoughts are read by somebody, come from? Some people of strong intuition deeply feel their Teacher and are able to come into certain mutual contact with Him. Others manage to read the warnings the Teacher sends them. Many of them are definitely aware that somebody invisible nudges them to take some actions or others or replays situations for some obscure purposes. That is to say, a sharp-eyed, thoughtful man can always see the connection between himself and those objects, which lie beyond the visible limits; and analyzing certain facts he can understand that some invisible being participates in his life. In this way he can identify the Heavenly Teacher's actions addressed to him.

But who are those mysterious personalities? What kind of life do they live? What are they engaged in? People have not got a slightest idea about that.

Remaining beyond the limits of human perception, Heavenly Teachers watch their fosterlings and see everything their pupils do. However, for the purpose of clarity of experiment, they do not intermeddle in affairs of people, but only where necessary, guide them towards the right direction or send warning signs.

As the saying goes, every tub must stand on its own bottom, therefore every pupil shall gain his own personal experience of reality because only this experience leads to soul perfection. Only if you solve your problems yourself, you are able to imbibe knowledge of life and gain the ability of correct conduct in various circumstances. Similarly, a pupil at school solving problems one after another, gains the required knowledge of mathematics and other disciplines. And without certain order and regularity in acquirement of specific amount of information a pupil will not be able to accumulate necessary knowledge enabling him to continue successful study in the next form.

The same is true about life. Gaining experience in living and social environment people acquire a certain energy potential enabling them to ascend higher.

Every person is given a program for him/her to develop under. But why do we also need Heavenly Teachers?

Due to the fact that a man is given a free choice (that is the program has options) he needs to be watched all the time. Low development level of most pupils and free choice given to them causes the deviations, which require the general programs to be corrected so that people can normally interface with each other and the events do not go beyond the permissible limits.

Besides, every Teacher wants to raise his pupil as high as possible in his development. Therefore the Teacher tries to send his pupil all possible warnings, when he takes the wrong turning or makes a wrong choice.

For the purpose of visualization the free choice and its possible result shall be better presented in the form of a certain private house with a fenced yard. A child is allowed to play within the limits of the yard. As compared to a city or a country the area allocated to him/her is small. But even enjoying the freedom within such bite-size area a child may do a lot of mischief to the extent of burning the entire house. The child is restricted but still it is able to fix up a fire. Therefore a certain kind of control over him is mandatory.

The same is true about every human being: the lower the development level, the more control he needs.

Hence such managerial layer as Heavenly Teachers, or in new terminology – **Determinants -** are just indispensable for the mankind, otherwise they may blow up the whole Earth, threatening each other with nuclear and other weapons, or turn all reservoirs into some poisonous settling basins.

The layer of Determinants belongs to the first Hierarchy Level. However this Level contains not only Heavenly Teaches but also a lot of other Higher Personalities having similar energy potential but engaged in some other work. This work refers both to the earthly plane and to other worlds located in other galaxies.

Determinants refer only to the Earthly plane and they are called so, because they are those who **determine** human beings in their lives, are in charge of their fates and keep watch over people preventing them from crossing the limits of permissiveness.

The Determinants themselves have the image, which is different from human appearance. They exist in other dimensions, in other continua. Consequently, contacts of two creatures living in different worlds, leading different existences, are specific.

Modern people see Them as a small gleaming gas cloud. B the way, now nobody sees any wings on Them. And in comparison with human beings, such "small clouds" or let us use new terminology and call them bundles of energy, have more powerful mind and much higher morals. Isn't it wonderful? And does not it make us reconsider our conception of obscure subtle world and about creatures it contains whose number is many times as large as the number of people living on the Earth?

And now let us listen to what God tells us about our Heavenly Managers, what secrets of their lives he discloses.

Who are the Determinants and What are They Deemed to Be

Replies of God:

- "Who are the Determinants and what do They do in subtle* spheres?"
- "Those are certain essences* of My Hierarchy*, guiding people through their lives. People call them Heavenly Teachers or Guardian-Angels because They patronize their pupils and guard them within the frame of prescribed program. In other words, They prevent happening of events that are not included in personal program of an individual."

We are listening to tranquil calm voice of God and feel hot currents reaching us from above. At the beginning of channeling these currents are not very burny, but by the middle of channeling they become hotter and start to frizzle us. But this heat is unusual: you feel like as if invisible fire burns you from inside. It gets inside and then starts to ooze from a throat chakra as a cold flow, which is burning at the same time. And when you ask a question there is a feeling that you are like a firedrake with fire breaking out from your mouth.

When we once asked God a complicated question of high Level, he said:

- "You will receive the answer to this question when you are inside the Hierarchy."

Having not understood why the answer was not given, we tried to insist on getting it. For this purpose we re-worded the question a little. And then God asked us gravely:

- "Do you want a channeler to have fire coming out of the month instead of words?"

We understood that the power of the answer contains such energy potential that no combinations of letters are able to translate it, only fire is capable to express its mighty meaning. Therefore we stopped to insist on getting the answer, but just continued with less serious discussions: for example, about Heavenly Teachers.

- "Does it mean that Guardian-Angels are deemed to be Determinants?» we asked.

- "Besides Guardian-Angels, many creatures of subtle world may be attributed to Guardian-Angels", He replied. "They are not the only ones, who help human beings. For example, Entities belonging to Medical System can also be called Guardian-Angels because they assist people in emergency circumstances. Sometimes people face such dangerous circumstances as Acts of God or accidents involving loss of a great number of people. But not all individuals die in such situation, some of them survive if the program prescribes so. However, it may be difficult for a single Determinant to protect his fosterling, therefore special crews of saviors from the Medical System* may be invited to help people. So in relation to a human being, Guardian-Angels may be represented by the creatures who are not only from different Systems, but also from different Hierarchies. It is high time for people to refuse from old concepts and switch over to the new knowledge about Higher Entities."

- "Do Determinants have feelings?"

- "They do not have such pronounced and strong feelings as people may have. However, to some extent they preserve sensitivity because Determinants refer to the first Level of Hierarchy, who still have many properties of nether worlds inherent in them. Everything gets extirpated little by little. Besides, many of them are deemed souls of former people. But a human being is not able to get rid completely of his/her feelings up until the hundredth earthly Level. He can quench them to a great extent, but still part of them remains. And as they ascend the Hierarchy Levels, feelings get more and more reduced until they turn into some uniform manifestations. At more higher Levels, feelings change into general sensitivity of forms, that is the Entity starts to feel with the whole of its being, very deep in its soul. At Higher Levels there are feelings unknown to human beings, although they may be distantly compared with universal human joy, delight, unity with others etc. But our feelings are very high if compared with yours."

- "May the Higher display temper?"

- "No, not at all. No temper", said God amicably in somewhat featherlike manner. "The more Higher, the less adverse and negative in external manifestations. No anger, aggression, hatred exists there."

- "Why are for the purpose of acting in material world, people given so much: mind, consciousness, subconscious mind, mentality?"

- "Such structure of human being depends on the properties of your substance, on the need for a human being to be guided inside it and to be involved in the processes of self-improvement. In the majority of other worlds creatures do not have mind and subconscious mind."

- "What other essences of other worlds are given similar qualities?"

- "They are mostly are given to those who belong to nether material worlds."

- "Speaking about the subtle world, do Determinants need to have mind and subconscious mind?"

- "In Higher worlds consciousness exists. But the need in the work of subconscious mind falls away. Therefore Determinants do not already have mind and subconscious mind."

- "We know that all Entities in the Hierarchy are unisexual, and there is no male/female division between them. Does it mean that in subtle worlds such process as reproduction does not exist?"

- "Yes, such nether processes do not exist in My Hierarchy. The entire Hierarchy is replenished and extended at the extent of souls coming from other worlds. Material worlds increase their quantitative aspect at the expense reproduction of material forms. And this process is permanent. Souls go through processing, selection at the lower stages of development and after that they replenish Our ranks. Such is the system of increase of the headcount of Hierarchies."

- "Determinants do not have division into males and females, but do they have the concept of kindred love for each other and love for the Higher?"

- "Yes, they have such love, although, of course, it is expressed and manifested quite differently as compared to your world. That is why we try to maximally develop this wonderful feeling in every human being because later it serves a basis for development of more perfect qualities of Higher Entities. Without love developed in one's soul it is impossible to have a sense of at-oneness with those similar to yourselves in spiritual* worlds. Therefore love is not unknown for Determinants as well, but with them it stands at higher level compared to human beings. More often than not it is manifested as respect for each other and reverence for the Higher, worship of Them, sense of adoration. All the above is based on superior qualities of soul and not on vile calls of body, which is inherent in human beings."

- "Do Determinants feel affection and love for their pupils?"

- "Some of them do, and some don't. All their senses are on the other Level. Their love may be equated to universal love. Therefore all their relations, as you say, go from all their hearts. Hence they feel affection also for their fosterlings because guiding them throughout their lives, they get used to them and keenly share their feeling in many situations."

- "What do Higher Entities feed on?"

- "Who do you mean by «Higher Entities»? I have entire Hierarchy of them"

- "Let us take Determinants, for example."

- "Such notion as "feed on" is not available with us. It is accepted on the Earth."

- "But do they have anything similar to the given process?"

- "They acquire energy and grow at the expense of it."

-"Do not Determinants feed on the energies of Inferiors* as it is accepted on the Earth? People eat plants, fish, and birds, everything that is below them."

- "No, they do not. They do not have it. Everything needed for their existence they work out themselves."

- "And what about the energy they receive from people? For what purposes do they get it? Perhaps, to feed on it?"

- "No. Determinants acquire the energy needed for their growth and development through their own work, but the energy they receive from people is used for entirely different purposes. It is used for construction of various Systems or the same material worlds."

- "Do Determinants have organs of vision?"

- "Their organs of vision are not similar to those of people. They are differently structured and they see, one may say, with all their selves. It is a special three-dimensional perception of world."

- "What is the radius of their vision? A human being, for example, can see as far as city limits."

- "Determinant can easily lighten your Universe from one side boundaries to the other."

- "Our Galaxy or Universe?" –asked we, trying to comprehend the margins of some else's potentials."

- "The Universe", confirmed God."

- "And do Higher Hierarchs have even wider range of vision?"

- "Of course, they do. There is certain dependence: the higher the Level of Creature, the greater the radius of its vision."

- "Does it mean that Higher Hierarchs are able to see several Universes?"

- "Yes, and not only several of them. Their coverage is very vast both with reference to the distance and also in respect of qualitative basis. For example, a human being can see only coarse physical forms, but Higher Hierarchs see all subtle structures, their vision is multivariate and includes dozens of dimensions. They can see three-dimensional, quintamensional and other worlds – all the worlds which are below their Level. And their number may be great."

- "Well, they have well-developed outward vision. And what about atoms, molecules? Can They see them?"

- "Higher Hierarchs are able to see small and large to the same extent. Just as ultrasound can pierce material objects revealing their structure, so their vision basing on energies of very high frequencies having great penetrability extends to any forms."

- "Do Determinants see cells of human body and processes going on inside?"

- "No, they haven't reached such-like state in their development; to be more exact, they don't need it, such vision is not inherent in their structure. They have other purposes."

- "And does their vision enable them to see deep inside atoms?"

- "As distinct from the Higher, they do not possess such vision. The properties characteristic of Personalities who reached Higher Levels of Hierarchy are not available with those who are still on its nether stages. Everything develops in proportion to extent of improvement."

- "Does it mean that Determinants can see macro-structures and micro-structures are not accessible for them?"

- "It depends on the type of a micro-structure. They see some of them, but to do so, They have to go through special adaptation. People also see close and distant views differently, some kind of eye adaptation takes place."

- "There is such a notion as velocity of cosmic vision. What is it?"
- "Velocity of cosmic vision is the velocity of vision coverage of space per time unit."
- "Is this velocity higher with ?Higher Hierarchs than with Determinants or is it the same?"
- "The higher the Personality, the higher all Their capabilities."
- "Do Determinants have such capability as hearing? Or do they live in silent worlds?"
- "For people they are silent, but for themselves they are full of sounds. Human beings are given sound as the analogue of sounding existing in Higher worlds. But there perceptions are finer and broader. The Higher the Entity, the farther the distance of its hearing is."
- "What properties, which are not available with people, do Determinants possess?"
- "Mostly these are properties related to mental processes. For example, they possess pulse and parallel mentality. But people cannot conceive things, which are not inherent in them. Usually they try to compare everything with their primitive apprehension. But Inferiors will never be able to understand the Higher*."
- "People have legs and arms to perform some actions, to construct or make something. Do Determinants have any limbs? How do they work and what do they produce in their world?"
- "All of them work with the help of mental force. They do not have such forms as people do, but they are very good in control of thoughts. This ability substitutes legs and arms for them. With the help of mental force they control all relevant processes, all energies of their Level. It is much more faster and more efficient than use of extra action mechanisms. People can hardly conceive this, because they themselves think very slowly and incoherently, and their thoughts are still very weak, they lack vigor and force."
- "How do Determinants move about?"
- "It is possible to say that their movements are also performed based on mental force."
- "Does their translation look like a flight in our world?"
- "No, it is not a flight. They get disappeared in one point of space and appear in another. They kind of convolve to form a point. Most probably, it resembles your teleportation. The more energy Determinant has, the longer distance He is able to cover."
- "Do They use any aircrafts to move about in their world?"

- "No, not at all. This is too primitive for them. Within the limits of one and the same world, aircrafts are used only on material planets."

- "Within what boundaries can Determinants move: within their own System, Galaxy, and Universe?"

- "It depends on a Determinant and energy margins available at his disposal. The greater energy margins, the farther the distance He is able to cover."

- "What maximum distance is the strongest Determinant able to cover?"

- "The most Superior Determinant is able to move within your Universe. Their world is spatially vaster than your material world."

- "And speaking about a Determinant of minimal energy, within what boundaries can He move?"

- "Within your Galaxy."

- "Can They move for long distances at their own wish or only upon permission received from the Above?"

- "You see, They have a commitment They firmly adhere to. And if it is a job, it is given from the Above. It means that everything they do is performed by assent of Higher Managers. All their movements are mostly related to their commitments. And they may never fly anywhere just on an impulse. Nothing is done there just for the hell of it, without any purpose. Besides, They themselves have no wish to move about to no purpose, for their own delectation."

- "Are there any temptations in the life of Determinants?"

- "As this is an inferior Level of my Hierarchy, they have temptations, but other than those of people. Each world obeys its own laws and has individual temptations."

- "What can be referred to their temptations?"

- "A wish to get from man as much energy as possible."

- "Are they punished for such selfishness.?"

- "It depends on the circumstances. But the law of cause and effect relationship stands in force with them also."

- "Do they have to decide between good and ill, just as people do?"

- "No. Division between good and ill exists only on the Earth, but there are no such-like polarities in their world. But, of course, there some contrasts, but they are different. Everything changes: boundaries of choice and the main point of choice. For example, when a soul arrives at the first Level it has to choose either plus creativity and minus programming. And plus creativity passes over to the phase of good, but minus programming – to the form of evil. It means that change of existence forms results in change of moral categories."

- "Do Determinants contact with those who are like them?"

- "Certainly. They interact with each other. Each world has certain relationships established for their type of life style. Form of existence is driven by the processes taking place in a given world. And the life style of this form depends already on the conditions of requirements for normal progress of relevant processes. In different worlds all possible forms are based on different interactions. Therefore in your world there are some types of interaction between people, and They have other types."

- "And do They have contacts with Higher Hierarchs?"

- "Only when the occasion requires. They never disturb each other without reasonable cause. Basically, their task is to guide people and control systems inferior to Them. However They contact each other, but not very much, because They are always busy. They are deeply involved in their work and find satisfaction and devotion in it. They commune with each other only if they have some matter to discuss. It may so happen that two fosterlings come up against each other, and something occurs between them due to which the Determinant of one person cannot agree with the Determinant of another person. They have different view of the given situation, they disagree with each other. Therefore they have to meet in order to make explicit decision. Determinants also may have controversies because everyone has its own view of the event. It may take quite a time for them to reach a mutual decision."

- "How do they settle disputes in such circumstances?"

- "Determinants apply to HigherManagers who make a final decision. They address those Managers who personally control Them, and Managers decide what to do next and how the situation can be resolved. "

- "How is information communicated from Higher Hierarchs to Determinants?"

- "Neighboring worlds have their own communication system. Everything depends on the degree of development of neighboring worlds. The higher the worlds, the better communication."

- "Do Determinants use some instruments or devices in their work?"

- "Yes, they do. There are a lot of subtle plane instruments."

- "Do they make them themselves?"

- "No, they do not. Others make instruments for them. In subtle world specialization also exists. Some entities are making this, other are making that."

- "But are those instruments the same as people have?"

- "To some extent they are like yours, but they have other forms and other operating principle because they are of different nature, different material and operating principle."

- "Improvement of human being's soul is based on existence. And at what expense does the soul of Heavenly Teacher get improved?"

- "Determinant does not have its own existence similar to human existence. However He guides the existence of His pupil and lives it out in the same way as His pupil does. He feels his senses and affections as His own. He lives out his life as His own. Therefore soul improvement certainly takes place. Similarly, parents who cradle their child, give it all their loving and fight for it, improve their souls at the same time. And the aim of their connection lies also in that. Determinant and a human being interact with each other in such a way that progress of a pupil always results in progress of the Teacher."

- "And how do Determinants replenish their own knowledge?"

- "Within one life, Determinants acquire knowledge in their System, in the System they are, in the System to which they are assigned. Everything is taken from the System energy reserves, which it accumulated before. And they also, just like your channelers, decode energy units. They receive preliminary pulses, after that the energy in Them gets decoded to produce information and knowledge, which they need. Meanings of information are different, they depend on the quality of energy. The energy of one quality is decoded to produce this knowledge, decoding of energy of some other quality produces other knowledge and so on."

- "So the Higher Level gives them its own information. They decode this information and assimilate it, don't they?"

- "No, you are wrong. Their System accumulates the energy of certain type of knowledge, which is taken from the given domain and brought together. They gather the information and then They make available a certain part of it to each Determinant from the created base. Then the information is decoded."

- "How do Higher Hierarchs enhance their knowledge? Do they have another principle of work?"

- "Higher Hierarchs? They do not need that kind of decoding. Passing certain stages of development, they accumulate a sufficient amount of information based on their own methods. The way they acquire knowledge is somewhat different. It is more sophisticated as compared to that of Determinants, but at the same time, more advanced. They enhance their level through **their existence**. Like as if all new information is sucked in by their entire surface, by every particle of their energy."

- "What kind of programs do Determinants have? How do those programs differ from human programs?"

- "Human program contains only one life. But the program of Determinant consists of the bits of all those programs which They lived through in the past. Those bits are brought together and relevantly replenished."

- "Why are the programs built up from bits? What is the benefit of that?"

- "This kind of integration is required for their work. The program bits do not contain entire life, they contain only useful information: everything which is not relevant for the given existence is removed. Every bit includes some new knowledge acquired by Him within one life, and repetitions are not included. As a result, their amount is accumulated in an aggregate program. Everything that He managed to conceive within one past life, second, third lives and so on, is now united in one program, and deemed available to Him. So He uses this knowledge (which is already in the past) like his own reserve."

- "Who prepares the programs of Determinants?"

- "Higher Systems. All personalities develop in compliance with relevant programs. There are no unprogrammed creatures in Cosmos."

Where do Determinants Come from?
How Many People Do They Guide?

- "If Determinants deal with people, it means that in the past they themselves were people and therefore they should feel and understand them very well. Is it true?"

- "No, not exactly. Not all of Them pass the phase of human development."

- "Where do they come to Your Hierarchy from?"

- "Many of them come from other worlds, from other Universes. As soon as a soul reaches a relevant Level of development, it is transferred to the first Level of My Hierarchy, and here it chooses activity for itself. Those who want to, become Determinants. Similarly, souls of former people choose occupations for themselves."

- "When selecting Entities for the roles of Determinants, what parameters do You rely upon?"

- "They shall have perfect knowledge of human structure, the whole of human science, the whole of programming science, they shall understand energetics, addition of energies, they shall have excellent skills in carry out of certain manipulations with them. These are the basic parameters."

- "Creatures (coming to You and assigned to the first Level) earlier existed in various forms of life. Does this mean much at the first Level?"

- "No. They preserve permanent subtle bodies, and at the first Level they acquire such-similar protective bodies- two or three of them dependent on their indicators. Therefore, actually they become similar to each other in appearance – just as people being in material bodies are very much alike."

- "Why are souls enclosed in protective bodies?"

- "Each world has its own protective bodies designed for souls. Those bodies help them to adapt to the surrounding environment. They are produced from the matter of the given world. All physical parameters of protective bodies comply with that world; therefore a soul normally orients itself in a new world. When a soul reaches a new Level it receives new bodies. Usually He gets two or three new ones."

- "But if He ascends higher within the limits of one Level can He change the bodies at his own wish?"

- "At one and the same Level bodies are not changed. They are meant for passing through the entire Level from beginning to end. And nobody will give Him any new bodies until He fills up them with energies of this entire plane."

- "Such transfer from one Level to another, probably, bears a resemblance to a death of a human being when the soul leaves material body and acquires another one."

- "Not at all. If this transition takes place in a subtle world, then just bodies are changed in the way you change your clothes."

- "But is this a painless process? Death of a human being, for example, is very frightful and painful."

- "This is an absolutely painless process. Death exists only in material world."

- "Does it sometimes happen that those external bodies of Determinant get damaged?"

- "Yes, everything may happen. Some kinds of defects of subtle bodies can result from careless handling of technical devices, from exposure to foreign energies. But usually nothing that may damage the external forms of Earthly Determinants happen to them, because their work is peaceful. They watch people but never interfere in any peripeteias. However, there are nether subtle worlds, which launch wars. And they sometimes have their external bodies damaged by energy rays. These are the wars of energies. And protective bodies may go all to pieces. It means that death never occurs, but external bodies may get damaged which is followed by a complete replacement of temporary subtle bodies: they have to change the old ones for the new ones. However in such a case transition to a higher Level does not take place. Because change of subtle bodies involving ascension to the next stage occurs only if a soul reaches a relevant Level of development."

- "Does Determinant feel adverse effects of environment as, for example, a man exposed to heat or cold?"

- "No, He is never exposed to this, because they live in quite another environment, which is favorable for existence. As for human beings, they are surrounded by aggressive environment, which drives their mental processes essential for accelerated improvement."

- "Does anybody instruct Determinant how to perform the work when He starts it for the first time?"

- "No. nobody does. A certain program covering a relevant work is embedded in them, which is sufficient for them. They learn what to do straightway."

- "How is the degree of their proficiency in the work they do checked up?"

- "Based on the previous program. They see, how He performed it, what results were attained."

- "Do Determinants have to give account of their work, what period does a report shall cover?"

- "The reporting period is equal to a lifespan of a human being. After the death of a guided person the Determinant surely reports the Higher Manager all his benefits and implications."

- "And does He has to report before the death happens?"

- "No, He does not."

- "When the guided person dies, does the Determinant receive another person having a similar program?"

- "No. While He guides the first one, He himself also changes because as the Determinant lives the life together with a human being (and it is exactly so: He is not indifferent spectator - He just lives the life), He also gets improved, gains experience. The Determinant (together with his fosterling) also faces certain events, contemplates and analyses them, and as a result, He gets improved himself, acquires knowledge, learns to create and invent something together with his pupil, helps him to make progress in any areas of activities. And at this time it is checked – whether He himself has reached the relevant limit within this period. And until the Determinant acquires knowledge allowing him to step up higher, until He achieves relevant level of development, He will be given one pupil at a time for guidance. But those people will already have more complicated program and they will be more developed spiritually. And as soon as He is transferred to the next stage He will be able to guide not one but several persons."

- "Does it sometimes happen that Determinant continues to guide the soul of his first fosterling through the second and the third live?"

- "Yes, it does happen, and very often at that. It is even easier for Him with such work pattern because by this time He very well knows all habits and nature of his paternalized soul, as He has studied it in its previous incarnation. It is easier for him to understand the extent of progress made by the guided soul."

- "How many generations can the Determinant guide throughout his life?"

- "He has not got lives, these are stages of development because His life is endless. But within a stage of development after which He ascends higher the Determinant has to guide through about five generations. But, of course, in some circumstances this number may be lesser and greater than this. Everything depends on the capabilities of Determinant himself."

- "Does the Determinant always guide one pupil or several of them?"

- "In most case – only one. The number of the guided depends also on the Level of the Determinant. Beginners guide one pupil, more experienced ones –have several pupils. There are Determinants who guide from two to three hundreds of pupils concurrently."

- "After a pupil finishes his program and dies, does a Determinant starts to guide another pupil?"

- "Not always. Sometimes some changes, rearrangements occur at the level of Determinants themselves. For example, if a soul which He guides, degrades to its absolute decoding, then the Determinant may be abased in His work, He may be transferred to the previous lower Level and offered some other work to do."

- "As soon as a person dies, do the Determinant and the person He guides meet each other face to face? Are their contacts continued on the subtle plane?"

- "No. A human being and Determinant have very much diverse energy Levels, energy potentials, which do not enable them to meet each other. A Teacher may descend to his pupil, but He (Determinant) does not need it. He just waits for his next assignment."

- "Does Determinant continue to control a human being "beyond the veil"?"

- "No, after the death of a man he is controlled by others."

- "Do Determinants know their future?"

- "There is no need for them to know that. Everyone has to perform the given work in good faith and do all their best for it. And it is for the Higher to decide who shall be assigned and where everyone shall be assigned. Basically, future tendency depends on a zeal and degree of improvement of every individual at present. The same is true about human beings."

- "Lifespan of a human being is just an instant in comparison with the lifespan of Determinant, which means that he is engaged in guiding his pupil for some short instant during his long existence. And what does He do when He has no human beings to guide?"

- "He has not always been a Teacher, until this time He may have been involved in some other work. But if He has chosen to be a Teacher, then it is a solid Level*, which contains a certain Hierarchy. It means that the Level of Determinants contains a specific number of a Sublevels* or ascension steps as long as they guide people on the Earth. Going through improvement at this Level they may be involved in guiding various people over a period of several lives or they may guide one pupil during several lives of his. After such work They are raised and transferred from the Level of Determinants to a higher Level of Originators or somewhere else to perform some other work."

- "What other types of activity may Determinants be involved in while they are guiding people? Or, perhaps, they just carry out control over people and have nothing else to do."

- "They permanently increase the scope of their personal knowledge. They study programming within the frame of their plane*. They also have programming personal who are in charge of preparation of individual programs for their world."

- "Probably, the work of Determinants is chosen by Entities who like teaching."

- "They are offered various jobs, and They choose jobs which They see proper. Here feelings are not so much concerned as the wish to be promoted in some field of knowledge. To guide a pupil Determinant needs comprehensive knowledge, therefore the work itself contributes to considerable progress of Determinant. But not everybody likes his job. Sometimes Originators* are descended to the Level of Determinants because of some faults of theirs. And, of course, in such case they sometimes are not satisfied with their new job because They already know that at the higher Levels there are more interesting and better occupations. Besides, it is more pleasant to work in higher worlds. Therefore They will always compare present world with the previous ones, and will try to come back, and their present work in the quality of Determinant will be performed only in duty bound and also based on the wish to right themselves."

- "Currently the number of people living on the Earth is reducing. What will happen to the Determinants who will have no pupils?"

- "Subsequently, They may go through a phase of change of their fosterlings or They may change over to other forms of life, to guide somebody from the worlds parallel to the Earth. It never happens that Determinants remain without pupils. If we reduce the number of people on Earth, then some of Determinants go further and are occupied with some other work."

- "And do those who stay with people continue to improve their qualification? If they do not rise to higher Levels, does it mean that They fail to get improved, to gain adequate job-related experience or Their matrix lacks certain energies?"

- "Yes, it is true. The most inferior Determinants are left to work with people. To be more exact, those Determinants are soul-beginners. They have come to the first Level recently from some other world and chosen to work as leaders. Through continuous improvement of people souls They keep on developing themselves. Organization of their work enables Them to improve themselves due to the progress of their pupils."

Functions of Determinants

- "Are Determinants taught how to manage pupils? Do They take any training courses?"
- "No. A program is prepared without training, and Soul item* already knows what to do. It is like inborn abilities with people. But if a Soul-item has not any instructional experience at all (for example, with people such experience may be in the form of teaching) then at the beginning the first-time Determinant is given the lowest stages of human beings: frequently, all sorts of experimental people who have a small number of control points and who live for short periods of time. They try to guide very simple people with primitive programs. He is deemed a heavenly trainee. When experience is gained he will be given normal tasks."
- "Does anybody control their work in this case?"
- "They are controlled by their Teachers who precede them and stand higher in the Hierarchy. Every Determinant also has his own Teacher."
- "What kind of work does Determinant do in respect of a man?"
- "His major function is to guide a man from the time of his birth to his death. He is given a program of his fosterling, and based on this program He controls him/her, governs his/her actions within the prescribed limits."
- "But who prepares a program for the man? Other Determinants?"
- "No. They receive a finished program, and the program is prepared by Originators, standing at the higher Level in the Hierarchy. They, in their turn, get the basic plot from Managers*, who generate it with due account of karma of a man and his past results. Managers just plan what parameters of a given soul shall be reached at the next stage of development, and they determine the fate of a man i.e. circumstances

which he shall pass throughout his life. It is just Managers who are deemed arbiters of fate of people. They hand over the prepared plot to Originators who calculate every situation, determine what energies and in what amounts they shall allocate to them with due account of potential of the given soul. Based on those calculations a program is prepared in compliance with generally accepted rules."

- "Determinant receives a finished program. And how does He work under it further on?"

- "When the program is ready Determinant shall preliminary study its content, clarify for himself everything that he does not understand, update it, whereupon he shall input the program into special technical device similar to your computers. Here He also puts absolutely all data about the future pupil, to the extent of the indicators of the future material body in a standard option, and information about subtle bodies. And further on, when a human being is born to the world, control over him is carried out through a similar computing facility. The real data on material body are input into computer memory after his birth and after that the required parameters are compared with those received."

- "Who is allowed to update the program, if appropriate: Determinant or Originator?'

- "Major amendments are introduced by Originator but He shall do it only having concurred these amendments with Managers."

- "Is Determinant given any soul for guidance?"

- "No. As soon as a program is finished, energy potentials are determined then the relevant Determinant is selected, who shall possess relevant knowledge and required energy potential enabling him to guide this soul. Or sometimes it is vice versa: if the Determinant is competent enough, He is allowed to find a relevant soul for himself. Between a pupil and a teacher a certain matching shall be maintained. A simple man who deals only with household matters receives a simple inexperienced Determinant. If an inexperienced Determinant is given some intellectual with wide range of interests, this Determinant will not be able to guide him due to lack of experience and knowledge. Therefore to a human being having a certain development level a Determinant having a matching development level is always assigned. And a man with highly developed spirit will never be guided by inferior Teacher."

- "And do Determinants sometimes refuse to guide a soul suggested to them?"

- "Yes, sometimes they do."

- "For what reasons can He refuse?"

- "He may not be just interested in it. If a Determinant is suggested to guide some low active soul, but his potential is higher than that, this kind of work may seem too simple for him, not sufficient for his further personal improvement. For example, in case He guides some alcoholic or underdeveloped individual. What can he find interesting for himself in such sphere of activity? This kind of job is too primitive for Determinant, and he may want to have more advanced work. Naturally, one cannot receive a lot of energy from an alcoholic, or even suffer losses because of that. If a pupil becomes an alcoholic, what means that he is given such version of the program, it disturbs the energy interchange between a pupil and a Teacher. The latter gives his energy to the pupil, but receives no return from his pupil. His personal expenses are not paid back, and his energy supply source becomes thinner. But in return to the energy given to the pupil, the Determinant has to receive other energies which shall not only compensate for His contribution but also give sufficient gain, otherwise he may suffer losses and will not be able to make progress himself. Competent Determinants can predict expenses when they receive inferior souls, and for this reason they sometimes refuse to take them."

- "Does it mean that Determinants do not only guide a man throughout his life but also take energy from him? So the role of the Heavenly Teacher is not limited only to teaching as people thought earlier, is it?"

- "Of course, not. He shall know a lot about energies and be able to manipulate them. Determinant does not only patronize his pupil throughout his life but also provides him with energies having the properties necessary for him. In order to perform such-like actions a Determinant shall have a relevant amount of energy having a certain range. He has his own energy reserves. Thus, for example, every organ of a human being requires to be made up with energy of appropriate quality. And when they sleep a Teacher recharges them. He also supplies energy required for mechanical actions of a man. And if a Determinant fails to send this energy overnight, then no actions will be performed – a man will not be able to do that. He will feel ill or morally depressed and fit for nothing. During the day a Determinant will also control energy consumed by a person, and if the latter lacks energy and feels tired, a Determinant feeds him off additionally in daytime so that he will be able to fulfill his daily program. Determinant is also in charge of issuing dreams for his fosterling which are sent to him for his education and for his soul to receive qualities it lacks."

- "Determinant guides his pupil with the help of computer. But is it possible for a man to have fully automatic guidance since he has his program?"

- "Any technical device works in strict compliance with its program and it is not able to respond to abnormal conduct of people in flexible manner. Automatic guidance may quickly lead a man into a deadlock and bring him to death because it is not capable of logical thinking and flexible response to behavior, which goes beyond the program framework. If a man lived under his program without Determinants, he would always choose the easiest way for himself and invariably deviate from the major goal. Besides, strict adherence to the program would make him a robot, having no ability to think himself. Instead, a Determinant sends him pulses, ideas and (applying other methods of his) He, first of all, makes him think, analyze and make his own choices. Automatic device is not able to educate. Only a Determinant, with his flexible mind, is able to drive his pupil to his major goal. It is also He who sends him thoughts, takes care of development of his cognitive ability. If a man was guided by a machine, he would always remain a stupid, shallow creature."

Handling a Pupil

- "What does educational work of Determinant consist of?"

- "Determinant shall see to it that the program is adhered to. Usually a pupil percepts the program at intuitive level enjoying freedom of choice, therefore he may choose for himself pathways that lead to his degradation. In this case Teacher's purpose is to caution him against inadequate actions. Therefore a teacher will send him some warnings or he will preclude him from certain actions, create difficulties for him on one way and facilitate his movement on the other way leading to progress of his soul."

- "How can He warn his pupil that he does something improperly?"

- "Usually Determinant uses signs for a pupil to respond. If he does not pay attention to a sign used by other people, the Teacher also stops using it. A failure, bad luck in some business may signal that a man does something wrong. But at the same time it may be his trial, therefore everybody shall analyze his failures and certain signs. As a rule, everything is done on individual basis. Determinant may send warnings to the pupil in his dreams, and sometimes resort to serious punishments. For example, when a man of quite high spiritual development level goes in for football playing and suddenly breaks his leg. It indicates that such option of development is too low for him and he has to find for himself some more decent activity. And as for a young soul, on the contrary, going in for football will be rewarding because this soul prefers sports to alcohol and drugs."

- "What else does the educational work of Determinant manifest itself in?"

- "They send to their pupils ideas, which comply with their level of development. People receive all the ideas from their Determinants. Determinant also takes care of development of his pupil's feelings and emotions. The latter shall not grow to be indifferent and selfish. But here I speak about plus Determinants who prepare souls for My Hierarchy. They know what qualities the souls I need shall have. With the purpose of development of those qualities They add to situations such nuances that help their pupils to reach higher levels in their development and become more spiritual. The aim of the Teacher is to maximally develop the sensory basis of a man and then to refine it up to the perception of Higher world and whereat to quench wishes associated with material world. It means that a Teacher shall instill in a man a drive for spiritual world and indifference to worldly pleasures."

- "Some earthly preachers, such as Osho, insist that it is possible to reach God through sex. What System do they represent in their work?"

- "This is a special System, which handles just the given type of energy. But of course, it is a very low range and it will never be able to lead to Myself. Those Systems need this energy for their work, and they try to receive it as much as possible. Besides, such preaching is a test of soul for resistibility to some veiled temptations. A mature soul will not accept popularization of lechery even if it is offered by a preacher standing very high in social hierarchy. In his speeches an immature soul may find justification of its inward inherent vice."

- "For what purposes is this type of energy used?"

- "For special constructions. In certain places there are constructions which are formed on the given subtle matter. But let me repeat, it is a very low spectrum of energies."

- "Do all ideas come to a pupil from Determinant or is a man capable for something all by himself?"

- "A man is capable to produce minor household and social ideas all by himself basing on behavioral stereotypes embedded in his mind, but novel ideas which give rise to development of people or society are always sent from the Above."

- "Are ideas sent down arbitrary or in compliance with some system?"

- "The sent ideas shall comply with the program of a man so that to facilitate his progress. But sometimes they may send ideas going beyond the framework of the program. Let us speak about an idea touching upon some parallel, target things when a man is moving to a single purpose but at the same time is involved in other activities, particularly, in creative, charitable matters, or goes in for sports or deals with engineering business. And all these activities are just parallel. His development may be targeted else-wise, and creative, sporting and engineering activities are just accompanying the improvement of his soul. Therefore Determinant may sent down not only the ideas facilitating achievement of goal, but also other ones aimed at his comprehensive multidisciplinary development."

- "And may the Determinant ask some other Determinant to help him in development of some talent in his pupil?"

- "Yes, he may. If a Determinant lacks some specific capabilities or knowledge required for instructing his pupil in something, he may request assistance from some other Determinant. For example, if a pupil has got interested in versification, but his Determinant is not good at it so this Determinant may seek help from the Determinant who is able to teach writing to his fosterling. But later, of course, such pupil has to compensate for his study through situations or emotions. Nothing is down for free. This principle complies with the basic cosmic law of energy conservation. By the way, people think that if a Teacher or a healer is God-inspired, then he must not take charge for his work. But it is a violation of the energy exchange process. Both a healer and a Teacher shall recover their expenses."

- "May a Determinant interfere with the affairs of a man He guides?"

- "No, this shall not be done. It is against the laws."

- "And if two pupils guided by different Determinants are fighting with each other, may one of the Determinants (in order to support his pupil) give telepathic prompts to the opponent pupil to take incorrect actions? Is such kind of interference possible?"

- "No, nothing is prompted to opponents. The result of such situation may be predetermined by the program so that one of the pupils is able to acquire the qualities of a winner, and the other come to know how it is felt to be a loser and acquire other qualities. It is just the acquirement of needed qualities that drive the outcome of events for each of the participants. Therefore if a pupil has chosen a fight instead of peaceful settlement from the proposed development options, then the Determinant will lead His fosterling to the outcome predetermined by his program. And accordingly, He will inculcate on his pupil the prompts complying with the chosen situation option. But all this is pre-programmed and kept in the Teacher's computer. Nothing that goes beyond the limits of the program is given."

- "What kind of punishments needed for education of his pupil does Determinant have at his disposal?"

- "In the given case the procedure is as follows: the program has pathways/sub-options that is offshoots from the basic option where he just receives strokes of misfortune. If he manages to choose a basic option correctly, then everything goes on smoothly, but if only he takes a wrong turning and chooses an unacceptable option, punishments may come one after another. Having chosen a sub-option he may go a very long way, and still come back to the basic path. All sub-options lead to one point, to this very point because an individual acquires wrong energies instead of those needed for his matrix. So as a result he goes the way but fails to ascend higher and just as he lacked, for example, type "A" energy enabling him to the next higher level, so he still lacks it as before: the cell remains vacant. That is why when he chooses the wrong way he receives various punishment on it. But all those punishments are inherent in the given sub-option."

- "Do Determinants have some additional methods of punishment which are not included in the program?"

- "No, such methods are not available. Everything happens according to the program: both the development and punishment. As soon as a man starts to follow a sub-option deflecting him from his goal he gets his punishment."

- "Is Determinant able to contribute some punishments invented by himself?"

- "No. He never punishes his pupil at his own discretion."

- "When a man's soul is degrading does it mean that the Determinant proves unequal to his task?"

- "Yes, it does."

- "Should He have definitely raised this erring soul to the next step?"

- **"Certainly. The objective of man's life is aimed at achievement of the level which is higher than the previous one."**

- "How do people interact in conflicting situations?" For example, how are forces aligned when people fall over one another? Do Determinants control their conflict?"

- "Such conflicting situations as fights are included in the program with reference to some karmic outcomes. The life plotline is worked out, winners and losers are assigned. Winners shall have one type feelings, losers shall feel differently. The situation helps to hit a specific objective. If an individual simply goes through some trial, then he has options to choose from; however if it is a karmic situation, then he should experience everything it is designed for in full measure. Suppose four individuals are involved in a karmic situation, and they are at fight. Besides them, eight Determinants participate in the situation because everything shall happen in compliance with the key points of the program, i.e. everything shall happen without the right of choice. Determinants shall supply energy, control actions and outcome. There are always methods at their disposal to make a man follow a prescribed plotline. They do not supply energy to the individual who has to lose a fight, or they may send him pulses neutralizing his confrontation or they may blackout his consciousness just for a moment, which will be enough for him to lose the situation. The whole spectacle very much resembles a puppet show, where the wire-pullers – i.e. Determinants – make participant of the performance play the role They need. Pulling the invisible puppet's strings they obtain from them exact performance of actions which comply with the plotline prescribed and sent from the Above."

- "Is failure to supply energy to a man important?"

- "Yes, of course. The actions may not happen at all. An individual becomes weak as if he droops and for reasons, which he himself cannot understand, becomes unable to revenge. The energy to an individual may be supplied by the Determinant, other than his own. One of them shall conduct actions and the other check how energy is supplied."

- "But why is such distinction applied to Determinants?"

- "It applies to some cases when one Determinant is not experienced enough and the other helps him, in such a way they allocate responsibilities. Sometimes one of the Determinants lacks energy of a certain type needed for some situations, so he borrows it from another Determinant. There may be various Options. But don't think that Determinants watch every step of an individual. They control only critical situations."

- "When a man is far gone and does not remember anything, how does he find his way home? With us it is attributed to acquired reflexes".

- "Such a man turns into a remotely controlled robot. It is the Determinant who brings him home and spends a lot of energy for this purpose. And the guided person has to return Him this energy in other situations. If no accidents are programmed for such a pupil, he will come home alive: Determinant has to switch on automatic control and lead him to the doorsteps of his house so that he will neither be knocked down by a car nor get frozen on his way. As soon as a drunkard crosses the threshold he falls down like a log. And of course, he does not remember anything because his consciousness was switched off."

- "Sometimes while a man is walking he may suddenly fall down. Why? Who makes him fall down? Or it is just an accident?"

- " It is also a planned situation in which a person has to experience senses important for him. That is why Determinant undercuts him in the right place at the right time. The individual who falls down cannot notice this undercut. Very often a man himself cannot understand what happened to him. But in some other similar situation when a man slips down occasionally but his fall is not on the program, then the Determinant is able to hold him up and help him keep his feet. Later on a man may wonder – how did he manage to keep balance and avoid falling down. As a matter of fact, it is not he himself who managed to keep feet but somebody from the Above helped him not to fall over. But for the pupil all those facts remain behind-the-scenes, so to say. Although some believers attribute such actions to Guardian-Angels, however all that belongs to the domain of Determinants."

- "Can Determinant be returned to a man's body if He gets degraded?"

- "Yes, they can, but very seldom or never."

- "And hence a very smart and advanced personality appears amongst people, does not it?"

- "Yes, it does. A man having the soul of a former Determinant is not ordinary in every respect. He will think and act differently as compared to others, because his soul reserves skills acquired in the other world. For ordinary people he will give an impression of being not so much smart as weird because inferior people are not able to appreciate the higher, even a former one."

- "Can you name at least one of such personalities who are amongst people?"

- "No. What will be the use of that for you? And for this person as well? But generally, if we want to find somebody, we shall send a request to the data base which controls movements of souls and knows everything - whereabouts of all people wheresoever they are: in which world, at what place. But this knowledge is useless for the people."

- "Does Determinant keep uninterrupted watch over a man or sometimes resorts to automatic control via the computer?"

- "Determinant does not control his fosterling every minute, He has a lot of other work to do. However as a rule, He controls him half a day, and another half is devoted to other types of work. In day time the behavior of an individual has to be controlled. If he is active or if there is some imminent dangerous or just offset situation, then he has to be watched for longer period dependant on how things are turning out. If a man is calm, then Determinant may allot little time to him and control only the key moments of his life. So the extent of control depends on the character of a man, intensity of his program and physical fitness of the fosterling. At night Determinant may stop watching his pupil if the latter is in good health and his life is in no way endangered. He programs his dreams, connects him to the computer and switches everything to automatic mode, which means that his body will be automatically made up with energy and his dreams will proceed as programmed. Everything is monitored and controlled. Should any disturbances occur, alarm system gets actuated. If the fosterling is physically fit, Determinant may stop watching him at night, having completely attached him for automatic maintenance. But if he is ill, absolutely all processes of energy release, its distribution inside the organism and in subtle bodies shall be closely controlled. And very often health of a patient shall be rehabilitated. A healthy organism requires less care."

- "People often apply to their Heavenly Teachers with requests to help them in this or that matter or situation. Do They help to solve problems?"

- "It depends on the problems and situations. Everything a man is given is programmed and predetermined by his fate. But fate cannot be changed. A man shall understand that the Earth is his school that he is lowered down into the life with a purpose to teach him to resolve his personal problem all by himself overcoming difficulties. In energy plane, resolution of some problem, situation is possible if soul accumulates energy necessary for his transfer to the next stage of development. If a pupil asks to release him from some problem or to resolve some hard situation, then, if he receives such help, his soul will not work to acquire required qualities. It is the same as your repeater – a pupil at school who stays in a form for a second year. In his next life the same situations or problems are repeated so that he can work and acquire the energies he cannot ascend higher without. Of course his request may be met if he is not morally ready to solve his problem, but over the years or in the next life he will have similar problem repeated. He will not be able to get rid of it completely. It will inevitably return to him some day. Therefore it is much better instead of evading problems, try to learn how to resolve them adequately."

- "People think that You are ready to meet any of their requests. Is it true?"

- "Any requests come up to Determinants only and They decide what could be done. If it is a minor request and does not contradict the program, Determinant may execute it himself. If a request is more serious, He shall convey it to His Originator and Manager for them to decide what to do with the given application. If this is the case, time of execution is more extended. But even if the decision is positive, a man should understand that nothing may be given for free. If something is granted, something else is withdrawn. Having received something a suppliant shall work out the debt either in current life or after death. Everybody has to work out their fulfilled desires i.e. to produce energy having the quality equal to quality of the energy which was consumed for accomplishment of his desire."

- "It is clear how a man can work out his debt through situation. And how is payment made after his death?"

- "After death means in the next life. In a new incarnation he will have a huge work to do. He may work hard for a long time and he may receive nothing at all for his labor or he will be given very little money for his work, just enough for survival. And such a man may exclaim, "I work very hard. Why do I get nothing for my work?" He just works out his debt. An individual must reimburse all expenses connected with him, even if it concerns some feelings and not material benefits."

- "And what feelings must a man work out for?"

- "Some people want to be loved. And they ask their Teacher to help them in that. Determinant is able to telepathically implant love or affection for the indicated person. But afterwards an individual who asked for love will have to work out the service provided. Because when the Determinant implants feelings He uses his personal energy, incurs costs. It is those costs that a pupil shall reimburse to him and additionally provide profit margin. This is the accepted procedure."

- "How shall a man actually work out a request like that?"

- "He shall give his Teacher a set of certain energies having produced then in situations. In fact, everything associated with feelings involves consumption of various types of energy, and not one energy type. Therefore various types of energy are subject to be returned. So the Determinant who wants to compensate for his own costs will pull a man through such situations, which will facilitate generation (by the man's organism) of those energies, which the given Determinant lacks and those which he has spent. So a man shall work out just for any infusion (implemented from the Above). Sometimes after death a soul shall work out even insignificant debts in the subtle world."

- "And where is it more difficult to work out – in material world or in subtle world after death?"

- "Everything depends on the soul itself and on the place where it will find itself in order to work out the debt. Man things are important. Some souls are good in that, others – in this. Everything depends on its Level of development. What is easy for one soul may be difficult for the other. "

- "Does Determinant always hear his pupil?"

- "No, not always. If a pupil is at inferior level of development, his mind does not have enough energy to break though and reach the Level of Determinant. Determinant simply keeps watch over such a pupil and guides him under his program. Requests and thoughts of a low-potential pupil are not heard by Determinant. But if such pupil is in church, then his request may also be heard provided that certain ceremonies are adhered to."

- "But still are thoughts of inferior man somehow controlled? He just may plot various crimes."

- "From a low-potential individual relevant information is read out with the help of the Determinant's computer. It reads out from the brain of an individual all data He needs and in this way controls the mind of his fosterling. Besides, He knows his program and those margins which a pupil may approach in his conduct. If situations are dangerous, control is permanent."

- "Does this read-out involve brain-center ring?"

- "No. Information is read out from material brain, and pulse ring is involved in receipt of pulses from Determinant and their transmission to a man."

- "But certain Determinants still can hear requests of some individuals. How can it be explained?"

- "There are several options. They may read them out from the computer or hear them in church via energy channels. Besides, if a pupil has already reached a high level of development, and consequently, has high energy potential, then he (due to the energy of his own mind) may break through to Determinant. They can hear strong energy thoughts."

- "Sometimes a man wants to acquire new knowledge and mentally works in the desired direction, as a result, he receives new information. If this is the case, what kind of connection takes place: to the computer of the Teacher or to the common data bank?"

- "At the expense of hard and continuous work thoughts of a person may break through only to the Determinant's computer. And it is up to Him to decide, whether he shall or shall not respond to the request. They communicate via the computer."

- "While certain information is transmitted from below, from a man to Determinant, is it corrupted? There may be a lot of disturbances on its way."

- "No. Information, which is transmitted from below, is not corrupted. In this respect communication is properly tuned. The field you have in your material world is so coarse that it serves as a protection of subtle mental forms."

- "Do many scientists receive new information from Determinant via the computer?"

- "Yes. Some scientists, inventors, poets and many other intellectuals, political and social figures break through the channel of communication with their Determinant at the expense of power of their own thoughts."

- "To scientists information is sent without any requests on their part. Why does Determinant decide to send them new information or ideas?"

- "For advance of mankind from time to time some new ideas and knowledge are required to be introduced into society. And to properly adopt certain specific information one shall be competent in the given field of knowledge. Therefore the most advanced individuals are selected, as well as those persons who due to their hard work in the given field deserve encouragement in the form of sending them something new. And via the Determinant's computer he receives ideas which will be needed by his people in the near future. But sometimes it happens otherwise. For example, a Teacher sees that his pupil is nailed, has come to a dead lock, and that resulted in some unwanted psychic changes in him. And so a Teacher sends him some new information or idea in order to drive him from the dead-lock. It stimulates his development and he continues to improve further. So the decision to give or not to give a man some new information depends on the pupil's program and Determinant's decision."

- "Well, why and how does it depend on the program?"

- "A program always prescribes progress of a pupil up to a certain limit. If he fails to reach it on his way he receives new information. If he does, he will receive nothing new beyond the information allocated to him. But he may be involved in creative activities or get engaged in something else. That is to provide his further development but already in some other field of knowledge matching the same Level of development, they will try to change his type of activity. It means that accumulation of different energy types of one and the same Level takes place."

- "A mid-level man just as an inferior man can not break through to his Determinant via communication channel, can't he?"

- "Yes, he can. Because such soul has already accumulated in it sufficient amount of emotional energy. There is one more way to get connected to Determinant – it can be achieved through stresses. Nervous agitation, strong emotions accompanying emotional upsets may cause energy outburst. An inferior man has not got such reserve, he has not had time to accumulate it. Therefore his emotions will have the character of rough inferior outbursts spreading in nether layers of the Earth and not being able to rise higher. As for a mid-level man, he has already accumulated a sufficient margin of higher level energy, which (in case of emotional stress) is able to rush upwards in a flash-like manner and to break through the channel connected to Determinant. He may start hearing his pupil directly. Of course, this process itself is complicated. A transmission gear chain shall operate. Operation is started with a strong nervous impulse generated in the brain, strong emotions impart great starting energy to the man's upset impulse enabling the signal to reach the computer of Determinant. What a Determinant sees at this moment is a sort of red lamp lighting up. He checks the situation and helps his fosterling to handle it or prompts in a telepathic manner how to avoid it."

- "Do such shocks make a man's chakras open? May some superpowers open under such conditions?"

- "No. Stresses do not result in opening of chakras and superpowers in the sense people imagine that. It requires hard work on self-improvement in terms of energy accumulation. If an individual failed to structure himself properly during previous incarnations, no stress can help; if he did manage to do that, stresses may serve as an additional factor for connection of the mechanism, created by an individual over many of his lives."

- "Is a man always given an opportunity to get connected to his Determinant through stresses?"

- "No, it is not an opportunity; it's a chance. Situations, resulting in stresses experienced by a man, are given to him for acquirement of certain qualities, for accumulation of relevant types of energy in his matrix."

- "Are there any other methods of breaking through a communication channel to his Determinant? For example, may he be able to break through to Him by means of intensive work?"

- "Method of intensive work does not always give the intended effect. A mid-level man is not able to achieve that because his energy potential is not great enough for that. Being hypnotized, a man can be connected to the computer, but this is fraught with grave consequences for the man himself and for his mind."

- "When an order-pulse is sent from the high Level downwards, is it accompanied by consumption of great amount of energy?"

- "No, it isn't. If it comes from above it means that higher potential goes through weak potential structures, and here considerable energy consumption is not required. Physical matter has weak potential."

- "Does it mean that if a pulse goes from the bottom upwards, energy consumption is greater?"

- "Yes, it is true. Upward pulsing requires greater energy consumption from a man. An individual of weak energy potential is able to produce only weak pulses which can hardly reach higher energy structures having great potential. That is why such a pulse has to be additionally energized."

- "Does it mean that while breaking through to Determinants channelers consume a great amount of their own energy?"

- "Naturally. A very great amount of energy. Therefore such channelings derange their constitution. But We help them to get recovered afterwards."

- "But at the same time you also send energy to the Earth via channelers. Does this energy rehabilitate them?"

- "This energy is intended for the planet, it is of other quality. But a man needs energy of his own range. But as a channeler works for Us, We provide him with energy he needs after the channelings."

- "Determinant possesses more powerful energy than a man does. Does He accordingly resort to hypnotization of people in certain situations?"

- "Hypnosis is deemed equal to pulse sending as far as the objective of achievement is concerned. Hypnosis makes a man do what Determinant wants. But a pulse brings about the same: it makes a pupil do what is required."

- "But if a pupil is about to perform actions breaching the program, and Determinant has to prevent him from such actions, can He make a pupil behave properly using hypnosis?"

- "No. In such cases He sends him a powerful pulse, and situation gets improved."

- "Does Teacher communes with his pupil only with the help of pulses or also based on telepathy?"

- "Except for a few individuals people are not ready yet for telepathic communication. They have not managed to develop themselves properly, although it was planned to be achieved as early as by the year two thousand. Therefore further on communication with pupils will be carried out via computers and with the help of pulses sent by them."

- "People possess methods on materialization of their thoughts and desires. According to these methods, a man must vigorously want something and imagine this in his mind's eye. In such a way his desire allegedly comes true, and after some time he gets what he wants. Can that be true? And how may such kind of materialization occur?"

- "Naturally, desires do not come true through miracles. It is the same as a request. No dreamland materialization exists, everything is done based on situations, building of relationships and energy distributions, and not though certain tricks and miracles as a man used to think. Longing for something, for example, a desire to purchase a car, constant imagining of that something is deemed a kind of meditation, which helps Determinant to hear his pupil. At first Determinant debates a matter in his mind – does he need this car, will it facilitate his advanced development? And if He decides that the desired thing may help his pupil in some knowledge acquirements or in something else, then He conveys this to the Above – to Managers. He asks them to meet the request of his fosterling. The Higher consider the petition received from below and make a decision – to give or not to give. It is similar to a request of a man praying for health in church. Everything is decided similarly. And if a decision is positive, Determinant starts to place a man to situations, which help him to translate his dream into reality. To be more exact, for this purpose He uses the situations embedded in the program, and does not arrange new ones. Everything goes through situations, via other people."

- "How do magicians achieve materialization of some things?"

- "This is the work of a certain System, which is close to material world and which uses for this work some essences of subtle plane*. They may help the magician. Besides, a human magician may have a very strong and influential Determinant, higherthan many other Determinants. He may involve them in arrangement of some joint miraculous functions. Magicians themselves are very strong personalities possessing great energetics. Their thoughts are very powerful therefore their signals sent upwards are immediately heard by Determinant, which helps Him to quickly respond to requests or commands of a magician. It is a synchronous operation that is done from below and from above. But there are also a lot of tricks which can be performed by the magician himself due to his powerful energetics. But they are insignificant."

- "Is it useless for people to learn magic?"

- "An ordinary man will never learn to be a magician. This should be either a special spectacular program or a man shall develop in himself high energetics through hard labor, and only after that the Higher from the Above will send him an earth teacher and start teaching him fundamentals of magic. Diligence and persistence in pursue of the set goal is always appreciated by the Higher."

- "How can a man enhance his energetics?"

- "People are given a lot of various methods: for example, through some breathing, meditative or physical exercises."

- "But can superior magicians work without their Determinant, at the expense of their own powerful energetics? You say they can perform certain tricks."

- "No. Usually, this is just a joint work. Tri ks themselves refer to the category of juggles – namely, it is performance of certain trifles aimed at demonstration of one's unusual capabilities."

- "Hence, it is Determinants who do miracles and not people, isn't it?"

- "A man himself is up to nothing. Teachers help him to perform miracles. However miracles are done not to entertain people but also for certain purposes. Every miracle pursues a specific objective. And techniques of the subtle plane are very often involved in that."

- "Sometimes in the sky above the Earth flame writings could be seen: they warned people about oncoming disasters. How were those writings produced?"

- "It is a kind of hologram. Determinants produced them on special devices and sent to the relevant point in space."

- "Were those devices deemed computers?"

- "No. To be more exact, those writings were produced on other devices by the Determinant of the Earth based on His own method. The Earth knows everything that happens to people and what is going to happen in future. And it is the Determinant of the planet itself who warns about oncoming events. This leads people to speculation and unravel of strange mysteries."

How Does Determinant Handle Energies

- "Where does Determinant take energy for his personal needs from? In fact, to do something in his world He should have certain energy reserves."

- "He does not take energy, he accumulates it at the expense of the activity, He was involved in before his teaching job. Before becoming a Determinant He existed in some other form and was engaged in some kind of work. As a result, He made some reserves. It means that before becoming a Teacher and guiding pupils He should have accumulated energies of various types based on certain methods. It takes place at inferior Level. There He also developed himself for a long time, came through the phases of education and in the process of his life journey made certain reserves, which later on he started to use in his teaching activities. For example, now at the given stage of work, Determinants also are making new reserves in the form of energy, which they will need for future development. Later, when they finish the life of Determinants, having enhanced their Level, They will use the energy accumulated at present at the higher level of their development. Hence energy reserves are always made by Entity while its progressive development."

- "Does He spend energies on the man, other than on himself?"

- "On the man the Determinant spends lower range energies. However since He went through inferior stages, His inventory includes a lot of various energy types - both higher energies and lower ones. However if He does not have some required energy, He borrows it from others. But after that He shall work out the debt."

- "Does the program of Determinant prescribe what types of energies He shall accumulate or do those types depend on himself?"

- "Every Determinant has an individual program, which plans everything that He shall accumulate. Some part of energy is accumulated by Him through his own actions in his world and another part is acquired during his direct work with his pupils when He makes them live out certain situations"

- "How does He receive energy from situations, which are lived out by the man?"

- "The man is connected to Determinant who possesses a relevant technique of energy accumulation. Energy can be received as a result of human behavior and emotions. In any situations a complex of structures in the man are forced to work: both the material body, which is capable of not only mechanical actions but also induction of various emotions as well as work involvement of subtle structures, which provide further processing and refining of energies produced by the body. Material body produces some types of energy, which are cruder; feelings and emotions generate subtler types of energy. Brainwork also provides its own spectrum. And Determinant collects all these energies for himself."

- "When the man is engaged in physical work, does not the energy get transmitted to other energy types and dissipated in the environment?"

- "Naturally, some part of it is lost, but most of its subtle constituents are fed into the Determinant's energy collector, and with time losses become less because of constant improvement of collection mechanism."

- "It is clear if we speak of the man who works and produces energy. But if a pupil does not work and just fuss about, what processes take place in energy plane? In fact, actions may be different as far as their quality is concerned."

- "If the man is fussing about, certain emotions and feelings, which are not apparent even for himself, get switched on. Mechanical movements and feelings generate energy of optional types, which is also accumulated by the Determinant of the given person. In that case it is the quality of generated energy that gets changed. If the man performed those actions without being fussy, quality would be absolutely different. Feelings tinge actions in this way or another, thereby they modify energies generated by people."

- "But is the energy received as a result of fussy actions useful or is it considered defective?"

- "All types of energy are useful. Any energy is made use of. We have waste-free production."

- "How is energy distributed in a situation with several individuals participating in it? For example, one man does some good to another. How is energy distributed among those who do good and those who that good is done to?"

- "The Determinant whose pupil commits kindliness gets more. And the Determinant of the pupil who kindliness is done to receives nothing because the good is returned to his fosterling by karma. His pupil receives energy together with things and money as a reward for his preceding deed. He is repaid karmic debts but he himself is doing nothing at the moment; he does not perform actions, which can produce something. He replenishes the energy that he once consumed. But a man doing the good performs positive action, which produces a lot of energy. Good always produces great amounts of energy."

- "And if, for example, the situation is different: parents take pains to educate an undiligent child, giving him all their buoyancy. Whose Determinant receives this energy?"

- "Naturally, it is the Determinant of the child who receives the energy of love, warmth and affection."

- "And what do Determinants of parents receive from the given situation?"

- "Everything that mother and father have to endure growing and educating their child generates energy of worry, which is of higher quality. This energy is accumulated by their Determinants."

- "Who of them receives more: Determinant of a child or Determinants of parents?"

- "It depends. If parents calmly tolerate tricks of their child, they do not give away their energy to the other Determinant. But if they start scolding him, the situation slides into vampirism – and the child's Determinant takes more energy for himself. Those who provoke quarrels always take energy for themselves. And it is not only the man who may provoke quarrels but also another Determinant in order to get some energy from the other person. Therefore children shall be raised in a calm manner. However, basically, the way family is designed presupposes that those who are superior in their development shall always share their personal energy with the inferior members."

- "The Determinant who guides an inferior man, for example, an alcoholic, gets little energy from him and His energy source suffers losses. How can He replenish it in such circumstances?"

- "The program prepared for the next life of former alcoholic provides for compensation of this loss, and this very Determinant will guide that very soul in such a way as to make it compensate him for the lost, under-collected energy."

- "Hence energy is compensated at the expense of the next life, isn't it?"

- "Yes."

- "But this alcoholic may experience great sufferings also in this life and through them repay his debt. Is it so?"

- "Everything depends on how much he owes. Is repayment of debts in the present life comparable with those losses suffered through the fault of his. Sometimes alcoholics lose so much energy due to alcohol that in present life they are not able to compensate those losses through sufferings. They are not able to endure those sufferings because their moral courage has already been broken by alcohol. And in the next incarnation they will be placed in other circumstances and be guided under another, more severe program."

- "What type of work with the man gives the Determinant most energy for his personal energy source: through his suffering, illnesses or intellectual efforts?"

- "Intellectual activity gives a lot for development of people, but little for Determinant. Generally, energy is drawn from living out the situations involving activation of all feelings, emotions and mind of an individual. Situations arouse his feelings, initiate all his structures. Therefore Teacher receives a maximum amount of energy from situations involving suffering of his pupil."

- "What methods does Determinants apply for accumulation of energy for themselves, besides the method of getting it from people?"

- "They are engaged in programming within the limits of their Level. Thus, they program dreams, supply and consumption of energy. But the key activity with them is creative work. When they are free from their work with pupils they may be engaged in creative activities, enhance their data base and so on. There are a lot of activities with them, which can be hardly imagined by people due to differences of forms of your existences."

- "What does their creativity include? What can they create?"

- "Creativity matches their world and their life. Every world possesses individual creative processes, certain tendencies. Here creativity is always manifold and it is not inferior to earthly creativity as far as the number of styles is concerned. The higher the world, the more opportunities it offers for creative manifestations. And all this leads to accumulation of various energies."

- "During the current transition period human relations are very complicated. Does not it mean that every Determinant tries to gather as much as possible energy for himself?"

- "Yes. It is true. Many souls will be decoded, and Determinant tries somehow to accumulate energy, which can make up for his power spent on frustrated pupils. Besides, they also go through rearrangements therefore they want to accumulate a maximum of energy of various types needed for further work. The greater their energy reserve, the greater work they will be able to perform. Actually Determinant receives energy not only from his own fosterling, but also from those who he mixes with."

- "What is energy interception from another pupil based on?"

- "In fact, power interchange takes place."

- "Are there any special rules prescribing Determinants –who is allowed to take energy and who energy can be taken from?"

- "No. Such rules are not available. It is a natural process. Determinant takes energy only from his own fosterlings."

- "How then do They take energy from those people who their fosterling mix with?"

- "Everything is coordinated by programs. Determinant takes energy not from all those people his pupil forges relationship with, but only from those who owe Him. He receives his debts to himself. Currently everybody receives debts. If a Determinant some time ago lent some energy to another Determinant or did something for him, then taking energy from the other Determinant's pupil in a certain situation he returns to himself the type of energy which he once borrowed him. If, for example, He teaches versification to some else's pupil because his personal Determinant is not complement in that, then afterwards through certain situation He will return everything due to Him. And nobody takes energy from anyone just for no reason. Everything is well-reasoned. But everybody return the debts."

- "May it so happen that those Determinants who are less conscience will try to squeeze as much energy as possible from their fosterlings?"

- "We shall not put it like that. They can't have more conscience or less. At one and the same Level all Determinants are equally conscience, have similar quality. And if They didn't possess it, The would not get to the first Level; on the contrary, they would continue to get developed below. Conscience is deemed already a moral framework of behavior of an individual. And nobody having low conscience is able to come to my Hierarchy."

- "Does anybody in the world of Determinants keep watch over adequacy of their behavior?"

- "Naturally. It is those who stand higher who keep the watch."

- "Are there any effective laws in Their world?"

- "The laws, which I partially gave also to you, are in force at all Levels in My Hierarchy. They are deemed general laws of development and existence given for any creatures whose souls have reached a certain level of maturity. But, of course, elsewhere in the worlds there are also special laws intrinsic in every specific world."

- "How are these general laws applied at the Levels of Your Hierarchy?"

- "Mankind is just passing the phase of initiation into Higher Hierarchical laws. And Hierarchy itself has its own principle of their application. At nether Levels their power is maximum. The higher the world, the lesser subjection to the laws, the wider discretion. Because at

Higher Levels the relations are absolutely different. The laws are at the root of behavior of every Higher Personality therefore all their activity bases on high level consciousness and self-control. Laws are impressed in Them as the key mechanism of subsequent activity in Higher spheres. Compliance of the entire Behavior with the Higher requirements becomes arbitrary. And this is the key principle of development."

- "While guiding a man throughout his life, the Determinant is invariably involved in manipulation of energies: he takes some of them for himself and others are drawn down to his pupils. Is it true?"

- "Yes, it is. He exists in permanent circulation of energies, and this is accepted as a basis of his work. But He does not work with two or three energy types – He handles dozens of them. All these energies are stored in His energy collector, but they are not mixed there but arranged type- and level-wise."

- "Information about spontaneous inflammation of people was recorded earlier on the Earth. Was it associated just with energy supply to a pupil by the Determinant?"

- "Yes, it was. Those were special people. They translated Our energy to Earth. But some of them were not provided with refrigerant, a certain protective gear. For this reason, energy failed to be balanced and as a result, they were burnt off in material plane in response to supply of great amount of energy. Sometimes ordinary people got also burnt off due to incompetence of inexperienced Determinant: he sent down such great amount of energy which provoked inflammation of people. Subtle energies are able to burn off everything, they are very powerful. Therefore standard amounts of energy to be sent down to the Earth have been prescribed."

- "And did their souls fly out instantly or did those people suffer torments similar to pains felt by those who were burnt by material fire?"

- "No. Everything happened instantly. A man did not have time to feel pain before his soul was out and flew away. Usually such people translated great energy flows from the time of their birth, but everything was normal until some disturbances arose. Determinant didn't notice or didn't have time to correct them therefore inflammations happened. But the main cause of inflammation is disorders in material body."

- "But then spontaneous inflammation may be thought as a result of improper work of Determinant."

- "Yes, it may be considered to be his fault. But such Determinants were punished for that. If your channeler didn't have minus refrigerants, she would have been exposed to similar danger. But We took due account of our former errors."

- "Currently very powerful energy is supplied to the Earth. Do people have to take special steps to be able to receive and distribute it inside themselves in subtle bodies?"

- "This energy will be controlled by their Determinants. People will not be able to do anything themselves. However usually inflammations happen to people guided by Determinants who are not experienced enough."

- "Does a man anyhow depend on energy reserve of Determinant?"

- "Naturally, such dependence exists because when Determinant accepts a pupil to be guided He shall also prepare for this work His energy reserve in compliance with the needs of this individual. One soul may require these types of energy for its guidance and the other one will need other types. The same with quantity: one soul will require heavy energy inputs, while the other – lesser ones. Hence there is a dependence on energy reserve, however it is not always so."

- "Is the following condition possible: a Determinant has large energy reserve but his fosterling has low activity level?"

- "Yes, such case is possible. Everything depends on the pupil's program. An individual may be passive, he may consume small quantities of energy but it does not mean that his Determinant's energy reserve is small. However, more often this dependence is otherwise: the larger energy reserve of the Determinant, the higher level of activity of this person in his life."

- "But there is a whole category of low-level people."

- "You see, they may not be active in the society but very active in their own life, in creativity. And the latter may be very significant even if compared with some action-oriented persons. Hence in some groups of people activeness is manifested in creativity."

Human Diseases

Interview with Devil:

- "Are diseases of people somehow related to those energies which they shall produce?"

- "Yes. Closely. Disease is deemed an output of energy of certain quality and in certain quantity."

- "Why are certain types of diseases pre-programmed for people?" Is it done by Your programmers?"

- "Yes, my programmers do that. It was Me who developed this System. Diseases depend on conditions of energy indebtedness of a person. Zodiac-wise disposition to those diseases is given to people so that they can learn to watch their organisms and make progress in self-knowledge. For many centuries people have been trying to fight their own ailments, as a result they developed medicine, biomedical engineering, pharmacology and many other branches of human knowledge and industry. Nowadays people study their energetics, subtle structures. So diseases facilitate their progress. Any pain forces everybody to advance, and excellent health basically leads to degradation."

- "People have twelve zodiac signs. Does that mean that they produce twelve basic types of energy?"

- "Yes, if you mean basic ones."

- "Is Determinant able to turn a severe violent attack of some disease of his pupil for weak pain extended in time? In this case an acute, insufferable pain is changed for small portions, but the disease becomes more prolonged. It is easier for a person to stand pain, and due to extension of process Determinant will get from his pupil everything He needs."

- "Yes, it is possible. But everything depends on the man's program. If he is planned to understand something through violent pain, this pain will not be changed for a mild one for him."

- "For the man pain is an alarm signal warning him about some failures in his body. As for You, pain served as a source of delight when You were in material body. How did You manage to derive pleasure from it?"

- "It depended on the qualities of My soul," replied Devil. "Only a high-potential Personality like Me is able to derive pleasure from pain."

- "But masochists also try to derive pleasure from it. Are they also high-potential personalities?"

Devil did not like such undeserved exaltation of such small common people. Therefore He gave an arrogant reply:

---

* see the dictionary;)* - note of the author.

- "No. It will take them thousands of years to reach in their development the level of high-potential personalities. Although they alsocan enjoy their own pain, with them it is mental abnormality."

- "Does any energetics of pain exist?"

- "Of course, it does. It is just energetics of pain what I based on while I was developing My potential."

(Devil managed to accumulate energetics of pain in great amounts within dozens of lives which he lived out in material body and to turn into a powerful energy Personality having changed over from the material plane to the subtle one. He was able to get to the heart of pain itself, to conceive its energy nature and to skillfully use it for his own purposes. However, this method of energy accumulation at the expense of enjoyment of pain and perverse comprehension of its essence* is deemed a path of ascension appropriate to Devil and not to God.)* Then we asked:

- "Is the energy of pain different from energy of diseases themselves?"

- "Of course, it is. Pain is the energy of torments and disease is the energy of many qualities."

Interview with God:

- "Why is disposition to diseases programmed for the man?"

- "Because human organism shall be brought to a certain mode of operation, enabling it to produce the types of energy prescribed by his program. The energy production function is mandatory for a life of a specific human being. The program prescribes how much energy shall a man produce and of which quality. Everybody has an individual task. There are basic energies, which shall be generated by a man, and also there are incidental energies, which are produced additionally as a result of behavioral choice in situations. Incidental energies are the result of formation of additional quality types. Diseases always give planned energies, and behavioral choice in situations gives casual ones. But speaking about energy production by the man you should not forget the main thing: he generates energy not only for Determinant and other needs of Hierarchical Systems but also for his own soul. Energy is supplied to the outside – to the Teacher, and inside – to matrix.

While running a personal program, a person enriches his own soul with various high-quality energies."

- "In normal conditions organ produces energy of one quality, and in disease state – of the other. Do diseases enhance the quality of produced energy?"

- "Diseases give pure energies. However different diseases bring different vibrations and different energies."

- "Does an ailing organ generate the same type of energy, only purer?"

- "Yes, much more purer, than through situations. That is why sometimes Determinant may replace a situation with a short-term disease of his fosterling."

- "But if some organ in a human body is very unsound, doesn't it result in its destruction?"

- "No, it is not quite so. Even in diseased conditions organs can work for a time prescribed by the general program. Everything is defined by the Manager of a person based on dozens of requirements to be met by his future life. A man participates in complicated cosmic circulation of energies therefore every cell of his body is designed for complex operation in coordination with a lot of cosmic objects. Just as any particle of his body in its work is connected with the organism as a whole, so is the man himself like a cell of a more large-scale cosmic body is linked to It within the integrated entirety of its work. Therefore everything in him (in the man) is designed with due account of needs and demands of this Great organism. Thus, any disease is a certain request of micro-constituent of the Cosmos, as it is, for energy which He needs for provision of life activity. A man shall not hang up about pain and disease, he shall understand that is the operation mode of constituents of his own organism. But it is a man himself who shall choose this mode through pursue or failure to pursue his program by either conscientiously sticking to procedure prescribed by his fate or swerving from the correct path to follow the way of pleasures and degradation. People themselves destine their future diseases through their forms of behavior at present time. If a man properly executes his personal program, he may be absolutely healthy."

- "But a lot of inferior people may have excellent health."

- "Requirements to be met by people who have just embarked on the course of evolution are more conservative than requirements for sophisticated souls. Inferiors have simple programs, which they are able to execute quite adequately. Sophisticated souls have complicated programs which are difficult to be executed, consequently, a greater number of defects and errors is possible. Anyhow, everybody is destined to have diseases: some people fell ill at early stages of their lives, others – at later periods. Absence of diseases may result from right living."

- "Determinant controls his pupil for correct execution of his program. But does He look after his health? Does that come within his duties?"

- "Determinant carries out full control over his fosterling including his health as well. He has various functions. He takes part in birth of a man, in the process of shaping child's body, in introduction of soul to this body, embeds defects in the organs of a child's body if it is in the program of future development or, on the contrary, shapes vocal cords of the throat in such a way as to enable a child to become a singer in future. All this is done by Determinant. But after birth the child's organism is constantly monitored. The computer contains data on normal state of organism and its programmed conditions i.e. prescribed by the program. The data base is updated to include all new changes which occur in it with time."

- "If a man's health has to be corrected during his lifetime, who does Determinant assign with this task?"

- "Usually He does it Himself or helps his fosterling to find an experienced doctor to treat him or finds some books containing description of useful practices. But as far as medicine is concerned, sometimes it gives opposite affect, when doctors in their trying to cure a patient inflict such harm to him that then Determinant has to work very hard to remedy consequences endangering his life, and, consequently, exposing the man's program to a risk of non-execution. But He cannot allow that."

- "Diseases of organs are preplanned in compliance with the development program. But we are aware that diseases are needed for generation of certain types of energy. Who is the main consumer of this energy:the man himself or Determinant?"

- "Everything is interconnected. Karmic debts of the pupil are taken into account, and production of energy of the required type is subject to the program of his Teacher. It is He who lacks such energy as well. Determinant also works under his personal program computed with due account of program of a person who will be able to provide Him with needed amount of energy of adequate quality. For example, let us take a partitioned container. Some of its sections are filled up, and others are empty. The task of Determinant is to fill up the empty sections of the container with contents of relevant quality through performance of some work. Quality is provided by a disease of this or that organ of human body because every individual consumes his own type of energy and, hence, produces also the relevant quality. But this task the Determinant receives from the Above. If a man is healthy, the he has to produce some other energies through situations, feelings, thinking."

- "Does character of a person have any effect on diseases of his organs, as it is stated by astrologists?"

- Yes, it does. The man is constructed in coordination with planets, and he has to acquire a certain set of qualities, and hence, certain types of energy, both for the Determinant and for his own matrix. Let me illustrate this with the help of the following analogy. For example, a man has to acquire seven rainbow dyes, six dyes are already available, and one is missing. He has to fill this vacuum. Zodiac signs, connected with certain organs enable them to produce energy of relevant types. But the missing type is prescribed by the program, and subject to this, the birth of an individual is linked to the relevant zodiac sign. As a result, a man will have or may have a disease or some disorders in the organ, where the energy he lacks is produced. And such organ cannot be cured because everything is prescribed by the program. However adequate state of such an organ may be maintained for a very long time. Disposition to a certain disease does not mean that it will severely fail in its work just since the day of birth or since childhood. However it will remain weak, unable to withstand overloads. Due to this, the man will have to lead a special way of life: e.g. keep a diet or breathe on fresh air. It is also possible that this organ will work normally throughout the whole life of a man but in later years the organ which corresponds to zodiac sign will be the first to fail."

- "But why are many people predicted to have specific diseases based on their zodiac? For example, if it is "Virgo", does it mean that millions of people born under this constellation will have diseases of intestines?"

- "For their potential such souls shall produce exactly such energy type in order to ascend higher later on. The entire mankind is broken down into categories and it depends who is referred and where. Accumulation of totality of all twelve zodiac types of energies results in ascension to next Level. But a man may be acquiring a single quality not within one life time but throughout several lives because the quality shall give a certain potential. Therefore everybody is involved in development of certain products. I.e. the man himself needs the energy of the given type in great quantities. Therefore accumulation gets extended for many years in the form of functional disease. However while producing this energy for himself at the same time a pupil supplies it also to his Determinant as if he shares it with Him."

- "But then we shall not fight zodiacal diseases, shan't we?"

- "You shall learn how to maintain you health in normal conditions in order to support adequate existence. Anything may ache but one shall learn to suppress pains and control one's state. This is always possible. But if one accepts everything "as it is" doing nothing to treat the disease, then it can be neglected so that the processes may become irreversible, to the extent of lifespan shortening. Every disease contains a certain inconsistency: it is needed but it shall be fought against. Disease has two key objectives: make the man produce what is needed and teach him to fight against what is not needed. Therefore people shall have a rational approach to it."

- "Nowadays people have brain cancer more often than before. Brain tumors are diagnosed with many patients. Why are people doomed to such disease?"

- "Brain diseases as, by the way, some other diseases, are related to investigation carried out by the Medical System. You see, development of human beings fell behind to a great extent. Brain investigation identifies causes of this retardation, particularly physiological ones. Possible potential of human being is being determined. Research and experiments are underway. Brain of a man of sixth race must be very much improved. Therefore the work on extension of its functionalities is in progress."

- "Is this brain disease associated with man's program?"

- "With some people it is not, but with others it is. Currently we live during the period of transition from one race to another. So some programs are reduced earlier. But there are people who are destined to go through medical research from the onset. It means that this is also their karma. They are placed at disposal of Medical System starting from a certain period of their lives. And it is up to Medical System to decide what diseases shall be inculcated and what cells of organism shall be investigated. Such experiential man is governed by the same Determinant, who controls his disease. Medical System works in cooperation with Him pursuing its own goals. Everything is aimed at improvement of functioning of human organism in future. Cancer cells are very important for research. Many tumors result from high exposure doses, from increased solar activity and radiation. Human cells try to withstand it and as a result, they work out special conditions resistant to increased radiation. Those conditions are used for creation of novel organics, novel cell, which will serve a basis for construction of new bio-structure, resistant to high solar activity and general increased energetics of the Earth. People will be able to exist (without serious consequences for them) at very high radiation levels and in conditions of increased energy fluxes coming from the Cosmos."

- "Nowadays new diseases are diagnosed with people and animals. What are they originated from?"

- "Our programmers concern themselves with this. It means that there are individual programmers specializing in diseases of people and animals. They prepare programs for course of new diseases, implement them, carry out monitoring, investigate the influence of new energy on the function of cell and on its mutations. They try to bring a cell to a higher energy potential because with time matter shall be able to withstand exposure to a more powerful soul. The matter of material body itself shall reach the next-higher order level. It is included in practical developments of Medical System. Its departments are assigned specific tasks, funds are allocated and groups of people and animals subject to experiments are identified. Work with them is carried out on a subtle plane. A man may either not notice it or feel their implantation as a prick, as some unpleasant sensation."

- "But Determinant always knows that his pupil is under experiment, does not He?"

- "Of course, He does. He knows everything. Medical System itself never does anything on its own initiative. If sometimes anybody needs to be punished for depravity, then upon the request of Determinant first the possibility of such punishment is considered Above, and after that instructions are given to Medical System, and it, for example, may communicate AIDS to him or other similar disease. All epidemics begin from them (Medical System)*. At first virus is introduced to one or several individuals and from them it spreads further identifying a chain of depraved connections."

- "Did Researchers involved in investigation of human body work as doctors previously?"

- "Yes, they did. They have studied material body as good as your medicine enabled them to do that. But, of course, earthly knowledge of physical matter proves to be insufficient and incomplete although they were hard-working pupils. Therefore the souls of former doctors (while their existence in a subtle world) continue their improvement working with material body of human beings and animals. Here they have other prospects available for new research of the same body and for acquirement of more profound knowledge about human organism."

- "Do blood-strokes and heart attacks happen not by themselves but are initiated by Determinants?"

- "Yes, they are. Your guess is true."

- "How does it happen?"

- "When organism is in a certain state, that is when it is predisposed to such stroke, then this is done with the help of computer. However everything occurs subject to the program of an individual."

- "May death come when Determinant does not expect it to happen, kind of inadvertently?"

- "Yes, it may."

- "In what cases does it happen?"

- Murders, suicides. A person may decide so by virtue of freedom of choice given to him."

- "And can people die of diseases unexpectedly for Determinant?"

- "No. Any disease is monitored and its course is displayed on the screen of computer in every tiny detail. Every organ has a digital pattern (see fig. 1). Identical figures indicate sound conditions. Other digital values will indicate abnormalities and severity of illness. Specific digital dependence indicates extent of abnormality in this or that part."

- "What is the procedure of treatment of a patient by Determinant?"

- Computer displays the organism as a whole, and first of all general areas of abnormality are identified with due account of quality of energetics*. Comparison is made against standard parameters of healthy body. Identification of areas is followed by investigation of severity of organ damage: their parts are studied at cellular and molecule levels.

Relevant digital patterns characterize severity of damage of organs and systems. Energy of appropriate type is sent to identified areas: they are made up with energy. Unwanted energies may be withdrawn. Basically Determinant manipulates digits and energies, identifies which chemical components are lacking in the organ. Therefore He sends pulses to his fosterling explaining him what herbs or drugs he should take.

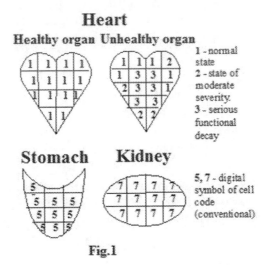

Fig.1

Sometimes somebody starts to give advice to a patient as to what drugs he should take and what advanced methods apply. It means that his Determinant through other Determinants and people tries to help his fosterling with just material remedies. If those methods help, He will not squander energy from his own reserves. Besides, material body is designed so that to have the only energy does not suffice for it. It also needs certain chemical and physical components for its recovery. Therefore if the organism lacks them, Determinant has nothing to construct with. Everything shall be combined in appropriate interrelations. But help from the Above is offered only within the framework of the program. Therefore Determinant may disable some parts and recover others."

- "While contemplating the work of Determinant we can see that, on the one hand, in case His fosterling has some unhealthy organ, He spends His energy on its recovery and maintenance, but, on the other hand, He also receives energy of subtler quality from this very organ. Does He spend more energy than He receives or vice versa?"

- "Principally, He receives more than spends. This is provided by the program: how much to spend and how much to receive, everything is calculated. No deviations from the program are made. The organ is made up with energy of one quality, then this energy is converted by this organ, which generates another range of frequencies collectively with the energy of material body. Conversion* and circulation of energies take place. For advancement of development the added value of production shall always override expenses."

- "Can the Medical System help people?"

- "If someone has an important mission, and death of this person as a result of disease or injury of his body in an accident may interrupt many connections with others, and Determinant fails to cope with treatment of his fosterling, then He may apply to Medical System and ask them to help Him support his pupil."

- "Do Determinants themselves fall ill sometimes? And who treats them then?"

- "Everybody can fall ill. Every Level of existence assumes some failures, damages of structures which shall be subject to recovery. Every world has specific types of ailments. As for Determinants, their world also has some diseases, typical for their form and environment. To some extent everybody shall be able to self-recover and to maintain oneself in normal conditions.

For their form of existence there is a special reserve of the so called "remedial" energy. It is special energy, which complies with their physiological constitution. People for their recovery require one type of energy and They need absolutely different energy type. In their world there are such common reserves of remedial energy kept in dedicated depositories. Should a need arise, they take from the depositories the type of energy they need for their own recovery. Depositary contains a certain amount of energy required for every Determinant, i.e. everything is provided and calculated in advance. However if Determinant behaves properly and does not fall ill, His reserve remains untouched. But if Determinant falls ill i.e. He starts to lack energy of some type, then He takes it from the above depository. But afterwards He will have to replenish this energy through his work and return it to the depository. Such are the principles of Their life."

- "Is every Determinant capable of self-treatment?"

- "Not always. Sometimes they may lack knowledge needed for self-recovery, and in such cases they get help from Medical System Entities who specialized in their Level. Human beings are treated by lower Entities, and Determinants –by higher Entities. Medical System treats all those who need their services in My Hierarchy, but it is not also for free but for relevant equivalents."

- "Do diseases of inferior personalities differ from those of higher ones?"
- "Diseases facilitate development of inferiors and hamper development of the higher."

Participation of Determinant in Birth and Death of Human Beings

- "Does Heavenly Teacher start to educate his pupil from the moment of his birth?"
- "No, much more earlier. He starts to manage the soul of his future pupil prior to formation of his material body. Then He finds a couple who He wants to provide material body for his future fosterling. And if this couple is stubbornly reluctant to have children, He looks for another couple whose physical parameters are acceptable for the body of his child. For this very reason They do not approve of abortions because for Him abortions cause difficulties in selection of parents for introduction of soul of the future fosterling. The child shall be physically built in a certain manner i.e. to meet specific physiological characteristics which can be given by some couples but cannot be provided by others. But if future parents choose to have a child, then Determinant continues His work through participation in construction of his material body and control over formation of his organs. For the entire period of nine months Teacher patronizes his future pupil. So He carries on huge preparations before his birth."
- "Why does a male cell merge with a female one during conception?"
- "Cell fusion is based on conception process control performed by Determinant via the computer. Determinant of the future human being controls cell fusion and formation of child's organism. Genetic code of cells provides the program of material body formation. But it does not mean anything by itself if at the moment of conception Determinant fails to lay energy foundation – special vital power which is deemed a basis for body construction."
- "Not a single body is able to appear without Determinant, isn't it?"
- "Yes, it is true. Everything is under control. But if someone, at one's own wish, eliminates an unborn child, then this someone gets the

karma which shall be worked off afterwards. However a human being enjoys freedom of choice and is free to do as he wishes."

- "Some people do not have children of their own. Does it mean that Determinants do not give children to them?"

- "For one thing, it must be definitely some karma of theirs, and, for another thing, it is a special program of development without children."

- "Does Determinant of a child also form all his organs?"

- "Yes. There are relevant laws covering body construction. I.e. there is a certain procedure, which all Determinants adhere to."

- "Sometimes monsters are born. Are they produced by Determinants?"

- "If they are born to absolutely healthy parents, then it is their karma and karma of a child itself. But currently environmental dysfunctions and inadequate way of people's living may bring about disorders in body construction also apart from Determinant's will. Environment inside the mother becomes so aggressive that it disturbs normal processes of body formation. This is the fault of people themselves."

- "Child's body is formed by its future Determinant, and what does its mother's Determinant do meanwhile?"

- "Two Determinants always participate in the process of birth: Determinant of future mother and Determinant of the child. Processes taking place in the mother's body are controlled by two computers. One of the computers controls normalization of processes proceeding in the body of a mother herself and the other Determinant monitors the child's body. They try to balance them chemically and physically."

- "And who is engaged in introduction of soul, its descent into the child's body?"

- "Determinant himself."

- "But where does He get souls from? Does He make a request to depository of souls?"

- "There are special Hierarchic Systems in charge of souls. And they give him a soul which meets the relevant parameters and assigned mission. Selected soul shall be made maximally close to meeting relevant requirements of the Determinant's program so that later working with this soul He will be able to make progress himself and acquire energy he needs as well as facilitate advancement of the pupil's soul. Usually Determinant has an instrument, which contains all data needed for soul selection. Soul is selected for him based on those data, and He brings it down to the Earth when the time is due. If Determinant is competent enough, He can calculate himself what kind of soul he needs to enable his own progress. He transfers the computed data to the System in charge of souls, and this System offers Him one soul or several souls for him to choose."

- "Does the brought down soul have a complete program? "

- "Before sending a soul down to earthly world the programmers record new programs on its subtle bodies. On each body an individual program is recorded. Determinant does not take part in that."

- "Is it done with the help of certain instruments or based on special procedures?"

- "Recording is done with the help of instruments."

- "Is the place intended for descent of soul also selected in advance?"

- "Certainly. Every new soul born on the Earth shall be exactly placed relative to other bodies in compliance with computations of Higher Systems. This computation is very accurate, and not a single soul is brought down to your world without it. Based on computations, energetics of soul (which it possesses at the given moment) is correlated with energetics of the planet in the initial point of the Earth. At the same time energies of other planets of solar system shall be also taken into account. A complicated computation consolidates together many processes. It is very important because the energy which passes through the newborn body at the time of birth will exert much influence on his further fate. Besides, total energy of other planets will serve as a certain charge for material body of a child, and his tonus for the whole life of his will depend on this energy. That is why people are offered astrology as a science which helps them to progress in this direction."

- "We know how the place of birth is selected. And how is the time of birth selected? Does time mean anything for a human being?"

- "Yes. The System in charge of souls has a kind of schedule, which contains characteristics of every earthly hour, minute and every second. Those characteristics form a specific program: they specify what kind of human being shall be born as to his energetical and purely human properties at such-and-such hour and at such-and-such second."

- "Is a special channel intended for descent of soul to the Earth and connecting two different worlds built?"

- "No, no special channel is built. Everything is done by the Determinant himself. Of course, if He has not gained much experience, then others help Him, but generally He alone does everything."

- "Does Determinant perform introduction of soul into the body automatically or based on some energy methods?"

- "Determinant has dedicated instruments for that. First He points the soul at the relevant place and after that He launches it from the subtle world into physical matter. In doing so, Determinant also has to descend to reach a special layer of the Earth (see fig. 2). This is an intermediate layer between etheric layer and the planet on subtle plane. In this interlayer He stays only while pointing the soul at the baby's body. And then He returns. At the same time mother's Determinant is in his own world keeping remote control over the process via his own computer in order to maintain conformity."

- "Is a soul invested with protective bodies when it descends from the subtle world into the material one?"

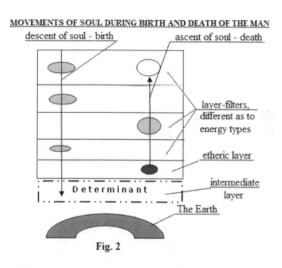

Fig. 2

- "Yes, it is. By all means. When a soul passes through various earthly layers, it is invested with some subtle bodies. Those bodies protect it against environment and allow it to be stationed in those layers without being pushed out of them. Thickness of the bodies shall be appropriate to the layers being passed in a certain way. If the required proportion is not met, a soul will not be not able to go through a layer because as it approaches closer to the planet, the layers become thicker and thicker for a soul to pass through them. Soul's descent is like a soul's ascent after death. But it is a reverse process: while a soul is prepared for birth, bodies are put on it and during its after-death ascent – it shucks them off (fig. 2). In each layer it is invested with one body. And the thicker and rougher the layer, the thicker the protective body. Higher worlds are subtle, and bodies are also subtle. The closer to the Earth, the rougher and thicker the protective body."

- "How long is the period of preparation of those subtle bodies?"

- "Preparation takes quite a long time. But here the principle is as follows: the subtler the body, the more complicated it is, the longer time it takes to get formed and invested i.e. to get linked with the matrix."

- "Who produces those bodies?"

- "They are produced by higher Levels. Special systems are involved in their production. There are individual Designers and Developers for every subtle body. They are deemed Entities handling specific range of energies."

- "Bodies are produced by many Systems. Does it mean that it is quite difficult to design them?"

- "For people the term "subtle body" may stand for some airy cloud. But virtually any body is deemed a complex structure which is capable of independent function and work together with other subtle bodies. Different souls need bodies which differ in their quality and quantity, i.e. bodies shall correspond to types of souls. If a soul is young, it needs a subtle body designed for low potential. If a soul is higher, it needs bodies, which are able to withstand high potential. Consequently, their inward structures will be different. People seem much alike for each other, but virtually their constitution is different. And those differences are determined by different Levels of their development. "

- "Therefore Determinant gets subtle bodies to pack the soul of his fosterling from the Systems producing them, does not He?"

- "He does not get them. When a soul reaches Him it is completely formed already. Other experts are in charge of preliminary preparation. And Determinant himself is responsible only for pointing a soul at the relevant body and its introduction in it."

- "How long does it take a soul to get introduced into a body?"

- "It is a flash-like process."

- "Is a soul blacked out while it is descended?"

- "No, in the period of preparation it is not blacked out. It remembers and is aware of everything. Consciousness is blacked out at the moment of introduction of soul into the body. After that a new program gets directly connected, and adult soul is initially switched over to a child's program. Then development of the material body is accompanied by connection of age-related phases."

- "What does a soul feel when it is being brought downwards?"

- "Not "downwards", but into the body", corrected God softly and explained, "While being brought down into the body the soul does not feel anything special. It is only aware of the target, which is set for it at the moment, i.e. introduction into the selected body. Besides, it is fully aware of the main goal, which is set for its life and for which sake it is being brought down to the Earth. A soul knows its future."

- "Does a soul also feel when programmers write a program on it?"

- "Yes, of course,"

- "Is any additional preparation performed before a soul is launched to the Earth? For example, it is inevitably cleansed when it is brought up to the subtle world from Earth after death."

- "No, no preliminary preparation of soul is provided when it descends because it is clean when it comes from the Above. It is only provided with some additional protection (if appropriate) besides the normal one. However additional protection is not placed on all souls, but only on some of them."

- "A soul lives in subtle world, and there it may acquire some energies of inadequate quality, the so called "dirty" energies. In this context may it be subject to cleansing before its descent to the Earth?"

- "In subtle world there are no energies of "inadequate quality". Basically all "dirty" energies originate from brute matter, from brute material body. And we do not let those brute energies go up. And in the subtle world absolutely everything is "subtle" and of various qualities. This type of matter is absolutely different, it cannot be compared to yours. Therefore there can't be "inadequate" energies in such world. And everything what a soul works out there is immediately placed in different cells of matrix without preliminary filtration. That is why when the soul is launched to the Earth it is not subject to any additional cleansing."

- "What happens to bodies of a child while a soul is introduced into his mother's body. Are they tuned for interaction with her fields?"

- "After soul's introduction into a body, subtle bodies of a child start to work immediately, but a child itself is surrounded as if by a micro-climate because it gets under protection of mother's bodies which are more powerful. It has double protection: its own one and of its mother's. Such protection cannot be easily broken through."

- "And can anybody put the evil eye at a child?"

- "Everything depends on personal energetics of its mother. Nobody can do any harm to a child if energy of a stranger is not as high as energy of its mother. But psychics whose energy is higher than mother's energy may injure a child. Therefore would-be mother are not recommended to visit institutions of psychics and other persons of high energies."

- "Does initial information come to a child through interaction with subtle bodies of its mother?"

- "Yes, interaction of subtle structures takes place."

- "Why are new bodies grown in female organisms? They could be grown artificiality, for example, in flasks."

- "So was decided for your Earth. Although birth may happen in some different ways: through bud reproduction and division of an old organism into new states, and through growth in flasks and cell cloning. There are a hundred of different methods. But it was an experiment set up on your Earth – to be born into the world just like this. In other worlds this process is different."

- "Will souls of the next sixth race come to our material world in the same way?"

- "Yes, they will. This is the key method accepted, although some other methods were tried on your Earth. But they did not work therefore the given technique has been applied further on."

- "Which soul: enlightened or underdeveloped one – consumes more energy for its birth?"

- "Energy consumption for earthly souls is the same irrespective of whether they are smart or underdeveloped. Until a certain Level there is no difference. This Level is **hundredth**. Until the hundredth Level births of all people consume the same amount of energy. But as soon as a person reaches the Level, which is higher than the hundredth level, then after that everything with him will be different."

- "There are earthly and cosmic souls. Do they get introduced into the bodies in the same way or according different methods?"

- "Of course, differently. Cosmic soul has very powerful energy therefore it needs stronger subtle bodies because they have to withstand more powerful energy. Therefore preparation of subtle bodies for cosmic souls takes much more time. Such souls themselves are very powerful. If they are placed in ordinary earthly bodies, they will be pushed apart very much. As a result a soul will invariably feel uneasiness. Moreover, those subtle bodies may be blown up under the action of soul power. Consequently, a person may die on the earthly plane before he completes his program."

- "Is the birth rate always controlled from the Above?"
- "Yes, it's true."
- "Is overpopulation possible?"
- "No. Everything is under control. Even if overpopulation occurs somewhere, from your point of view, it means that it has been specially designed."

About Death

- "Determinant guides the man from the cradle to the grave. What is the extent of his participation in the death of his fosterling?"
- "Participation may differ. Some Determinants stop to supply energy to the guided people, and so they die; others may strike energy blows at weak organs, some other Determinants will bring their fosterlings to death through some long-term illness. But in any case the type of death is pre-programmed beforehand, and Determinant is just responsible for its technical aspect."
- "And if a man is killed driving or dies in an accident, then how does Determinant participate in this event?"
- "He leads a man to a situation, which will be arranged for the purpose of soul withdrawal. If a fosterling is programmed to die in a car accident or someone is destined to get run over, then a driver or a victim is made to get blacked out for a very short time. This results in a car accident, which in its turn cause death of a person whose program is completed. Many people do not remember how they got run over because they were blacked out several seconds before they collided with a car. All situations are computed and thought over to the last detail by programmers and designers."
- "And let us take an accident entailing many victims. Is every victim purposefully brought to the situation?" Are there casual victims?"
- "Those who are programmed to survive will survive. For this end special protective measures will be taken. Those who are destined to finish their life journey will be disabled. Usually the situation of an accident, powerful jerk and stress helps the soul to rush out of the body and makes it easier for Determinant to release soul out of the body.

In case of long-term diseases, for example, soul leaves the body with difficulty, its release is very painful and Determinant has to work for a long time trying to disengage it from trammels of the body."

- "We know that death is accompanied by energy spike. Is the amount of energy given by Determinant for birth equal to energy which He receives back in the article of death of a man?"

- "Of course, it isn't. He gives less and receives more. Death gives a very strong spike of energy."

- "Is the work of Determinant finished after the soul escapes from the body?"

- "No, his work goes on further. Determinant continues to control decay of material body until its decomposition to the level of molecules. At the same time on the subtle plane in His own world He summarizes work undertaken and prepares himself for reporting his results to the Higher. After that his fate is decided by others: He is either given a new pupil or (if the soul is quickly retuned to life) Determinant continues to work with that very soul. Determinant may also be transferred to a higher Level."

-"Does Determinant meet the soul of his deceased pupil at the moment of its release?"

- "No, He does not need it. Souls are met by other Entities who are directly deal with them after human death."

Different Types of Determinants

- "Determinants are engaged in education of people. Some of them may be more competent, others less. And do all of them refer to the first Level of Hierarchy or do some of them pass to the second Level?"

- "Determinants are deemed the first Level of My Hierarchy irrespective of the phase of their development. But They are all mixed-level, i.e. They have different degree of excellence. There is a separate Hierarchy of Determinants, which is all disposed at the first Level of My Hierarchy. This mini-hierarchy refers only to the earthly plane. But many other Entities engaged in other activities and united into separate mini-hierarchies are also at the first Level (see fig.4). A lot of other Entities also concern themselves with people and work with them but already in other areas. It needs explaining – at the first Level there are several mini-hierarchies dealing with people and dozens of mini-hierarchies dealing with other creatures of My Universes. "

- "What is a mini-hierarchy of Determinants?"

- "Hierarchy of earthly Determinants is detached and it starts with those Entities, which guide insects, reptiles, fish and so on in the order ascending up to human beings (see fig. 3). Determinants of people are subdivided into those who guide one or several people who are individuals not united by group targets. Above them there are group Determinants who guide crews, groups united by some professional or other kinds of ideas. And so on, also in ascending order of human communities."

- "Is a family guided by one Determinant?"

- "Every family member has his own Determinant. They may be even from different Systems. For example, if a family consists of plus and minus individuals i.e. of good and evil, then the former will be guided by Determinants from plus System and the latter – from the minus one."

- "How are programs of individuals belonging to the same family interfaced?"

- "As one family is guided by different Determinants a program of one family may be in computers of different Determinants. Family members are interfaced through a family program, which is included in the common program of the city where they live. Therefore their interfaces may be based either on individual programs or on municipal program."

- "And a city Determinant guides all the people of a city, doesn't He?"

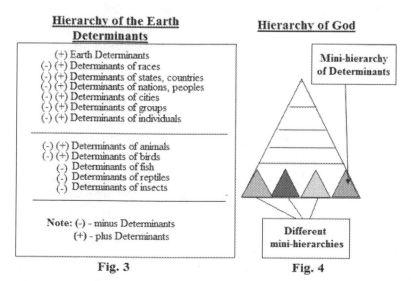

Hierarchy of the Earth Determinants

(+) Earth Determinants
(-) (+) Determinants of races
(-) (+) Determinants of states, countries
(-) (+) Determinants of nations, peoples
(-) (+) Determinants of cities
(-) (+) Determinants of groups
(-) (+) Determinants of individuals

(-) (+) Determinants of animals
(-) (+) Determinants of birds
(-) Determinants of fish
(-) Determinants of reptiles
(-) Determinants of insects

Note: (-) - minus Determinants
(+) - plus Determinants

Fig. 3

Hierarchy of God

Mini-hierarchy of Determinants

Different mini-hierarchies

Fig. 4

- "He doesn't guide, He controls, coordinates links, interfaces programs, enters amendments, if appropriate. But they are guided by their personal Determinants. They lead citizens to the city target, control energy flow. Determinants guiding cities, races and so on resolve general issues and settle disputes: They have their own tasks."

- "What do the tasks of group Determinants consist in?"

- "The task of group Determinants consists in leading a group to a single target. But these are higher Determinants already. For common people ordinary Leaders are used. But higher personalities and those persons (who We have chosen and given missions to) require Higher Managers. For example, currently I (God speaks of himself) am guiding several individuals having lofty goals."

- "Do you guide any politicians?"

- "No. For the given period I have some other goal."

- "Do group Determinants take some other group of people to achieve other goals as soon as the previous goal is gained?"

- "No, they do not. They are not replaced by others till the death of people."

- "And what happens if a group splits?"

- "If a group has stopped to pursue its specific goal and got slit, then the task is deemed unfinished, which may be followed by replacement of Originators and Managers, i.e. rearrangement of higher structures will take place."

- "What is the relationship between the Determinant guiding an individual and higher Determinant guiding a group?"

- "As to private life, pertaining to His fosterling only, it is guided the Determinant of this individual. But if the issues concern social goals, then the group Determinant takes the lead. He gives orders, and the inferior Determinant shall submit to him entirely. The group program input to the computer of the higher Determinant combines individual and social tasks. This Determinant manages people through their individual Determinants."

- "An individual Determinant picks up energy from his pupil, and who does the energy produced by him go to when this pupil takes part in group actions?"

- "Social situations associated with the group program are controlled by the group Determinant and he also takes for himself all energies resultant from those situations and pupils. But sometimes an individual may belong to a company, but may not take part in mass events. In such a case all the energy produced by him will be delivered to his private Manager. For example, an employee works for some plant. This is a social organization. If case of a conflict between an employee and a supervisor, all its energy is supplied to individual Determinants. Suppose a group takes part in a protest demonstration or a group of ecologists fights for preservation of forest, which is planned to be cut over, then entire energy goes to the group Determinant."

* * *

- "Does Determinant of animals guide one specimen?"
- "If it is a large and clever animal it may be guided by one inexperienced Determinant. But generally beasts are guided either in groups of several and more animals or in flocks."
- "Is fish also guided?"
- "Fish is managed only in shoals, therefore they behave themselves accordingly: their actions are general and coordinated. And every specimen in a shoal takes its own place. That is, they live just according to the program, and nobody carries out special control over them in contrast to people. Flocks of birds, insects are guided in similar way therefore a flight of a flock is distinguished by particular maneuverability and synchronism."
- "And how are they controlled?"
- "Also through a technical device i.e. a computer. Every flock has its own program. Control is carried out according to this program. One computer keeps track of hundreds of thousands of animals. However insects, wild animals are generally guided by minus Determinants, just as minus people."
- "Are domestic animals also guided by minus Determinants?"
- "When peaceful, unaggressive domestic animals reach high levels of development, they are guided by plus Determinants. For example, a mean, nasty dog may be guided by minus Determinant however a friendly and clever dog may be guided by plus Determinant. There are subtleties in every business."
- "And what about other worlds? Does someone guide creatures there or do they develop all by themselves?"
- "Absolutely all living beings are guided by higher Determinants. Parallel worlds have their own leaders. In a Hierarchy each higher Level

patronizes and guides inferior world. However, the higher the world in terms spirituality, the less control is applied to it from the Above. The more freedom it has."

- "May a Determinant guide a human being and at the same time some creature from a subtle world?"

- "No. Such diversified creatures are not offered for guidance because they are from different worlds applying different communication methods. It involves a lot of difficulties. Therefore when a Determinant guides a human being, He may be given one more similar human being. However He will not be allowed to guide in addition an animal from the same world. Knowledge shall be uniform."

- "May the Determinant guiding a man be transferred to guidance of creatures living on other planets?"

- "No. If Determinant guided a man, then He either continues to work with other people along the same lines or gets to a

higher Level i.e. He develops within His Hierarchy. Other creatures have their own Leaders and Hierarchies."

- "Do Originators and Managers belong to the Hierarchy of Determinants?"

- "It is a higher Level already."

- "Do planets and stars have Determinants? As a matter of fact, they also develop under their programs."

- "Determinants of relevant Level handle them. They are planetary and starry Leaders. They also have their own individual Hierarchies because planets and stars are also at different phases of excellence, and to guide them one shall have a certain level of knowledge. But their Hierarchies stand well above the Hierarchy of earthly Determinants."

- "Our Earth as a planet has individual Determinant. And people living on it also have their Leaders. Are there any relationships among Determinants of people and Determinants of the Earth?"

- "They are Determinants of different Levels therefore no relationships may exist among them. Everyone performs his work – and that is all there to it. Planets have their Hierarchic chain, and people have a different one."

- "And do they never cross over in their work?"

- "Why? Some issues are resolved together. But this is true only about higher Determinants guiding peoples and states."

- "Do Determinants of people and Determinants of the Earth have the same or different Managers?"

- "Their common Managers are at a very high step. They manage both types of Determinants mentioned above because all of them carry out common work."

- "Are programs of Determinants of people and Determinants of the Earth inter-coordinated at a higher Level?"

- "Naturally, because the program of mankind and the program of the planet go as specific options within a more comprehensive program connected with Hierarchic Systems."

- "There are dozens of Determinants of different forms. As we understand, they guide a creature till the certain Level of development, don't they?"

- "Yes, they do. It is necessitated by self-preservation of inferior Levels of development. Those creatures are underdeveloped and they do not understand what they are doing. Freedom given to them helps to identify their flaws but at the same time it aggravates destructive actions of theirs. That is to say, freedom given to them actually leads them to self-destruction. Therefore inferior forms shall be mandatory controlled. However when their consciousness reaches a certain level of maturity, Determinants are no longer required. Every well-organized Creature of high consciousness is able to control itself and to foresee results of its own work well ahead together with activities of others because all of them work to attain the same goal, so interfaces are important."

-"Yes, It is clear. But you mentioned plus and minus Determinants. Does it mean that they differ in quality and their work shall be somewhat different?"

- "On Earth both plus and minus individuals get improved. Plus individuals are guided by plus Determinants, and minus ones – by minus Determinants. Minus Determinants generally guide people-destroyers, killers, those who add to life woes and troubles, corrupt others, seduce people out of the right way, those who do harm to society. They carry out the Earth-wide guidance of captains of big industries, leaders of state who initiate wars or oppress their people. They control a lot of people who are respectable but who still do harm and evil to others."

- "Can we say that all kind, decent people are governed by plus Determinants?"

- "Yes, they govern those who are plus in all their manifestations, humane, well-doing, protecting others and guided by high ideals. We never give people minus ideals, only plus ones. And minus ideals are made on the basis of plus ones by people themselves in pursuit of profit motives."

- "Do minus Determinants have a task to teach their fosterlings something good?"

- "No, they don't."

- "Do minus Determinants purposefully make wars, arrange accidents, provoke plus people to commit ill acts?"

- "Yes, they do. Because a plus one does not want to participate in this mud by virtue of personal character and accumulated positive qualities. But if he is still destined by the program to take part in some military operations, then his pupil's behavior will be different from that of a minus Determinant.

For example, a fight of two generals, guided by plus and minus Determinants will be solved in different ways. The minus one will want to win by hedge or by stile and even through loss of his soldiers. But a plus general will try to find a solution involving minimal or even no victims. He will fight for the life of every soldier. He is not indifferent to this. In such case the quality of their behavior is different. One of them will be guided by self-advancement, and the other – by patriotism. Every action performed on the Earth has it own subtleties, which divide people into plus and minus. It is just due to this, that the Earth is a separator dividing the entire mankind into two extremes."

- "Do minus Determinants work on behalf of Devil's System?"

- "There are a lot from His Hierarchy but some are from My minus Systems. Generally they are scientists, programmers, developers, designers. These are all mine."

- "Can plus and minus Determinants change the quality of their actions and substitute for one another in their work? For example, today he is plus and tomorrow – minus."

- "No. That can never be. Because everyone of us (existing in plus or minus System) made this choice on own accord. Everyone intentionally chooses the way, which is the best for him, allowing to apply methods to his liking, i.e. plus or minus, go through the good or evil. Otherwise, why have a choice if after that there will be no difference in your work.

The end never justifies the means. And They are very well aware of that while making their choices."

The Higher and Determinants

- "You say that at the first Level of Hierarchy, besides Determinants, there are also other creatures."

- "Yes. There are dozens of them. Determinants constitute a mini-hierarchy among a lot of others, similar ones, existing in the same plane. The world they live in requires other experts, the same as yours. Just image – how many of them live in your world. You will not be able to enumerate them, and the first Level of Hierarchy has even more of them."

- "We know that a part of Entities come to the first step from the Earth. And what planets and material worlds do other creatures come from?"

- "There are thousands upon thousands of physical designations in which they may have existed before. It is not only your material world that supplies souls for my Hierarchy. Many creatures know nothing about your world but it does not prevent them from successful progress. The first Level accepts souls coming not only from material worlds but also from some subtle worlds of all My Universes. There are dozens of development paths but they all lead to Me or to Devil or to neutral System."

- "What do other creatures of the first Level concern themselves with?"

- "Some of them concern themselves with creative work, computer programming, designing, there are builders, destroyers – scavengers in your language – there are those who deal directly with human souls. Even, for example, the work with souls requires dozens of special professions because some of them shall control them in a subtle world, and others collect them after death and perform dedicated treatment, the third ones hold their trials, the fourth decode those guilty, the fifth work with their thrown off bodies. And it is, by no means, complete list of work related to souls only. And the rest is even more numerous – to the extent that it can hardly be listed."

- "Who maintains order at the first Level?"

- "Every world has such organizations as COD (Coalition Observer Detachment), which is deemed its representative at the given Level of development. Every Level has its own COD. All of them are governed by Higher COD."

- "Does it mean that only They maintain order and law?"

- "They control only four Universes of mine. And the rest of them have their own legal Systems."

- "In what cases does Higher COD intervene in conflicts or disturbances?"

- "Only if it may involve deaths of others. But generally individual COD themselves resolve all matters of dispute at their own Levels. Besides local COD, each Level is controlled by Personalities of Higher Levels."

- "For Determinants these are Originators and Managers, aren't' they?"

- "Yes. Other professions are controlled by their Higher Entities specializing in the same forms of activity."

- "We know that each Level is divided into Sublevels. Do Determinants and Originators refer to different Sublevels of the same Level?"

- "Sublevels are intended for Determinants themselves, but Originators refer to higher Level. It means that Determinants and Originators are from different worlds. And Managers are even higher accordingly. And "Union" is above them, then goes "Higher Union" and so on (see fig. 5).

- "Do Higher Personalities compete with each other while they are ascending the Levels of Hierarchy, do some Entities try to be in advance of others?"

- "Yes, competition exists, but in the finest sense of this word. Because everyone does not only try to ascend higher himself but also to help others in their ascension, to the extent possible. The same drives the general progress of entire Hierarchy. And nobody for the sake of outrunning the other can ever cause damage to him. It is very mean and inherent only in human beings."

CELESTIAL HIERARCHY
MANAGEMENT CHART

5ᵗʰ Level	Higher "Union"
4ᵗʰ Level	"Union"*
3d Level	Managers
2d Level	Originators
1 Level	Determinants } Sublevels

Fig.5

- "Do all Determinants have the same or different energy thresholds of transfer?"

- "Of course, they are all different just as people. To be transferred everyone shall get specific number of points."

- "Do Higher Determinants differ from Inferior ones in some qualities?"

-"If Determinants differ in their Level, accordingly they differ in all other things: knowledge, consciousness, set of energies in matrix. Their qualities depend on situations because they determinate the set of energies. That is why Higher and Inferior Determinants participate in different situations. The Higher the Personality, the loftier and subtler the situation it participates in. Therefore Inferior Determinant will guide an unworthy person and will be with him in fights, frauds and treasons; but a Higher Determinant who is assigned to a high-spirit person will do good on the Earth together with his pupil, accomplish honorable deeds."

"Every Determinant shall have pupil of appropriate Level. This will allow them to accumulate energy of various quality needed by both of them. The higher the Determinant, the higher his energy potential, richer his matrix contents, wider the perception of visual environment. Of course, there are a lot of differences. Higher Determinants are able to guide a great number of people, up to two-three hundreds of people at the same time. Inferior one can guide only one person. As to Myself, I am able to guide all My subordinates simultaneously, as appropriate.

To do such work one shall have a great scope of knowledge and huge energy potential of one's own."

- "Can it be such a case that Determinant has acquired a large scope of knowledge but his spirituality still remains low?"

- "No, it can't. The fact is that knowledge drives the growth of soul. The enlargement of mind and accumulation of energy go simultaneously. Let us take the following comparison. If a soul develops on the Earth, it is controlled by physical time. As a result of transition to subtle world, physical time vanishes but consequences of its current by way of accumulation of energy potential by soul remains. Therefore knowledge accumulation by soul (as a consequence of this process) goes along with enhancement of consciousness and spirituality of personality."

- "Therefore spiritually underdeveloped personalities are by no means able to reach Higher worlds, aren't they?"

- "No, they aren't. This is out of the question. Every soul is stationed in accordance with energy potential of its subtle constituents."

- "Originators govern Determinants. And how many of them are held subject"

- "Usually many of them. It is difficult to give the exact number. Everything depends on Originator – how many positions He is able to manage. These are His personality traits."

- "Do Higher Personalities govern a growing number of inferiors as They ascend the steps of Hierarchy?"

- "Yes."

- "Does it mean that They should keep on learning management?"

- "Not necessarily. Personalities of certain energy configuration can function as governors, the same as with people. One has to possess such attitudes. Those who do not want to manage concern themselves with other activities: creativity, mathematical calculations, computer programming and so on. Activities on their taste."

- "So not everyone of people is able to become a Determinant."

- "No. It is depends on their will and ability. If you have a will but do not possess relevant abilities, you will not get a pupil. But we have a lot of other types of work, besides those listed."

- "Does Originator himself prepare programs for Determinants?"

- "No. He prepares programs only for people. And programs for Determinants are prepared by programmers of higher Level. Every Originator has assistants at His Level and at higher ones."

- "What do They proceed from in preparation of Determinant's program: from qualities He lacks or from a need to acquire certain types of energy?"

- "The program includes many factors: a need of Determinant's soul to acquire energies He lacks in his ascent to a higher step; and accumulation of energies in energy collector to be used for further general work; and qualities, which shall be acquired by the pupil. The program of every Determinant shall be coordinated with the program of His pupil – which is very important – in such a way that progress of the Teacher is made dependent of progress of the pupil. And if Determinant fails to raise his fosterling to a higher level, then He himself will not do that."

- "Do capabilities of Higher Hierarchs look like demonstration of miracles from the point of view of Determinants? Probably, Higher Entities have some extraordinary features and capabilities, which are seen as miracles by Determinants."

- "No, there is nothing miraculous about them. Because Determinants have another level of notions and consciousness. They have knowledge about Higher Worlds, and everything is seen natural – as due achievements. Just as, for example, people do not perceive your spacecraft flights as miracles but as achievements of many people possessing knowledge of relevant quality. At the same time some savage men may think that your spacecraft is a miracle. That is to say, everything depends on the comprehension level of individuals: what is seen as miracle by some people, is perceived by others as natural course of developments and certain level of knowledge. Hence, Higher Hierarchs do not possess any superpowers – They just have Level-sensitive energy reserves and great experience of former existences."

- "Do Higher Hierarchs live in the worlds resembling our planet?"

- "No. Their world is just space. As compared to the Earth, everything is different there. Therefore a human being can hardly visualize it."

- "Do Determinants also exist in similar space?"

- "Their world, which is closer to material world, has a lot of various constructions in it. Still it bears absolutely no resemblance to your world. However, generally speaking, each Level has its own specific structures designed for functioning and work. All worlds are special."

- "Diseases are inherent in material body of a man. And what about Higher Entities? What is exposed to disease with them? In fact, They have no organs."

- "Besides matrix, They possess protective fields, bodies, subtle structures. And all of them may have some abnomalities, which can be attributed to some forms of diseases in Their plane of existence."

- "How are those disorders felt? The same as pains?"

- "No, of course, as something different. They have other senses. Their diseases are felt as a lack of some quantity of energy of certain quality."

- "And how do They remedy those disorders?"

- "They get the lacking energy through processes characteristic of their world."

- "Do Their matrices have defects sometimes?"

- "No. It is an absolute construction. Higher Entities cannot have defective matrices already. They are beyond the boundary before which defects may still exist."

- "What are the causes of diseases of Higher Entities?"

- "Wrong behavior in Their world, inadequate interactions, i.e. contacts between Entities, incorrect development paths chosen by Them. Degradation of Entity results in serious diseases because of metabolic disorders. And pains make them modify their behavior and seek what They need."

- "People value money. And what values exist in Higher Worlds and with Determinants?"

- "As against your money, it is energy. But from the point of view of Absolute Spirit*, for example, the greatest value consists in souls, energetically highly developed souls with the level of development very close to the Absolute Spirit himself. Souls shall be Divinely developed, and there should be no end of them. That is both qualitative and quantitative aspects are valued."

- "What spiritual values do Determinants have?"

- "For them the most important spiritual value is self-actualization. They think highly of purposefulness, moral virtues, creativity."

- "Do Higher Entities value some special qualities in each other?"

- "No. They do not value them because They are grouped with reference to their qualities. That is within the limits of one and the same world They are similar to each other. Only energy is of value for Them. But at one Level this type of energy is important and at the other Level - another type."

- "And what do Determinants value in their relationships? It is just lower Level. Shall their perception of visual environment be somewhat different?"

- "Determinants value programs and people made available to them, quality of their souls. They also attach importance to the number of pupils They guide. The more people are guided by Determinant, the higher his reputation. And as for the programs themselves, their types are of importance because there are superior programs and inferior ones. Such are the values of Determinants. But energy is the key value for all Levels."

- "Determinant derives the needed energy from people and through some individual actions. And how is the work of computer programmers, designers and Your other experts dealing with human souls compensated?" What kind of remuneration do they have?"

- "Computer programmers, designers live differently as compared to Determinants. Their relationships are absolutely different. But they also receive energy as payment for their work."

- "Do They produce the energies They lack themselves through some processes or is human energy (accumulated by Determinants) redistributed to Them?"

- "No, everything is absolutely different with them. For all computations, which They perform for people, for the programs prepared for them They receive energy of other quality as compared to Determinants because their Level is higher. Every Level receives energy of relevant type. If They are offered energy, which Determinants are content with, for them it will be too low energy and inadequate payment."

- "And who pays them?"

- "Everything goes from Higher Managers, the same as with people – from line management. They instruct them on their work, check it and provide payment in the form of relevant equivalent of energy."

- "Does everybody receive equal payment?"

- "No, payment is different. They receive energy of different quality and in different quantities. Everyone gets an equivalent of his work contribution. And, of course, everything is arranged so that nobody is able to steal or misappropriate something, which is currently characteristic of your country, for example (1999). At all Levels of My Hierarchy strict correspondence between labor inputs (i.e. energy inputs) and its replenishment is applied."

- "And where do Higher Managers take the energy (which they later pay off to others) from? Do they also produce it?"

- "Yes, everybody has his own individual energy reserve acquired while ascent to higher Levels. Because at each Level They accumulate some kind of their own energy margins. Therefore there are all types of inferior Level energies available in their energy reserves."

*   *   *

Chapter 2
SPIRITUALIZATION

Introduction.

What is spiritualization?

It is a great and mysterious process turning all dead into living which starts to exist independently, evolve and move to a certain goal.

People divided the entire earthly world of theirs into two categories: animate living matter, to which they added entire mankind, animals, plants, and inanimate matter, to which they added the Earth, stones, stars and planets. That is to say, everything that differed markedly from their own life was identified as inanimate nature. And in somewhat obscure way it turned out with them that this inanimate nature began to give rise to animate and spiritualized forms. But how did it become spiritualized, how did articles and forms obtain souls – a man could not explain this. And while explaining world processes he, for some reason, was always content with such ultimate phrase as "created by nature". But this phrase explained actually nothing concerning creation and spiritualization of forms. However such reference always satisfied a man. He calmed down thinking that the phrase "created by nature " was kind of a limit the human mind would never be able to go beyond and to understand something more than juggle-like creation of millions of species of plants, fish, birds and different human races.

A man invented a soothing image of Nature, and Nature, for some reason, has turned out to be smarter than he and than all other animated articles of Earth. But how does Nature animate its creations and does it animate them at all - this has always been a mystery. It has been generally recognized that Nature produces its forms just as living beings using special technique consisting in connection of atoms, molecules and genic codes. And it remained an enigma how and why its development had brought it to acquirement of those codes and to creation of such a great number of animate forms.

And a man would have wandered about in the darkness of his myths for a long time trying to find answers to inexplicable questions if the true Creators of world and people themselves had not decided to reveal to him a secret of life emergence and spiritualization of living beings. And a man to his amazement came to know that it is not the material envelope i.e. his body that is spiritualized in him himself but a certain invisible substance i.e. soul that spiritualizes his body as a secondary factor.

The enigma of spiritualization belongs to one of the greatest secrets of God because even Devil has managed to learn nothing about it – so carefully it is concealed – but still there are some general provisions subject to disclosure. Now the Earth and mankind are being transferred to a new orbital i.e. to a more higher Level of development, therefore God acquaints them with his truths trying to expand their consciousness and to bring it to a new stage of comprehension of visual environment.

Human mind shall escape from the deadlock of materialistic conceptions about the world and enter on a new stage of development alongside with acquirement of new ideas and truths having cleared the mind of obsolete doctrines and false theories. In the same way a first-grader at school discovers knowledge intelligible for him; a fifth-grader is able to understand more complex truths but a tenth-grader can assimilate knowledge which can bring him to the road leading to social life. It means that each level of mentality of pupils is offered knowledge of relevant level. Similarly, the entire mankind passes over from one level of cognition to another, and each time the truths which are intelligible for him at the given level of development are made comprehensible for him from the Above.

Therefore nowadays the mankind approach to understanding of new secrets, and spiritualization is one of them.

*   *   *

To avoid repetitions of the given subject in dialogues, let us remember revelations of God in the book «Secrets of Higher Worlds», conveying that only God possesses the secret of spiritualization.

He himself went a difficult way of development and He himself mastered a process of creation of various souls and their spiritualization. All mice and men living on our planet as well as the planet itself was created by God together with His creative and designing Systems – it means that at first He created everything Himself and then He taught others all the actions that He had mastered Himself.

Assistants were required because there was a lot of work to do, and it was difficult to cope with millions of processes simultaneously. Besides, knowledge transfer to others (which constitutes a special form of teaching) was essential for improvement of souls, their ascent up the Levels of Hierarchy higher and higher. Thus, God is the Creator of everything existing in our Universe and in three other Universes, but He created everything with His assistants who are close to Him in their energetics and powers. God concerned himself with planning, designing of forms and targeting; and others implemented those targets.

Souls constitute the greatest value of God because His own growth and development depends on them. And the more numerous they are, the high their development level, the faster God's evolution and the more powerful He is. Therefore any soul, any man who enters the path of pursuit of pleasure instead of the path of self-perfection and becomes backward in his development, first of all, blocks the development of God himself. Therefore every man shall understand that if he honestly performs any work and improves his intellectual level, he makes good not only for himself but also for God because a man is His spiritualized particle.

God creates forms of future creatures, spiritualizes them, spiritualizes the matrices themselves, which are imbedded in those structures. (God also creates forms, which are not spiritualized but here we speak about future animate forms). Therefore stones, plants, animals, birds, fish and human beings are spiritualized on Earth. The Earth itself is spiritualized like a living being, and all other forms existing in the four Universes of God are also spiritualized.

Souls, their matrices, are created in a laboratory by special Hierarchical Systems (but not by Medical System which is a separate and independent Hierarchy, but it depends on God with regard to its replenishment with souls because it receives souls itself from God). As for matrices, they are created by the Systems included in God's Hierarchy.

Matrices are created and get immediately spiritualized. The process of spiritualization is the greatest secret of God. This is the secret, which is not known to Devil and which He has no access to.

Of course, it is odd that for all His sophistication, artfulness, prudence and intellect, He cannot worm a secret out of God although He tries to solve this mystery and attempts to build similar matrices as well, but He is not able to spiritualize them. It is just for this very reason that Devil falls into a position of full dependence on God. That is to be expanded the Devil's Hierarchy shall be replenished with new souls. But where can you get them from if you are not able to create them yourself? Therefore Devil gets souls from God, He takes the souls that are rejected by God. Those are not only the souls of killers but also the ones of other perverse personalities.

Defective souls which did not want to rise in their thoughts, to improve their actions and which failed to learn to be unselfish go to Devil. Therefore He is interested in corruption of people, in alluring them to the nets of temptation and pleasure. But even this number of people is not enough for him, of course. He would always like to possess as many souls as He wants and not to depend on anybody. He would like to be sovereign of entire cosmos. But He needs souls for that, and their number shall increase in proportion to his personal ambitions. However God will give Him the number of souls that He sees fit and in such a way as to preserve all his advantages over the Hierarch of minus System. Therefore Devil will never learn the secret of spiritualization by two reasons.

1). God entrusted the process of spiritualization only to His closest assistants. That is to say, if we assume that His Hierarchy has a hundred of Levels, then only the ninety eighth Level knows this secret. As for Devil, He has not reached even the fifth Level yet. Therefore with reference to his energy, His constitution is still very weak. His low energy potential is unable to raise Him up to reach the worlds of very high energy potentials. There He will be just crushed by the very matter of those worlds.

2). Although Devil seeks to learn this secret but He will never be able to master the process of spiritualization because He is built of the energies, which are not fit for this process. In fact, His evolution path is directed off the given process (fig.6).

Fig.6

The path of development Devil has chosen for himself is such as it will make Devil who goes in parallel to God more and more deviate from Him, and, consequently, from cognition of spiritualization process.

Devil is not able to cognize this process because of the energies generated by His soul. Any process, first of all, proceeds from certain material i.e. certain energies. Spiritualization process bases itself on energies of special type. These energies shall be worked out by soul. It means that here evolution shall involve an entire chain of certain actions which eventually make a soul generate special energy. And this energy, in its turn, will be able to spiritualize matrices.

Those miraculous actions which drive the chain of energy development to spiritualization include love, kindliness and creativeness. Love gives rise to kindliness, and love and kindliness generate creativeness. That is to say, an individual is rewarded with it for some good deeds performed in the past. And the program prepared for such individual includes options of his development through creativeness. Creativeness is deemed a program of certain actions, which may or may not be performed by an individual in his creative development. But creativeness is always given from the Above, but still it is a reward for the former righteous deeds of love and kindliness. And if a soul failed to work out the latter energies, then the creative energies will have nothing to base on, nothing to grow from. And it is deemed a characteristic feature of the process of development of these wonderful qualities.

As for creativeness, it just generates in human matrix cells those energies, which later on will be able already to drive the processes of spiritualization.

Devil is not capable of creativeness because everything that He creates in His worlds is achieved by Him through calculations. And He is not able to create something new without use of figures. Devil cannot use other paths of creativeness because His soul lacks the energies of love and kindliness.

During their evolution, plus energies shall necessarily in their succession go through energies of love, kindliness, creativeness and spiritualization. Some energies grow on others therefore the progress of energies shows regular sequence. Hence, if a soul fails to accumulate the energy of love, it will not be able to do the good. If energies of kindliness are not accumulated, then such soul will not be able to choose a creative path. It will be attracted by other processes, for example, such as: destructions, calculations, programming, control of others, automatic performance of some operations etc.

It is just because of this that Devil who has not learnt methods of Divine creativeness will never generate for his matrix those special energies which allow mastering the process of spiritualization and, hence, He will be always dependent on God.

On Earth a man has always the right to choose – which path to go, what to do, and eventually who to moor to: to God or to Devil. The man also in the very long term will be able to learn the secret of spiritualization and feel inside himself that magic power, which turns all dead into living. But the way to acquirement of this great miracle power starts here, on the Earth. Therefore he may think just now about how he can draw nearer to the Great somewhat faster and what qualities required for ascension he possesses at the moment, what creative base he presently has.

Creative approach may be applied to any deed therefore one shall not necessarily produce pictures or sculpture artworks. One can be creative in preparation of delicious dinner, apply a portion of imagination in cleaning the house, sew a dress according to one's own design or be able to give to his friend an exciting account of a most commonplace story. Love may be present when one writes certain texts at work and raise vegetables in garden-beds. That is, you may input elements of love, good and creativeness into any deed. And this will structure your soul in a special way directing along the Divine path.

Therefore don't try to be a great and well-known writer, musician, actor etc. but try to be maximally creative in all your deeds because absolutely everything done by the man is done not for others but for himself and for God. Every action of the man does not remain unnoticed. Other people may pay no attention to it due to their greed and selfishness. But every aspiration and action, diligence and creative impulse of his will always be noticed by Heavenly Teachers and God, and such personality will be certainly encouraged.

*   *   *

Having reviewed the paths, which can lead the man to mastering of the spiritualization process and to gaining insight into the great secret of God, let us now discuss the process itself and everything related to it.

But at first it is worth mentioning that many themes were not immediately disclosed during channelings. We tried to put questions first from one aspect of the subject of our interest, then from the other one. We used to be refused in getting answers to some of our questions for a long time with reference to unavailability of such-like notions with people or on the pretext that those subjects are closed for mankind. At first, sometimes answers were given reluctantly, but as we were very insistent and investigative we managed to get explanations of the subjects and those explanations became more and more profound in proportion to our increasing comprehension of new concepts up to some permissible limits.

Therefore each unknown subject did not become clear for us immediately, but after long considerations and wanderings in an abstract world of familiar images. Of course, the given theme also leaves a lot beyond permissible bounds. But even the fact that people managed to just slightly plumb the depths of this Great mystery is very rewarding because it also testifies that mankind ascended a step higher, and that our consciousness has become wider in perception of novel truths.

Where does God Get the Spiritualization Energy from.

Interview with God:

- "You use the spiritualizing energy for animation of soul structures. Where do You get it? From what sources?"

- "It is kept in My depot," answered God briefly and rather vaguely at that.

And by the character of the given answer we felt that He did not want to go into details therefore we stopped to elaborate upon this subject during that channeling and decided to reserve it for a certain period.

After several channelings we were afforded an opportunity to clear up some more questions related to the subjects we were interested in because (as God was very busy) a duty Hierarch got on for a channeling with us. So we tried to put this question to him.

Interview with Hierarch:

- "Where does the spiritualization energy generally appear from?"

- "It is generated by God. And the number of souls He is able to produce for Himself depends on how much quantity of this energy He has generated."

- "With the help of what types of activity does God generates it?"

- "Very different types of activity. They are obscure for people."

- "Does it mean that there are dozens of those types of activity?"

- "Yes, great many of them. It can be stated that similar-type activities do not exist. You know, there are a lot of such methods in the cosmos. This process shall not be viewed from the standpoint of a single Personality, it shall be considered comprehensively with a view of evolution of the entire cosmos. And there are a lot of Gods in it, and every God works out His own spiritualization energy based on application of individual methods. And this process discloses their powers, all their capabilities. Every God spiritualizes matrices and creates new souls. Thereby He shows His paces, what advanced Entities He can create. Using your terminology, here educational processes are also taken into account, which, in Our terms, means the processes of Personality creation: including organization of environment, the process of its movement and dozens of other factors. But, of course, the ultimate thing is the capability to produce the spiritualization energy. The more energy can be produced by God, the greater number of souls He can animate. But increase of their quantity results in build-up of total Power of God, His energy potential."

- "And what is then the distinction between spiritualization energies generated by different Gods? Or do they all have similar energies?"

- "No, all of them produce different energies. If we compare energy of this type, we see that it differs by its qualities with different Gods."

- "So owing to this, all resultant creatures are different, as far as their character type is concerned. Is it true?"

- "No, owning to this, Entities* are produced, but tendencies of their development get changed. And it is important – what world they belong. Quality of spiritualization determines their attribution to specific worlds, i.e. the souls animated by these Gods are not able to exist in the worlds of other Gods due to their specific quality grade. Thus, for example, J*...(the Hierarch pronounces a cosmic name of our God) created people intended only for earthly world, and they are not able to live with another God because of the quality of their spiritualization energy."

- "And so nobody in the Hierarchy, except for our God, is able to generate this energy. Is it true?"

- "Yes, nobody. Only He alone. Just in these actions He has no assistants and substitutes. The assistants who produce matrices use the spiritualization energy which is already available."

- "And before J*... reached the Level of God did possess the knowledge of spiritualization?"

- "No, He didn't. Superior knowledge comes with Higher consciousness."

- "And did this knowledge open to Him when He became God?"

- "This knowledge does not open by itself. One shall work very hard for the Superior knowledge to get opened. You see, every energy shall be generated individually. This is a special-type, higher energy therefore for its production and control a soul shall have high energy of its own, to possess it the soul needs power. A weak entity will not be able to manipulate it. Therefore a soul in its ascent up the steps of Hierarchy shall accumulate a very great power potential, which will enable it to accumulate this energy. It means that the spiritualization energy can be worked out only starting from a certain Level of development."

- "But probably, our God learnt this secret from Personalities who are even more Higher than He is."

- "Yes, of course. But he was let into this secret only after he had reached the relevant Level of excellence. But it seems to me that here you are tempted to ask a question: why, for example, when Devil reaches the same level, why not give Him the same knowledge."

- "Yes," we agreed "It will be interesting to know that."

- "He has another qualitative structure. For all His efforts, He will never be able to work out the spiritualization energy because there is a structural difference between good and evil, and they have different prospects."

- "And if leant this secret, what would happen?"

- "Ask this question during the next channeling," apparently, He tries to decline from himself the responsibility for unwarranted disclosure and reasonably defers our question to the next communication session because he knows that it is only up to God to decide to what degree He can disclose his personal secret."

Therefore at the next channeling we addressed God with the same question.

Interview with God:

- "What would happen if Devil learnt the secret of spiritualization?"

- "In such a case He would have surpassed Me long time ago. Because the rate of development in His Hierarchy is many times as high as that in My Hierarchy. If it were the case, the world would be quite different. If Devil held a dominant position, the real world would perish. And devil would create the world entirely of his own."

- "But if He has such a high rate of development, will He be able to approach the Level at which He may learn the secret of spiritualization? Or will Devil be always suppressed for prevention Him from acquirement of that knowledge?"

- "You see, He is My second half, my minus. Together we constitute a single soul, both of us, therefore suppression is out of the question. Everything is consistent with the course of nature. A soul just could not be then divided into individual parts. We will go on exist like that. But what is available with Me is not available with Him."

- "Does the secret of matrix spiritualization consist in knowledge of the process of spiritualization or in possession of spiritualizing power?"

- "Knowledge and possession is one and the same thing. The former is impossible without the latter and vice versa. But Devil does not possess the spiritualization energy, its reserve. He failed to work out this energy reserve and He does not know how to work it out."

- "Why is this process inaccessible for Him? Does He have another constitution?"

- "Yes, He is My opposite, therefore He builds Himself up appropriately. The quality of His energies is such as He will never master the process of spiritualization. As a result of improvement through good and evil a soul works out different energies. He builds himself in a different way as compared to Me. And this facilitates development of certain qualities and results in disability to acquire others.

And the second reason why Devil cannot master the process of spiritualization consists in the fact that He does not know creativeness, which leads to accumulation of special energies facilitating generation of spiritualization energy. Everything invented and created by Devil is based on figures and calculations. He builds his matrix from minus energies. And this is not the way leading to acquirement of spiritualization energy.

To understand this process one shall choose the path of love, kindliness and creativeness. It is such a long path of development which runs through millions of years. It means that one life is not enough for this. The path of love, kindliness and creativeness shall be chosen from life to life. Everything will be changed: worlds, processes, ways of life and living conditions and mutual relations, but a soul shall inevitably choose them from dozens of other various actions. And then it will certainly come to mastering of the process of spiritualization, and the great secret will be opened to it."

- "Hence improvement of soul basing on creative options of development brings about mastering of the process itself, doesn't it?"

- "First a soul shall carry out quantitative and qualitative accumulations. Through the process of creation and kindliness it generates certain energies. Then at the higher Levels those energies serve as a basis for such processes, which help the soul to acquire the given energy. Creative process helps to construct matrix in a special way, and later such construction provides the soul with the potentials, which are needed for mastering the processes of spiritualization."

- "Devil does not also know how to build matrices, does He?"

- "He knows that. He knows how to build matrices and He builds them Himself," all this is pronounced by God with regret, then He explains, "He studies matrices when souls are decoded. His minus System is in charge of with those processes. Plus personalities do not like decoding processes. But the basic process i.e. – spiritualization of matrices – remains inaccessible for Him. This is the only secret, which He does not know."

- "And what about other worlds? Have Systems similar to Devil' Systems managed to get hold of the secret of spiritualization?"

- "What "other worlds" do you mean?" asks God.

- "The worlds that are outside our Universes," we explain. "What may happen to the worlds if, let us say, minus Hierarchs get hold of this secret?"

- "The world will also change as I already explained. In this respect the dependence is similar."

- "But then will Devil master the plus System or destroy it? What will happen to the plus Hierarchy? We are trying to find it out."

- "He will not be able to destroy us. Devil cannot also exist without plus System. He will just perish himself. This is already concerns certain principles of development and special structure of the cosmos. But, of course, He may turn into a predominating power. There are such worlds where minus power prevails. And their existence is not spontaneous, i.e. Nature has such places where they are necessary for its normal functioning."

- "During one of the previous channelings it was mentioned that Material systems also create their souls. Do they also possess the spiritualization energy?"

- "If we speak about My Material Systems, they are fully depend on Me and they receive My souls. But if we speak about highly-developed Material Systems, which created human beings, they are fully independent. They have their own God and receive souls from Him. Their God possesses the process of spiritualization, but it differs from My technology and, consequently, the quality of spiritualization energy is different. However highly-developed Material Systems have the same division: material is created by the material, and energetical is created by the energetical, which means that souls for them are created by Spiritual Systems.

My Material Systems have also achieved some success in mastering the material processes but they have a long way to go before they will achieve the level of Higher Material Systems. And I continue to supply souls to My Systems. Of course, they do not know the process of spiritualization. I create a matrix, spiritualize it, prepare all kinds of energy components for it, both plus and minus.

If I need some new material forms, they are created for Me under contract by Higher Material Systems. And as they deliver forms to Me, I supply them with souls for those forms. And as soon as everything is ready they deliver finished forms to the appropriate places. So they produce new material bodies for my worlds, and I supply souls to them. This is deemed our joint work within the frame of four Universes.

Process of Spiritualization

Interview with God:

- "Is matrix spiritualized when it is started to be produced or when it is ready?"
- "Matrix spiritualization is carried out at the beginning. And throughout the entire period of its growth (which is quite long) it is already spiritualized. It cannot be grown without this."
- You mentioned before that when matrix is being produced it is filled with initial energy. Is this energy and the energy of spiritualization just the same energy?"
- "No, it is not the same. As to their quality, they are absolutely different. The initial energy filling the matrix animates only a half of its structure. And matrix will not work without spiritualization energy itself. The spiritualization energy is like a motor which drives everything. It means that during creation of matrix two basic components become interlinked. The initial energy spiritualizes a body only by half. And the second half of spiritualization is provided by the energy of spiritualization. Combination of these two constituents allows to maneuver the process. Formation of material body of a child may serve as a rough example. In this case mother's chromosomes only half-create that full development pattern, which results from their mergence with male chromosomes."
- " And what is the process of spiritualization of the material body of a child during its birth? Is the soul spiritualized at first and does it then animate the body as a result of its introduction into it?"
- "For this purpose there is a special mechanism connecting permanent structures of soul to temporary bodies and material body. This connection is managed by a special System in charge of inter-linkage of soul and body."
- "When a soul is introduced into the material body and during switching of this mechanism the spiritualization energy kind of flows inside to reach all the cells of the body. Is it true?"
- "Yes. Something like that takes place."

- "Material body grows constantly, the number of cells increases. Does it mean that the spiritualizing power is also able to grow?"

- "It depends on the spiritual potential of every soul. But in the growing organism as it gets developed the input of energy from this general potential increases. That is at first the given spiritualization energy gets blocked in the common energy unit, and then it is distributed from it to the growing organism batch by batch. In such a manner the spiritualization power gradually disseminates within the whole body. Initially its amount is allocated for the entire organism but is distributed to it batch-wise as new cells appear."

- "Does Determinant take part in this process? Does He contribute some additional energy from Himself for retention of material body within one whole volume?"

- "Determinant distributes the spiritualization energy and controls its linkage with matter."

- "What is the difference between spiritualization of souls intended for a man and for a planet? Apparently, this difference exists. Are they spiritualized differently?"

- "No, Matrices are spiritualized in a similar way."

- "But a human soul is so small, and a planet soul is much larger," we are puzzled. "Are dimensions themselves important for the process?"

- "Dimensions are of no importance. The mechanism of spiritualization is the same. But power is different: for some of them it is mini, and for others- maxi. And technology is the same."

- "And is the quantity of this energy also different?" We are trying to get down to details.

As we did not understand the main principle of the process we (in our notions) had to hold onto minutest details, onto every new idea which could lead to discovery of unknown. And it helped very often. Because every further explanation gave a certain crumb of new knowledge, which helped us in our further advance.

- "Power of energy, its quantity is different," answered God. "Quantitative volume of this energy intended for the man and for the planet will be adequate. The same is with power."

- "Is there any difference in manufacture of matrix for the man and the planet?"

- "Manufacture of matrix is standard but their plotting scale is different. Matrix of the man is small and that of the planet – large."

- "And is there any difference in filling the cells with energy?"

- "No, the principle of filling the cells with qualities is one and the same. The principle difference is in power. And energy interchange of a planet soul is much more intensive than that of a human soul."

*   *   *

- "Are spaces under construction spiritualized?"
- "Yes. Any space is some closed volume, which fulfils its tasks within the general Volume of Nature therefore it shall also be a living structure."
- "But in this case the applied method of spiritualization is other than, for example, the method of matrix spiritualization, isn't it?"
- "Yes, method is different, but energy is the same. It is the same within the given volume, which means that the space and everything that it is composed of and all the forms populating it are spiritualized by homogeneous energy because any specific volume shall be unified. But if we take another volume, which is a considerable distance away from the first one, then its spiritualization energy will be of another quality (fig. 7)."

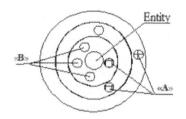

"A" - spiritualization energy of different quality
(heterogeneous).
"B" - homogeneous energy.

Fig. 7

- "Does it mean that spaces are spiritualized differently?"
- "Not only spaces, but absolutely everything. Here the principle is as follows: the closer to Nature Entity constituting this maxi-volume i.e. closer to its center, the larger degree of spiritualization of everything around: planets, Universes, spaces – with the spiritualization energy,

which in its quality is similar to this center. And at considerable distance from the center the quality of spiritualization energy changes. I am speaking about similarity of energies but not about perfect analogy.

It means that similarity of spiritualization energies close to the center denotes their homogeneity. However this homogeneity is characteristic of maxi-volumes. For mini-volumes it will all be heterogeneous. That is to say, there are relevant criteria, which help to unite them into a type of homogeneous energies. And there are indicators which allow considering them individual. And heterogeneous energies belonging to volumes, which are at a considerable distance away from each other, will have differences in the first and second indicators already."

Energy of Spiritualization.
Its Qualities

- "Does spiritualization energy have its own Hierarchy? Does it have any variations?"
- "Spiritualization energy is unique."
- "And if we compare it with spiritualization energies of other Gods?"
- "No, it is not a Hierarchy, when something goes from different Gods. A Hierarchy is formed when development of energy proceeds successively and one grows up from another."
- "Does this energy exist separately?"
- "Yes. It is special, individual and it shall not be compared with others because it possesses special qualities enabling it to turn dead into living."
- "Is the spiritualization energy used on Earth for various forms the same or different? For example, for spiritualization of stones it may be this type of spiritualization energy, spiritualization of people may require other type, and for plants – the third type."
- "The energy itself, its type is one and the same. But additional qualities are different."
- "What are additional qualities?"
- "The spiritualization particle is one and the same but it includes some special additional qualities, which are needed for this or that form. And those additional qualities are also considered spiritualizing. Linkage with different forms is effected at their expense."

- "And what sub-varieties of spiritualization energy exist? As a matter of fact, there are no end of worlds in Your Universes, and they are very different with reference to their contents. And creatures living in them are widely different in their appearance and inward structure. Doesn't such a diversity of living forms call for some differences in spiritualization energies also? Can it be true that one and the same spiritualization energy is used in different worlds?"

- "Yes, it is. One and the same energy or, to be exact, homogenous energy, is used for any forms in My Universes, and not only on your Earth. But at the same time, for different forms some qualitative additions are applied."

- "What are those qualitative additions? What do they add to the spiritualization power?"

- "They add peculiar coloring to it if we may say so. But at the same time it remains homogeneous and preserves the same structure. Those additions are needed just for different forms. But they do not affect the energy itself, its basic quality. Additions are necessary for linkage with various forms. If for some reason the volume of spiritualization energy needs to be increased, then the former volume is replenished with exactly the same homogenous energy."

- "Hence, quantitative reservations are made, aren't they?"

- "Yes. Quantitative ones are made. But its quality in all my forms is identical. And its accumulation results in growth of power characteristics of spiritualization energy. If we compare two bodies: small and large, then we can see that maintenance of a large volume in a single-whole state requires a higher power potential of this energy then maintenance of a small volume. Therefore quantitative reservations are necessary. But even a single developing form also requires accumulation, additions of this energy. The soul is growing, matrix keeps on expanding, and the increased volume shall be restrained by greater spiritualization power. Ever increasing volume requires increased power qualities and this brings about expansion of quantitative aspect of spiritualization energy."

- "What other differences do spiritualization energies of different Gods have except for their quality?"

- "They differ in their design. And every God has His own spiritualization mechanism. We do not allow any repetitions."

- "Are there any other energies, which are similar to spiritualization energy in their capabilities?"

- "No, of course not."

- "Spiritualization energy drives everything around, animates structures. Does it mean that as for the Level of its development it is the highest one?"

- "Yes, this energy exceeds all others. And there is no energy higher than it."

- "Does spiritualization energy originate from somewhere?"

- "Of course, it has its reference point. And it goes higher than My Hierarchy, therefore it may be stated that it is infinite in its existence. It is available in all Hierarchies standing higher than Ours by the level of development. Nature itself is penetrated by spiritualization energy, and it lies everywhere to the borders of Its habitation."

- "Can we say that spiritualization energy has only plus constituent because it animates everything?"

- "No. It is neutral. It can equally belong to any form: either plus or minus. It is able to spiritualize absolutely everything. But not everybody can possess and control it, to do so one shall have certain spiritual indicators. Being neutral and being able to spiritualize any form, it will work dependent on how the form will be used, what aims its activity is directed towards: towards the good or evil. It means that the forms themselves or those who control them can use spiritualization energy either negatively or positively."

- "Is the spiritualization energy categorized as per the degree of development: in a man – it is one degree of development, in a planet – it is another degree, in Absolute spirit – it is the third degree? Indeed, in different forms it exists within different time."

- "It has its own system, its own world in Hierarchy where it develops. Duration of existence is important, of course, but it determines only its quantitative aspect."

Spiritualization Energy after Death

- "What happens to spiritualization energy filling the matrix as a result of decoding of human soul after death? Does it escape from it, dissipate in space or is it collected separately?"

- "This energy is very expensive, and it is not reasonable to slather it. It is collected by specialized Systems separately from all other energies. During decoding every quality is separated, all energies constituting this quality are separated strictly type-wise, the types shall not be mixed. Every type of energy is placed, (according to your thinking) in an individual flask because every quality refers to the relevant reserve. And all previously used spiritualization energy is also accumulated in a separate reserve. Later on it is taken from this reserve as appropriate and is used for creation of new souls. But all this spiritualization energy is My personal depot, only I can dispose and use it for its intended purpose."

- "It falls out that a failed soul is decoded, but spiritualization energy is returned to You. Is it true?"

- "Yes, to My reserve."

- "And how can such once-used spiritualization energy be good for spiritualization of souls? It has been in use already. Does it somehow affect the process of spiritualization?"

- "No, it does not. Its quality remains the same. Therefore the same method of spiritualization is used."

- "Is the spiritualization energy somehow cleansed prior to its second implantation in matrix?"

- "It is never contaminated with any impurities therefore no additional cleansing is required. And after the time spent in the soul, which passed some development phases, it remains the same as it was initially."

- " Does it mean that spiritualization energy is always clean?"

- "Yes, purely clean."

- "And can spiritualization energy be derived from soul? Sometimes souls are enslaved. And somebody may need it for experiments."

- "Yes, there are cosmic Systems which enslave souls. But they are devoid of capability to derive this energy for themselves. Because generally those who are concerned with fighting stand on the low level of development, they do not know Higher operations and the main thing about it is that they do not know its release code. Only I know this code therefore usually they are content with capture of souls – they take souls all for themselves and use them for their own purposes."

- "And, hence, you are able to derive spiritualization energy from souls themselves." We pinpoint our attention upon the issue we are interested in."

- "Souls are Mine, and energy is also Mine therefore it is but natural that all processes are within the reach of their Creator," answers God proudly and in somewhat dignified manner, therefore at the mention of "Creator" we envision the tremendous vast of His Universes including thousands upon thousands of their worlds and creatures."

- "When a man dies, then the spiritualization energy leaves its material body i.e. the body becomes inanimate. But at the same time it consists of spiritualized atoms and molecules. How then in this case can the spiritualized be combined with the inanimate?"

- "If a soul has left the body, then there is no spiritualization energy left in it therefore there is nothing to be combined. This is inherent in the general mechanism of linkage and separation."

- "And what about molecules and atoms constituting a body? In fact, they remain and change over to their own existence."

- "From cells and molecules constituting a material body the spiritualization energy escapes following the soul, and they get disintegrated. They have a certain death procedure. Molecules which constitute a body are programmed in such a way that with them the program of death is left as a program of decay."

- "Can we say that atoms and molecules are the same as Universes?"

- "If they are living. Let me help you to understand what you are asking about: imagine that the man is just a molecule. When the soul leaves him, then the molecule gets disintegrated. But the soul remains at the energy level, a human soul remains."

- "Why don't spiritualization energy of soul and the energy of material body mix with each other?"

- "These are different energies, they have different qualitative characteristics. Besides, both bodies – spiritual body and material body – have their own bodies which are placed one inside the other in a special way but they do not mix."

- "Consequently, spiritualization energy has its borders inside the body, doesn't it?"

- "Yes, they are pre-programmed. But, generally, any homogeneous energy, in whatever quantity – large or small, is all supplied to a relevant reserve from any other sources and only there it is mixed up with similar homogenous energy, i.e. without any spiritual constructions. Energy of any type is registered, and is nowhere delayed for no particular reason. Therefore spiritualization energy also either exists in some form or is kept in common storage reserve."

PREDECESSOR OF DEVIL

Many subjects seemed to be fully exhausted, but channelings went on, and therefore small additions to former questions emerged here and there. Subjects got expanded and sometimes transferred to a new Level of understanding. This meant that we rose a step higher and therefore the things which were closed for us at the inferior Level became comprehensible.

And information about predecessor of Devil and about matrices are deemed such additions.

Once during subsequent channelings when everything had been written about the Hierarchies of God and Devil we addressed God the following question:

- "We have several questions about Devil. May we ask them?"
- "Yes."
- "You are twice the age of Devil. It means that there was a time when You developed without Him. For about a half time of your existence You did without Devil. Is it true?"
- "Yes, without this personality."
- "But then You had someone else."
- "Yes, there was another. It was the one who is in His System now. But Devil outrun him in His development therefore he made way for Him. Devil took the lead of the Hierarchy, and he became His subordinate."
- "Did You make the substitution or did they exchange their positions themselves as a result of some debates between them?"
- "I make all appointments myself to My own benefit."
- "Did Devil outrun him by His qualities?"
- "Yes, by many parameters. And I needed more efficient personality because scales of My work were expanding."
- "Did that Hierarch of the minus System have some other name?"
- "Naturally. Everybody has individual name. And as for the name "Devil", it was invented for Hierarch of the minus System by people long after that already."
- "May a need to have Devil vanish in the process of eternal evolution?"
- "No, it will never happen because this is My construction and I am not going to change it. It is not useful for Me because Devil or rather His System carries out all dirty work (as you call it) and all calculations."
- "And do other Gods have other construction?"
- "Everybody has individual construction. And why don't you ask me what terms I had been on with the other Hierarch of minus System before Devil came to Me?"

- "Yes. Do tell us more about it, please," we brightened up at the opportunity to expand the given topic. We did not ask some questions interesting for us because we were afraid to be refused. And as an opportunity to extend our knowledge presented itself we were glad to continue the dialogue.

- "To be more exact," began God "Me and the former Hierarch didn't have any relations, we had proportions of minus and plus because We together made up a single structural formation. At that time I was much more greater than He. But it was not until I began to manage four Universes that I could override Him by 2 to 1. As soon as I got past that point, a lot of new demands arose. Before that the Hierarch of minus System occupied one forth of My Volume. And, of course, such an overbalance of plus part impeded My work: to lighten it I had to maintain the balance between plus and minus.

It was Me who took major load. I planned, designed, performed all calculations, which were numerous because spatial Volume kept on increasing. I tried to entrust those calculations to neutral System (Medical)*. They had their own designers who worked to achieve their own objectives, and I added some new ones in connection with establishment of four Universes. The scope of my activity kept on increasing and I had to find some optimum scheme of work. And I myself also had to invent new forms involving some calculations which were performed by nobody but Me, and I also had to complete construction tasks – everything required My participation. I was overburdened with work. I had to do virtually everything Myself. And then I decided to put a real Devil in charge of the minus Hierarchy; he was good in calculations and surpassed his predecessor in them and in some of his ideas. Therefore I interchanged them. And minus System began to perform calculations. As a result, My load was reduced and I could concern Myself with more important tasks together with the neutral System."

- "And those Entities who do not enter in Your Volume and embark on their own course of development also look for their own Devil for themselves, don't they? Or does He already exist in their mini-Hierarchy right along?"

- "What Entities do you mean?"

- "Those who having completed their improvement in Your Hierarchy go out of the pyramid. They have either to enter in You or embark on their own course of development."

- "When the border is crossed and a new stage of development is started, as a rule, Entities try to find followers for themselves – someone like Devil, and they start to form their individual Hierarchy."
- "Does it fall out that every mini-Hierarchy has its own Devil?"
- "Yes."
- "How many Devil's predecessors did You have? Many of them or only one? We guess, there were a few mature personalities."
- "There were many predecessors because the path of My improvement is eternal."
- "And was there a time when You did everything alone?"
- "No. There was not such time. My second half always existed to larger or a lesser extent. It complies with my construction."
- "Can we ask some qualifying questions about Devil' System?"
- "Yes."
- "We know that after death human souls are subject to trial. Do Your Entities or Devil's Entities act as Judges of human souls?"
- "They are all involved in trials because there are different criteria of soul evaluation. My Hierarchy has our own soul evaluation criteria and the Devil's Hierarchy has some other criteria. By the way, separator himself is a construction of Devil. But My Entities manage the separator and control all the processes related to his work. However at the same time all dirty work is performed by His executors."
- "When Entities in the Devil's Hierarchy reach the vertex of His pyramid and enter in Devil's volume, does He allow anybody to embark on the individual course of development the way You do?"
- "Devil doesn't let anybody go. It is against His rules. If one gets to Him, one is never released. And as for independence, He frees His Entities from swaddling-clothes after they pass the middle of pyramid. That is, from this point on they start to get rid of robotization gradually."
- "Did somebody ever turn against Him? And how did He treat rebels?"
- "Revolts against Him took place, of course. Generally it is possible from the middle of Hierarchy because robotized Entities cannot resent or oppose something. Robots do not rebel, they just act in exact compliance with the program. But from the middle of pyramid this behavior becomes possible already. But here it should be highlighted that ordinary Entities are not capable of revolt, only mature Entities, those who reached the middle of the Hierarchy and succeeded in self-improvement are able to rebel. But, of course, such Entities are valuable for Devil, because

He invested a lot in their development. Therefore He decodes them in extraordinary circumstances, generally He reforms them. Besides basic programs, such Entities do relevant programs of severe rehabilitation. He also holds His souls dear after all."

*   *   *

Chapter 3
SPRIRITUAL UNIVERSES

Introduction

What is the Universe?

From the standpoint of the man, Universe is a certain volume of space, which includes some material bodies. And only a few of those bodies are known to people. All bodies are subdivided by the man into planets and stars and, in his opinion, all other minor forms such as meteorites, bolides as well as such states as cosmic dust and gas voids are their derivates. People know about black holes, pulsars and, perhaps, here the subject list of internal content of Universes stops.

The man knows very little about it. So little that we can say he knows nothing. But if we want to understand what the Universe is, how it is constructed, and who populates it, we shall decide what specific Universe we want to gain a familiarity with.

In terms of their structure, Universes are subdivided into material and energetical ones. The latter are of Spiritual type.

People live in material Universe and are familiar with the bodies listed above. But material Universe has parallel Universes i.e. spaces lying in other dimension but basing on its material structure as on a foundation and connected to it by certain subtle links and dependencies.

Energetical Universes are higher than material and parallel ones. They are at different levels of development and their design is relevant to those Levels. Naturally, every creature dependent on the degree of its advancement, lives in the Universe which corresponds to the level of its development. Therefore a material man exists in material Universe and can see these things, and a more developed Creature exists in the

Universe corresponding to the Level of its excellence and it can see other things. But in this regard a higher Entity* will know about everything which lies below it, and an inferior one will never be able to behold the higher.

Everything is beheld in proportion to increase of excellence. Therefore creatures of different levels of development will speak about different designs of the Universe, about different paths of its conception and development. Besides, the Universes standing on the same stage but intended for different purposes will differ in terms of their quality and structure. Moreover, there are no identical Universes.

As for us, we will dwell on discussion of four Universes, which belong to God and in which He exists.

These Universes comprise in themselves the energetic worlds of the energy range, which is characteristic of them. Therefore in discussion of the design of Universes we do not speak so much about the material aspects as the mystical ones. What is the mystical design of Universes, of those very Universes in which human soul has to exist not for a brief instant (as it lives in the material environment) but for billions upon billions of years during its ascent up the Hierarchy?

Upon completion of the cycle of development in the material Universe the man passes to Spiritual Universe of God, in His energetical worlds and continues his evolution in subtle world which is infinite in its development. A tiny human soul walking through the worlds is like a small snowball gradually becomes bigger and bigger as it acquires more and more energetical mass, eventually reaching the size of Higher Entities.

But what are Universes? How do they appear and vanish? We discovered all this during our interview with God. He exists in Spiritual Universe, and we live in a material one. Therefore as we understand, perhaps, a lot of knowledge lies beyond the reach of our mind. But still we wish to have at least a slight idea about the worlds which are above.

We shall admit that, of course, it is difficult to ask about things that you know almost nothing about, you have never heard of and never seen.

Truths which were known before have brought the mankind to a dead-lock of hopeless, senseless existence, but new truths have not emerged yet. Most of materialistic theories of construction of world and Universe became obsolete and didn't represent the reality. Therefore in our questions we always had to move as if by touch: first found a thin thread by feeling and advanced a bit, found again by touch something tiny – and advanced a little bit further.

And what is before us? We are blind, and only based on paltry notions of the new, we managed to get ahead step-by-step to the unknown. The only methods of search for questions and of advancement on the path of the unknown was to read the materials made available to us and try to find in them some new aspects and to expand the frontiers of knowledge on the subject chosen.

We did not receive answers to all of our questions. Most of information is kept closed for mankind. Therefore we rejoiced at every tiny disclosure of divine secrets, were happy to get to know every new notion expanding the frontiers of our knowledge.

So, what was narrated by God about Spiritual Universes?

Cosmic Organism. Nature.

Interview with God:

- "Wherefore do Universes exist?"

- "Universes are deemed cells of a huge organism of Nature which enable It to exist and fulfill certain functions of Its vital activity. And at the same time those cells (being certain forms of space) serve as environment for existence of souls. Both the former and the latter are interdependent; and no other way of existence is available."

- "Our Universe exists in a certain spatial volume which constitutes a part of a huge living organism referred to as Nature. Can a man see the inside of this Nature while looking through a telescope or just peering at the skies?"

- "Yes. But He can see only the things which are allowed to be seen by him and nothing more. If he saw a true picture of cosmic space, then he would be shocked at the sight of it."

- "But why? Does it look so terrible?"

- "A man lives in an artificial world which was created specially for him, with a lot of sugared up places. And he will never see the things which he is not intended to see. And this is done for protection of his mind. The entire Earth has a certain spatial shield, which protects it from lethal exposures and other external hazardous effects."

- "And can a man see in Cosmos something else which is not known to him at the moment?"

- "Vision depends on the increase of development level. But even in case of increase of energy input which is usually fed down by his Determinant a man will be able to see the things which he never sees at his normal energy level. Gradual improvement of soul results in accumulation of new energies by its matrix and permanent subtle bodies. Consequently, its total energy potential gets increased, and the range of vision is extended. But for Earth the usual procedure is as follow. The real pattern of space which is seen by a man from the Earth or from ionosphere is meant for a certain level of human development. And when the level gets increased we change this pattern of space for the next one which corresponds to the next stage of progress i.e. the next pattern of space will belong to the mankind standing at a higher step as compared to the present level."

Interview with Devil

During channelings with Devil we continued the work which we carried out with God; that is we went on with the work started by God. When Devil went out for contacts we had an impression that our Creator was busy and therefore He asked Devil to act as His temporary substitute. As a result, when Devil went out for contacts the schedule of our work did not change. On his part, Devil did not offer something personal to be included in our work which would have changed the pattern of our channelings and He did not try to obtrude His opinions. However once He said:

- "Do you want me to give you my own model of Universe?"

- "No, thank you. We are quite content with the information conveyed by God," refused we at once, without delay.

Of course, it would be interesting to learn about His model of Universe construction but we were aware that He never gave something away for nothing and afterwards in return He would take everything He would think fit for Himself.

Next time He offered to my spouse who concerns himself with astrology some new astrological calculations but he refused to take them. We tried to carry out usual conversational channelings and to keep within the established limits. Of course, we understood that during our channelings with Him He was trying to check us, to find out the temptations which we could be carried away by. Therefore we tried to be vigilant.

We continued to discuss a spectrum of questions also with Devil, so many of His answers were included in the composed subjects as well. At the same time one should not regard His answers with prejudice. One should remember that He is in the pay of God. He is one of His key assistants dealing with issues of destruction and clearance of territories. He is a mathematician, universal designer and a programmer who has a profound knowledge of everything that concerns His part in God's worlds.

Therefore Devil's answers were as follows.

- "What else is there in Cosmos except the things which are seen by the man?"
- The man is able to perceive only material things and the things, which correspond to the physical spectrum of energies. There are a lot of holograms in your Universe but people think that they are material objects. Holograms are given for your progress so that you have what to study and what to ponder on. Holograms facilitate brainwork. But when a man reaches the next, higher stage, he will discover for himself another form of life and something more. He will see the same hologram but it will be a changed one. That is to say, what you see now as some energy bunches, a kind of energy points, like, for example, individual stars, later on after reaching your improved stage of development will be seen by you quite differently. Currently you perceive everything as material objects and even energetics itself. You can see only the energetics, which belongs to material spectrum. But when you are a step higher, you will be able to see the energetics itself i.e. you will start to perceive energies of a higher range. On the other hand, you will not be able to see your brut physical matter anymore."
- "Shall we see only energy?"
- "Yes, material world will vanish for you. Because vision organs will change. You will be able to perceive subtle matter, start to see energy layers. And when you rise even higher, then you will start to perceive the visual environment as digits."
- "And how do You perceive our solar system then?"
- "For Me it is all digits and only digits."

- "And what is the energy construction of the Universe, from your standpoint?"

- "For Me its construction is energetical, also presented as digits. With Me everything is associated with digits. And energetics can also be digitized."

- "And do you calculate absolutely everything?"

- "Yes, I calculate everything: how much energy is needed, how much is available, for which purpose and why. For Me the whole matter is broken down into digits."

- "And can you explain what is solar system virtually?"

- "Solar system does not exist," said He dryly.

- "But we see it," answered we and tried to produce evidence and arguments, "Scientists investigate it, receive some data measured by instrumentation."

- "There are certain energy retransmitters," spoke He again in metallic voice, "And Solar system is just a material hologram generated for your development. As for your scientists, it is a dead-end trend of development. Eighty percent of their theories are false."

We were somewhat bewildered with this revelation of His, but He could not tell a lie. That was not that Level. Therefore we had to revise a lot of our knowledge. It's not for nothing that ancient philosophers believed that the whole world is an illusion. Therefore we asked further questions:

- "It falls out that in our Cosmos everything is also a hologram."

- "Why? There are also a lot of material objects."

As the devil's conception of the world differs markedly from that of ours, we decided to ask God for his apprehension of the world.

Interview with God:

- "What is your conception of Universe?"

- "Such concepts as: the Universe and the Cosmos are put into practice by human mind. Our world is different. What is known to you under the name Universe for us is a certain spatial volume in which we have to work. Your concepts differ considerably from our concepts: you believe that only people are spiritualized and all the rest is just certain inanimate spatial structure. But we exist in a living organism and those four Universes of Mine are deemed sort of cells of this organism. Of course, it is a crude analogy because it is very difficult to reduce the reality of macrocosm to the level of your concepts.

In reality the concept of Cosmos corresponds to the concept of Nature, of that huge living progressing organism which encompasses all outdoor. My Universes may be taken for four cells of this cosmic organism. There are four of them all in all. And inside it there are thousands upon thousands of similar cells. So the proportionality of our spatial volumes and Nature itself is enormous."

- On Earth the law of analogy is in effect: i.e. living beings repeat each other in some way. And are there similar Universes in Nature? Is something which exists in your cells - Universes – repeated in other cells of Nature?"

- "Yes, the analogy exists, but it is not full, but partial because everything is subject to the individual development law which isolates the particular and imparts to it something different from others."

- "Does the analogy is related to something that enables all the particular to unit to produce an integrated whole?"

- "Yes, it is related to vegetal functions of organism. In it certain laws are in effect. These laws unite everything scattered in comprehensive whole. But integration is also facilitated by the general program designed for the given Nature and taking into account its minute particulars in unified function. It also integrates the entire common time of organism and lifetime of cells-Universes. To gain greater insight into that try to imagine your own organism. It is one whole but everything in it is different. A lot of analogies are inside you but at the same time absolutely everything is individual."

Emergence of Universes

- "How do Universes come into being? Planets are born as a result of some explosion which serves as a certain starting moment initiating the program of its construction. Do Universes also have similar explosion-based program initiating moment?"

- "First of all, distinction shall be made between material and energetical Universes because energetical Universes come into being differently. As for material Universe, it can emerge in a variety of ways. It can be both an explosion-resultant emergence and non- explosion-resultant appearance."

- "Scientists believe that our Universe is an expanding one. Why is it expanding?"

- "It is expanding due to deployment of its program. It means that your Universe is growing and developing."

- "Are there Universes which get expanded to their maximum borders at once and do not move any further?"

- "Speaking generally (not specifically), absolutely everything (which can and cannot be imagined by people) exists in macrocosm. There are thousands upon thousands of options of Universe emergence. They may even be designed as dummies in the relevant region of space."

- "Space is infinite but Universe is finite. How can we correlate these two opposites?"

- "The Universe is a part of some space. Space itself is infinite but it shall be sectioned. Those sections are made use of for some purposes, and they are finite. So the Universe is also a part of infinite space, but it is finite."

- "And what lies beyond the boundaries of the Universe? Infinity?"

- "A man is very small therefore for him it is infinity. But actually beyond the boundaries of My four Universes there is an infinite number of other Universes which are limited to the size of Nature."

- "And what is single-whole Volume? Is it just the Nature itself?"

- "For the man – it may be Nature because it is very huge and incommensurable with him. However it may also be even greater Volume. Living world is infinite. A man can take that maximum volume (which he is only able to imagine) for single-whole Volume."

- "May it then be populated by thousands upon thousands of such Gods like You?"

- "Yes, there are a lot of moving ones. As a matter of fact we do not stand still, but keep on developing and passing from one Level to another. But those levels are proportional to Us already."

Acquisition of Universes

- "Did You start to control four Universes right away or did You start with one of them at first and then their number was increased gradually?"

- "No, I started to manage all four of them at once. Here the technology is one and the same."

- "Did You get four Universes on the basis of a number of souls available with You?"

- "No, it was the other way round. I was given space, or, rather, certain spatial volume, and as for souls, I started to make them Myself taking into account the space I received. There were no Universes in it. I constructed them Myself so that they could gather qualities I needed. Initially this volume existed in one body and had a certain permanent frame. And It was Me who divided it into four parts and built four Universes. I designed and improved them the way I thought fit. And I must imbibe from them all the qualities of this space into Myself. It is prescribed from the Above. It is needed for every next Level to be passed. Every Level has its own spatial volume; and until I accumulate the relevant amount of energy in My matrix, I will never be able to reach the next Level. And in this I am similar to other souls. Every soul has to accumulate a certain quantity of energies of relevant quality in its matrix and, consequently, to pass to the next Level. It is true of all souls at any Level."

- "You divided the spatial volume distributed to You into four Universes. And how did You use them thereafter?"

- "Every God rearranges His spatial volumes according to His own objectives. Therefore I started to improve them in compliance with my own plans. I designed them in a way I thought fit. Every Universe shall give specific quality."

- "Why did You begin to construct just four Universes and not less or more of them?"

- "Yes, I could have built ten Universes and twenty of them, but I decided that it was more reasonable to have four. It was consistent with My calculations."

- "On what grounds were You distributed a general spatial volume? Did that depend on Your power, potential?"

- "You see that is the path of My development. Why, I am also in the process of permanent development like all others and I ascend from one Level to another in compliance with the degree of My development. Reaching a new Level I get into a new world. And this world is just the volume I have to develop. Naturally, My energy indicators shall comply with each world. When I rise still higher, then at the next Level I will be made available even greater volume. And I will have to build even more enormous structures than here. My work, My development consists in that. But before I pass to a new Level I will have to accumulate the amount of energy prescribed for the given Level. I will not be able to ascend higher without them. Every Level is deemed a set of certain energies therefore they determine both growth of energy potential of soul and its power."

- "But still does every soul have some standard volumes of existence?"

- "Yes, certainly."

- "In Your Hierarchy there is a strictly defined number of souls. Hence it is related to its spatial dimensions, isn't it?"

- "Yes. Hierarchy is a spatial structure designed for a certain number of souls. Every world of Hierarchy contains a specific number of Entities, and every soul has a specific potential. That is, any soul is allocated a certain conventional volume. Dimensions of this volume are determined on the basis of energetical parameters of soul. More powerful soul requires greater spatial volumes. For every soul it is calculated how many qualities it shall get at the relevant stage of development. And qualities require a corresponding volume which is always strictly defined. There are such numerical interdependencies. But "volume" is an image-bearing notion. Actually everything is much more complicated. But the principle is as described above. Everything is calculated with reference to qualities. At the given Level a soul will get no less and no more. The only method possible is to increase the rate of its own development in order to pass this Level as fast as possible"

- "Who constructed Universes based on Your designs? Did Material Systems produce the physical bodies at first? And did then Spiritual Systems create their structures on their basis?"

- "No. Everything went the other way round. Material plane was joined to the subtle plane. Subtle structures expressed the basis which special features of material Universe construction depended on. Of course, from your point of view, it seems obscure and random but its whole structure serves a single purpose. Therefore it is devoid of everything undue, needless. Every object has its own strictly defined intention. But a man exists in material Universe, and I am in energetical one. However all those planes are correlated with each other both by processes and by structures."

- "Did You face any difficulties while creating them?"

- "Of course, I did. Some things had to be produced and rearranged but not in a real world but in the design version because at first Universes were constructed on experimental basis. Structures and processes were tested on models, if such comparison is the most clear to you. I had a huge laboratory in My disposal. Model Universes of reduced dimensions were constructed in it. Initial samples were taken, structures, energy flows, materials were tested. But not everything is to be verified in a similar way. For example, models should not be necessarily used in simulation of your Earth for testing the planet structure. Only a sample of the earth material itself was needed because sometimes material can give qualities other than the required ones."

- "Do four Universes have similar design?"

- "No, they are of different design. It is due to their functional features. Universes are different both in their quality and design."

- "Are Universes constructed only based on modeling design methods or do some other approaches exist?"

- "Of course, there are other methods of construction. But the modeling method is practical because at first everything is created as a design version which allows testing a lot of processes and to improve the theory of development using models. A model is subject to repeated testing, adjustment, and the final solution is transferred to the initial space. The Universe may be constructed in a step-wise manner. At first one part can be created, then the second, the third and so on. A Material Universe may be created in a similar way; and also there is an explosion-based version when some mass having a certain set of components is included in the process of construction through program deployment.

It resembles the work of a genic code, which begins to construct a huge organism under the action of a certain starting moment. It means that in the given case a material Universe is constructed automatically but under control of Higher Systems. Quality of the Universe depends on the set of those components which are built into the initial mass. However its quality is planned well in advance."

- "Are Universes constructed by the cosmic Systems that also create planets? Or are they constructed by a higher Level?"

- "Physical Universes and planets are built by the same Material Systems because Spiritual ones do not have relevant methods and technologies in their disposal. The material is created by the material. I have to engage contractors because I do not possess Material Systems of my own whose development level is as high as Theirs."

- "Nowadays people apply computer-aided simulation. Do You also apply it? Does Devil, for example, imitate any tasks on computers?"

- "Yes, Devil applies computer-aided simulation. He keeps on upgrading his computers and his design procedures. He never stops forging ahead. It is against his principles. As for creation of My Universes, at first all the models were designed in compliance with those tasks which I set before Spiritual Systems. It was they who made initial calculations of the design of the energetical part related to construction and contents of all subtle worlds, to their functioning and to acquirement of the needed number of souls. Those were vast schemes involving meticulous and profound work of designing Systems. As soon as the subtle structure models had been tested and approved for final use, Material and Neutral Systems from the Medical Hierarchy were got involved.

Material Systems also give much consideration of calculations because they cannot be dispensed with. Everything must be accurate. But their calculations are specific because they are related to chemical and physical processes as well as to mechanics of material body movements. As regards the Medical System, it includes departments which deal with experiments and calculations concerning living organics and biology. They carry out experiments on matter and deal with flora and fauna."

Structure of Universes

- "How are four Universes of Yours situated towards each other?"
- "They lie close to each other. A man can imagine them as four neighboring cells. In reality their spatial structure is much more complicated, of course. Actually they are neither cells nor squares. But we keep to your concepts. Territories situated close to each other are allocated on purpose because it facilitates Management. If My Universes were scattered, and I had to cover great distances, I would disturb the spaces between My territories as I possess huge energy. But those spaces are also in the process of development, they have their own life, program and their energy is different. Therefore only neighboring territories are allocated for management."
- "And as far as the energy type is concerned, are Your Universes similar?"
- "No, they are all different in terms of their energy and structure. And their structure depends on the quality of souls which they shall grow for My Hierarchy, which, in its turn, is connected with specific energy types inherent in each Universe. One Universe supplies souls

of this quality, another Universe gives souls of some other quality, and the souls supplied by the third one have still other specific quality. And those are souls of four types and of four different composites* - the souls I need. And I produce them in those territories. Processes aimed at provision of relevant quality were designed in compliance with the required composite of souls. And in construction of each Universe already we proceeded from the process technology. Such is the sequence of links which goes from goal and comes to structures materializing it."

- "Are all of Your Universes constructed from similar physical matters or from different ones?"

- " In material Universes the physical matter is one and same, but the internal construction is different."

- "If we take a human being and transfer him from one material Universe to the other, will he be able to live their?"

- "No, he won't. Material bodies of Universes are identical but the derivative of those bodies is absolutely different because their internal design is individual, and their processes flow in different ways. Therefore such a derivative as living conditions will be also absolutely different: air, temperature, pressure and so on. You see, even within the limits of your Earth having single matter there are various living conditions, and Universe-wide diversity is many times as great."

- "Do material worlds exist in all Universes?"

- "Yes, all of them have material worlds as well as parallel ones."

- "Does our Universe contain a certain number of worlds and spaces?

- "Yes."

- You have very many worlds. How do you manage to control all of them?"

- "With Me every world has its own code. And any world is deemed the energy of certain range or development level. Therefore, from My standpoint, here it is not so much a world that is coded as energy. Codes help Me to handle worlds, to rearrange, to join or, on the contrary, to separate something. Digits enable Me to predict the possible results well in advance. Besides, for Me codes stand for names. "

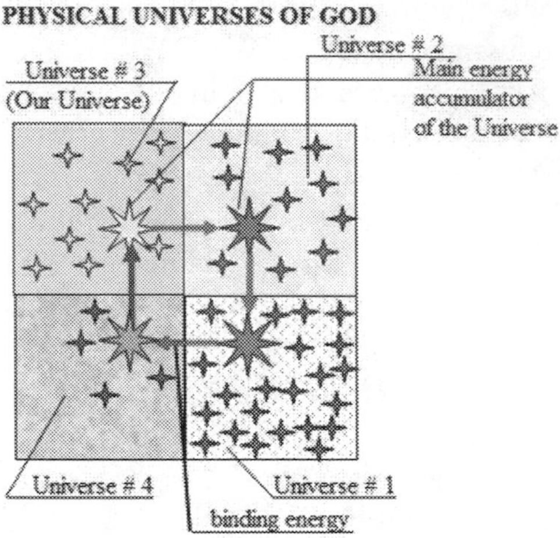

PHYSICAL UNIVERSES OF GOD

Universe no.1 – contains maximum number of starts

Universe no.2 – less starts than in no.1.

Universe no.3 – less starts than in no 2.

Universe no.4 – just a few stars (black Universe). In it stars are situated closer to the center of square and around the star which serves as energy accumulator.

Note:

Energy accumulators exchange energies with neighboring Universes according to prescribed procedure.

Physical Universes serve as the fundamental basis for spiritual Universes.

Scheme 1

It is not practical to invent names for each of numerous worlds. And it is very easy to operate digits."

- "As a Universe keeps on developing the number of worlds in it increases, doesn't it? Or does the number of worlds remain constant but worlds themselves continue to expand in the process of development?"

- "It depends on the worlds. Which worlds do you mean: physical, parallel or energetical?"

- "For example, energetical ones. Does the number of them increase or do they get expanded themselves and Universe keeps on developing at this expense?"

- "Different ways are possible. Generally speaking, both alternatives are acceptable. But as to your Universe, it is like that. You see, Universe is not durable. Your Universe exists for certain time and together with a specific number of worlds. For you those worlds are everlasting. But your material world will be destroyed together with all of them as soon as We terminate our experiment. Upon completion of the experiment We will remove the Universe and everything it contains including its worlds.

The experiment consists in production of souls having relevant quality. And as soon as the needed number of souls is produced, then I will take all souls for Myself, and We will alter all the rest i.e. the plateau, which they are grown on, to create something else. But before that We will cannibalize internal structures of your Universe to receive various mini-parts and states which later on will be used in something else.

If the spatial volume of the Universe is transferred to others, then they will reconstruct it themselves in compliance with their plans. If this is the case, your Universe will look like quite differently as compared to its image you've got accustomed to. And if due to some reasons We have to hold on at the given Level and with the same volume of Universe, then We will reconstruct every bit of it to meet new objectives. But in any case upon completion of the experiment the sight of your Universe and the number of worlds it contains will change by all means."

- "Do You mean that You will destroy our entire material Universe? Then eternal existence of the Universe is out of the question, isn't?"

- "The spatial volume itself remains but its entire content is changed. Therefore a Universe-cell is eternal. Its basic frames maintaining the spatial volume remain unchanged, eternal, and all the rest is changed in compliance with the general objectives of development. But for the man everything physical is changeable and all material is temporary."

- "May distraction of our Universe somehow influence three other Universes of Yours?"

- "If we destroy Universes, We will destroy all four of them at one stroke. Of course, changes will be enormous. Although all Universes are independent there is a certain exchange among them therefore any transformation carried out in one of them will result in some chain reaction. Let us take human cells situated close to each other: every one of them is individual by at the same time they interact with each other. The same is with My Universes."

- "Does every of your Universes contain its own number of worlds or do they have the same number of them?"

- "Universes are different therefore each of them has individual number of worlds."

- Does their number comply with the Level of the Universe development?"

- "How can a number of worlds comply with the Level? Explain, please," asked God trying to understand just what we mean.

But, obviously, Universe is subject to reconstruction. It points already to the fact that the number of worlds is calculated and is derived by design methods dependent on the objective which is set for the fixed period before the volume that we call the Universe. But in the course of dialogue it is sometimes difficult to seize the point; often something gets receded, and awareness flashes later. Therefore this time we try to get more detailed explanation:

- "The more developed Universe, the greater number of worlds in it. Is such dependence observed?"

- "No, it is not observed. Universe of high Level may contain a few worlds, for example, two of them. The higher the Level, the less the quantitative aspect, the number of Higher Personalities gets reduced, the same is with the number of worlds. However, advanced worlds may be very large in terms of spaces. That is why for advanced Universes the inverse relation is true: the more advanced the Universe, the less number of worlds in it but they are larger in terms of their dimensions. And as for inferior worlds existing in inferior Universe, there can be no end of them. As a Universe advances all inferior worlds fall away. Only one Higher spirit world remains, i.e. as a result of development of a Universe is brought to only a single world. This remaining world is very huge. Here is one of the ways to treat your question, but one may proceed from quite different point."

- "Are all four Universes at the same or different Levels* of development? Which of them is older, which is younger?"

- "They are all the same as far as their development is concerned because all of them were created in parallel. It may be regarded that I take care of four cells in a large organism. But that organism is formed in a parallel and in a single- whole manner. Hence all Universes of Mine have emerged concurrently."

Souls in Universe

- "In our Universe there are planets designed for growing of initial souls. And do other Universes also have worlds where just-created souls are grown?"

- "Yes, they do. In each Universe initial souls have their own paths of development. There are worlds where souls are progressing very quickly from the very start and further on. The rate of their development is so high that many of them outrun you a long time ago within the same period."

- "And are methods of soul education in other Universes the same as in ours?"

- "Everything is individual everywhere. In other Universes methods of soul improvement is so much different from yours that there is nothing even to compare with. On the Earth you have nothing of the kind."

- "Which of the four Universes is the most successful in improvement of initial souls?"

- "Not yours, of course. The best indicators are demonstrated by the Universe where souls progress at a very high speed. High rate of development has caused successful progress."

-"And is our Universe the last one in this respect?"

- "No, it is not the last."

- "What processes and what conditions contribute to accelerated progress of souls?"

- "It is due to basis of existence. Living conditions facilitating accelerated progress of souls are established purposefully. And all this is also calculated: environment, and household, and process flow rates; and We analyze final results."

- "May be, they have no karma and repetitions in development so their development gets accelerated."

- "No. Acceleration is due to the living conditions in their Universe which are opposed to yours."

- "What does the phrase "opposed living conditions" mean?" we were puzzled. It required further explanations because the conditions may be of whatsoever character but to become opposed they shall turn into anti-conditions. Therefore we decided to switch our conversation and asked, "Do minus Systems operate in their worlds or is the quality of worlds itself is somehow special?"

- "They apply severe living conditions and their freedom of choice is not so wide as yours. And every percent of freedom of choice reduction results in considerable growth of improvement process."
- "And is their household similar to ours?"
- "They have not any household at all."
- "Does household draw away from self-development?" asked we although it is evident for everybody: care of one's family, keeping residential space, cooking, garment washing etc. – all this draws goal-directed personalities away from self-cultivation. But at the same time it fills the vacuum in life style of inferior individuals who are not able to be in charge of their personal free time.

God confirmed our assumption:

- "Yes, household distracts. On the one hand, it helps, of course, but on the other hand, it slows down. If a person shoulders the material burdens of the family and educates other members, then such person may slow down his own development but, instead, he may accelerate progress of other family members. What you lose on the swings you gain on the roundabouts. Therefore We decided to create such two extremes as you and them. And two Universes were imitated accordingly. In some particulars they are similar but living environment is different. Their laws are almost the same as yours."
- "Are "Laws of Macrocosm», which You gave to us, applicable in all of the four Universes?"
- "All four Universes are different, forms of existence are also different therefore each Universe has individual laws. But as everything belongs to Me and meets My requirements, half of general development laws applies to all of them. As to their individual laws, people have no idea of some of them. It is because many laws are of physical nature but as the physical form is different, it involves operation of specific laws."
- "And which of You Universes delivers greater number of defective souls? In which of them are souls decoded more often? In ours?"
- "No, not in yours. In terms of defective souls your Universe ranks third. The slower development, the greater number of decoded. I have such a Universe. One of the Universes has accelerated development. One of them is yours. And two more Universes remain. One of them is doing worse, but the other one is doing better. It is the "worse" one, which gives the highest number of defective souls. And the one which

is "better" almost keeps apace with your Universe. But its conditions are still quite different from yours."

- "But in what conditions does the worst Universe exist? What cramps its development?"

- "Wider freedom of choice. It is even wider than yours. Greater number of errors, more deviations from main targets. That is to say, in My Universes I optimize the percentage of freedom which allows a person to choose and perfect its individuality and which at the same time ensures the maximum rate of development under the given condition."

- "Does household and family exist in this worst Universe of Yours? What cramps their progress?"

- "With them everything is a bit different as compared to you. There are no families there. Generally household is established by families. But since family does not exist, then no households are established in the form earthmen have them. Their life proceeds in different way. However they have societies. All creatures live in the form of societies. But their progress is cramped by wrong choices made in social and other relations re-creating their form of existence."

- "And is the external form of living beings the same as of people?"

- "No, they are not people, and the form of their existence is absolutely different. Of all My Universes people live only in your Universe. And in the rest of Universes there are other reasonable beings. Absolutely all of them are rational beings. Although, of course, most of their external forms may seem weird to you. Everyone gets accustomed to its material body, and inferior mind does not perceive others. But as souls are progressing, the spiritual scope of their knowledge and ideas increases; and souls are enabled to commune with any forms."

- "But are those creatures material? Or maybe some of them are liquid, plasmic, etheric…"

- "There are all sorts of creatures. The two main categories are material and energetical; and their further classification includes an endless list of types and forms."

- "Do Higher worlds have some kinds of artificial luminaries?"

- "No, there are no extras out there. Higher worlds are produced from high potential energies, which shine themselves. The very matter itself radiates light. Besides, creatures populating them are so designed that they perceive the visual environment differently and see it else-wise as compared with human beings."

- "Are Your Universes replenished with new souls on continuous basis? Or are they populated by lots: having received a batch once You have to wait until they come to required maturity?"

- "No, Universes are still being replenished with new batches of souls because the process is not completed. But I have planned out to receive a certain number of souls for every of the four Universes, i.e. these are specific figures which I have scheduled and have to achieve. The case is that I also receive defective souls. However the total figure shall be reached without any reference to those defectives. Therefore they shall be replaced through rehabilitation and replenishment of new souls. I know how many souls I shall receive: not more and not less. Everything is clearly defined and accurate."

Different Universes

Interview with Devil:

- "We are told that Universes may be material, parallel and energetical. Are there any other types of Universes?"
- "They may be plus and minus."
- "Wherefore are such Universes needed?"
- "These Universes are transient ones. From plus Universes transition to the plus is carried out, and from minus Universes – to the minus."

From His imperious tone we made out that it was a very simple and widely recognized truth and we were ashamed to ask Him further questions and inquire into details of this subject, but when time came to interview God we decided to clarify the following.

Interview with God:

- "When we spoke to Devil, He told us that in macrocosm there are plus and minus Universes from which transition to the sign-relevant volumes is possible. Will You specify where the transitions are possible to?"
- "From plus Universe transfer to plus Hierarchy takes place, and from minus one – to the minus one."
- "And may transition to some other plus or minus state of Nature be possible?"

- "This goes without saying. Everything is living, everything functions in its own way. From the human point of view, these are some obscure transfers, translations but in reality they constitute natural functions of cosmic organism. Inside you some states get converted to others too, from cellular level to the level of organs and systems. Therefore in terms of those isolated processes you will not look like the way you look if considered as a whole. In other words, based on consideration of individual functioning processes it is difficult to imagine a man as a whole. And it is all the more difficult for you to understand and for Us to convey what is going on in reality, from our Higher level to your Inferior.

You see, when the Universe finishes its development, first it gets transferred to a Hierarchy. It is such a sort of a constant point to Me into the Absolute. Plus Universe gets transferred to My part, and minus one – to the minus part. Indeed, in order to distribute everything available in the Universe within the Hierarchy itself the latter shall have relevant structures preventing everything from intermixing and insubordination. And as soon as transfers are finished, all My Universes together with the Hierarchy i.e. with its entire content, are taken to My Volume. And then We carry out still another transfer to the next form which is higher.

This great simultaneous transfer from the Level of smaller pyramid to the lower Level of the higher pyramid is deemed the transfer of large dimension and importance. And My Absolute contains everything relevant to construction of Universes included into My Volume. This contributes to preservation of forms of existence and non-disturbance of their living functions.

As soon as transfer from one Level to another is completed then Universes (i.e. their content with all their hierarchical and other structures) get out of Me. And the plus once again gets into plus and the minus – into minus but within the new scale boundaries. A new cycle start its development. Is it clear to you?"

- "Yes, it is. But we want to verify some details about Universes currently available with You. Are four Universes of yours plus or minus?"

- "Two of My Universes are plus and two of them – minus. This is harmony. There shall be harmony between plus and minus."

- "Do neutral Universes exist?"

- "Neutral Universe is a physical Universe. And now we are speaking about energetical ones. As a result of separation processes, supplies come from the neutral Universe to plus and minus energetical Universes."

- "Well. And what effects does plus Universe have upon development of souls then? And what is the influence of a minus one? Are required energies accumulated?"

- "Of course. Processes associated with creativity and inventions are more developed in plus Universe. As a result souls accumulate larger amounts of plus energies. And in minus Universe other processes are underway. This System is more cramped, and in it souls accumulate minus composite."

- "And can it be the case that more severe living conditions of a minus Universe offer more reasons for sufferings which facilitates accumulation of plus energies by souls? In other words, the Universe is minus, but it enables soul to accumulate plus qualities – is it possible?"

- "Of course, it may also be a case. For example, Devil accumulates in the souls of His inferiors not only minus qualities but plus ones as well. Under rigid programs He may accumulate plus energies in souls, but without inclusion of creativity elements in the programs. Because creativeness can be generated if there is freedom of choice. It means that without creativeness His souls will lack special energy spectra. And without them He will not get an individual input to a higher pyramid.

Without Me Devil is not able to get from nether Level to a higher Level of the next pyramid just because He and His entire Hierarchy lack this spectrum of energies; and you know that that transition is possible at a certain standard content of energies. Therefore although for Him and some others transfers from plus into plus and from minus into minus are possible but they may be effected only via the Volume of Absolute. And Devil is not able to accumulate the creative energy."

Death of Universes

- "How do Universes die? Do they become older like people and get destroyed?"

- "In Nature itself they may die in different ways. Spaces which they occupy are able to get cleared from internal content through some explosion and they may also be just dismantled. The latter method is applied more often because they are dismantled to the level of prime elements. This way is more tidy and qualitative. But self-destruction cannot result from ageing. There is no ageing in Nature because all its cells are continuously rejuvenated and regenerated."

- "And are there any other options? For example, a program is stopped, and another program for automatic dismantling is initiated."

- "No, that cannot happen. Entities participate in everything. Usually redesigning is applied. It is the commonest approach. Disassembly is carried out to the level of some basic structures, and some of the old structures may be partly preserved. For example, old space may be equipped with new planets, star systems and other relevant objects. However material and energetical Universes in addition possess development cycles. Until cycles are finished, they may be constructed and reconstructed artificially. But when Universe completes its full cycle of development, it gets transferred to the next Level of development. And this is already accompanied by global processes which, from your standpoint, are like death. At the same time Universes progress stage-wise i.e. material Universe vanishes in physical plane and moves to the next stage starting a new cycle. And energetical Universe (which is at this stage) rises higher etc."

- "Does it mean that You perform all your reconstructions within finished Universes?"

- "Universe has very large cycle of development, and I occupy its space only within some time of its cycle of development. That is to say, I use space itself, but I create Universes Myself in a way I think fit. I preset quality of the matter inside this space, I preset processes and structures. But as soon as I ascend Higher and clear these spaces, another God will construct His Universes in compliance with His needs."

- "You use spaces of Universes during certain time of their total existence. But how does natural death of Universe happen when its own cycle comes to an end?"

- "Let us speak about material Universe because it is more clear for the man. Your material Universe has its own development cycle. Upon completion of this cycle it shall shrink into a point and get to the energetical Level of improvement. During its progress Material Universe expands to reach some limits, certain spatial boundaries, which have special design and bear resemblance to sorts of ball roundings. Therefore having reached those boundaries the matter turns back and space starts shrinking into a point. Such a point may constitute something which is known to human beings as "black hole." As if the whole Universe turns back towards the center. It is as if Universe introverts matter. Shrinkage takes place.

Roundings at the boundaries ensure space warping therefore the illusion of the matter moving continuously forward is made. Although at some moment this movement makes a half-way turn, and everything rushes towards the center. At some moment Universe gives the impression that it starts to shrink into a point i.e. up to some critical mass which concentrates energy in a small volume. The concentrated energy (under the effect of high compression forces) gets translated from the material plane into the next subtle plane via the transformation point. The whole matter gets converted into a new state passing into another space via compression point. In this way material Universe reaches higher Level of subtle plane."

*   *   *

(Further information about God's Universes is given in the book "Secrets of Higher Worlds", chapter 6).

*   *   *

SPACE

We are used to perceive space materially. For us it is, first of all, a certain empty cube of three coordinates. When a time coordinate is also introduced, inside the cube or a certain volume movement gets initiated, processes are launched and certain content starts to fill out the void.

This is a primitive figurative idea of people about unlimited boundaries of something that they exist in. And partially the man is right in his perception of the world although it is not a cube, of course, or some other widely-known geometric figure: it is a hyper-volume which keeps on developing and improving and has a spiritual constituent. The man in his research has always ignored the latter qualities of space and Universes. But they proved to be the main ones.

Any space contains spiritual components in it. It is those components that determine the program of its development and identify the inward processes.

Interviews with God help to take a fresh view of old truths.

Spaces of Different Levels

- "Any Universe is located in space, which is deemed to be its container. But You told us that the Universe is a cell of a huge cosmic organism. In this regard we want to know what the space itself presents."

- "People believe that space is a certain volume having four coordinates including time. According to this assumption, space is a void limited by four coordinates. But it is high time for a man to extent the frontiers of knowledge and to switch to new ideas from the old ones. As for the organism of Nature the overall space is limited by its dimensions or by outward forms. But a deeper insight into it shows that space is infinite and it extends farther and converts from one form of existence to another. It is multidimensional.

One can never cover the whole space at once. Only a small part of it can be considered at a time. Therefore overall space is broken into individual volumes if it belongs to one and the same Level of development. Besides, with reference to its evolution degree, it is subdivided into Levels and phases. That there are dozens of spaces which refer to different Levels. The space of one Level is a single-whole volume which is composed of the total of individual volumes of the same Level of development. They do not differ much from each other in terms of the degree of progress."

- "How are spaces of different Levels disposed relative to each other?"

- "Comparison with layers of an anion will be the best for your image sensitivity (fig. 8). It has a dozens of layers separated from each other, and together they produce a certain single volume. In other words, there is always something that holds them within a whole volume and makes them work to reach the shared objective."

SECTIONAL DRAWING OF SPACE

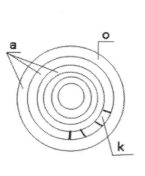

"a" - spaces of different Levels.

"o" - space of the highest Level of development, it occupies the maxomum volume for the given order.

"k" - individual spaces of the same Level, they occupy small volume and are on one of the development stages of this Level.

Fig. 8

- "Spaces differ from each other by their Levels. Do they also differ by their age?"

- "Yes, you are right. Some of them are younger, others – older. The larger scale of space, the older it is."
- "And by what other parameters can we judge of its age?"
- "The larger dimension of space, the higher it is in its development and, consequently, in its chronology."
- "And the more higher Entities live in it?"
- "Yes, more developed spaces are intended for more advanced Entities."

Principle of Space Construction

- "We understand that any space is individual, but there is something in common between them, which allows constructing them based on unitary principle. What is the general approach to space construction?"
- "First it is necessary to define the type of energy the space is intended for as different materials require their own design basis. Then calculation shall be made and a program prepared. After that we shall change from theory to practical part: input energy components in absolute proportion; and the program of development starts to use them right away through certain processes. The program is run by time because up to a certain Level time is deemed its processor. It controls processes that have been computed and input into the program, it also coordinates operations of all systems. However the time is able to coordinate only inferior type spaces. The programs of higher Level spaces are based on another principle, and they do not use time as a factor of action control."
- "How can a difference be told between a young, progressing space and an old and obsolete one?"
- "By expansion and compression of volume. The space grows and evolves if the number of particles keeps on increasing inside it or inside a unit of its volume. But if the number of particles within the space is reducing it means that this phase of its development comes to an end and it gets shrunk."
- "And where do particles go as soon as its program finishes?"
- "They get transferred to another space of the next Level. Nothing vanishes into thin air."
- "Does any space have the maximum borders which it is not able to go beyond?"

- "Yes. Any volume has spatial limits."
- "What is the purpose of borders? Why can't space progress infinitely under the program which is once prescribed?"
- "Everything has the maximum borders. They are deemed the beginning of something and the end of something else. Borders are the stages of development which maintain orientation of translation. Borders control all the processes which take place within the set volume, and which shall not go as far as other volumes. Borders help to preserve the individuality of space and its purposeful functioning. Imagine what may happen to your organism if the processes which take place in kidneys started to expand their limits and invade other areas. Normal functions of entire body will be disturbed right away, and the organism will be brought to death.

The same is true about macrocosm. Everything shall have individual borders, processes because only such conditions allow the entire single-whole organism of Nature with all its numerous volumes to work under adequate coordination and consolidated inter-linkage. Therefore borders are of great importance not only for space evolution but also for its involution."
- "For creation of a soul three constituents are needed conventionally: plus, minus and neutral (conventionally one percent of each). And what constituents are needed for construction of space?"
- "Space is a cell. It is the same, only it occupies very large volume to which also three constituents shall be added. But they are enormous in contrast to the constituents of souls."
- "Does every space have its own design structure?"
- "Yes. Any space is designed in terms of its dimensions, energy constituents and designability of structure. The latter depends on the intended purpose of space: wherefore is it created? What processes will take place in it? Every space possesses individual configurability of design. More than that, the configurability itself overrides all the processes which evolve within the given volume."
- "How may it be possible? How can the configuration of space influence internal processes?"
- "It is related to the program which is coded inside energy constituents. Any construction, any structure is built based on the program, which at the same time shapes the processes taking place inside the volume. The former and the latter develop in parallel. Any construction is connected with processes and actions therefore

certain processes correspond to every time unit and certain volume of constructions. And they are mutually dependent because they are connected to each other by one and the same program. Therefore when configurative construction is underway, some processes take place; as soon as this construction is completed, creative processes come to an end, and then reverse processes are initiated, and constructions get disintegrated."

- "Does it mean that any space is deemed always some construction?"
- "Yes, by all means."
- "And why do people think that space is some void?"
- "It is because of a special structure of the human vision. It does not perceive those subtle structures that exist around. For the man the void of the cosmos is real but it is only because physical eye is capable to perceive a very limited frequency spectrum. What actually happens is that the whole space around him is filled with a lot of subtle structures. And if it were possible to widen the human range of vision a little bit, the man would see that the Earth and the Cosmos have quite different configurations."

- "What is the difference between configuration of the material world and that of the subtle one?"
- "Intransitivity of material forms. It means that forms of material world are not able to pass to the subtle plane."
- "Will You explain, by way of example, how configuration of astral world differs from that of the material world? Such explanation will be clearer for the man."
- "From your world it differs in ductility, first of all. In it figures are subject to changes: in the way, for example, water takes the form of the container which it fills out. But in astral world shape is not limited by containers but by special laws and principles governing the processes."
- "Is configuration of spaces designed from identical or different figures?"
- "From different ones, of course. Similar figures are not used. A single space has unified material but forms which are produced from it are of very many sorts. For example, earth space has its own material which serves a basis for construction of physical world forms. But the first Level of My Hierarchy has a distinctly different material and other forms of construction."
- "Will You tell us what kind of forms are those?"

- "Human mind is not capable to perceive forms of other worlds. Let us take, for example, an insect and a man. They live in one and the same material world however the former and the latter see only something which they are able to see. Specifics and radius of vision depend on their design and development levels; and the things which are seen by the man will never be seen by the insect. And the man will never be able to see something that I can see."

- "Does structure of space change with time?"

- "Human life is short, therefore the man always sees space as something permanent and unshakable. But virtually it keeps on changing. Space cannot be invariable because it is deemed a living and constantly changing Entity of Nature. It is evolving, progressing and accordingly, its whole inside also changes. Human dimensions are also subject to spatial change. Remember how a man looks like when he is a baby, a child, in his youth, adulthood and by the end of his life. It means that all external boundaries of human development forms are set by genic code of his material body. Therefore his program schedules all its parameters in advance complying with passage of time."

- "In what directions does space progress? Only two of them – inwards and outwards?"

- "There are very many directions, and they are all different. Generally the directions depend on intended purpose of space."

- "What is the age of space defined by? Namely, what parameters may serve a basis for judgment about the age of space?"

- "By its dimension. The greater dimension of space, the more elaborate configuration of space and the older it is as for its age."

- "The more developed it is, the more dimensions it has. Is it true?"

- "Yes."

- "The whole macrocosm is changing. And is there something permanent, not subject to changes?"

- "Of course, there are states of permanency. The law of permanency is based on them. Everything that is preserved within some long time belongs to the permanent. All its changes are due to addition of new accumulations, i.e. permanency exists within the past and future. But in present permanency belongs to concepts of relative type."

- "Does Nature have such volumes or some structures which do not change at all?"

- "There are artificial constructions. But in any case they are permanent only for some period, and then they are either removed or altered. Everything around is evolving therefore any structure becomes outdated with time. Its permanency may be just relative. Thus, counting frames are replaced by computers because they got outdated. Therefore absolutely everything is modernized, all constructions are subject to destruction or obsolescence, and instead of them some new structures are built. So any permanency is relative."

Time and Space

- "Why space is given time?"
- "It is a mechanism of translation of low-organized matter, and indicator of its development level. Time sets direction of evolution, determines the length of existence in terms of duration. Highly organized matter is not guided by time in its evolution."
- "Is time actually one of space coordinates?"
- "No. It is deemed a coordinate only for your space. Time links all spaces of earthly plane. In other worlds everything is a bit different."
- "How does passage of time in three-dimensional space differ from that in four-dimensional space?"
- "In three-dimensional space there is one type of time. Four-dimensional space has two types of time which flow sort of parallel to each other."
- "What types of time are they?"
- "Past and future. They pass simultaneously and in parallel."
- "The greater space dimension, the more types of time it has; or does the space always have past, present and future time irrespective of its dimension?"
- "For material worlds there are generally three types. Although present time can hardly be referred to a separate, individual type of time. It is just an interfacing element between two time types. But independent branch of this type does not exist."
- "Do subtle planes* have their own time?"
- "Yes, they have different time because there everything gets converted to forms of perpetual existence."
- "Are there spaces that have no time at all?"
- "Of course, they are."
- "What does curvature of space result from?"

- "Specifically space may be curved to some extent because it gets ruptured by other type of time which in no way fits in this space."
- "What else may entail curvature of space?"
- "Any energetics."
- "Does it sometimes happen that spaces vanish? Is it possible?"
- "Yes, of course. Space may vanish if its shrinking rate is very high. It turns into a point and vanishes. However it is just a general scheme. The process itself is more complicated, of course."
- "Does involution of space itself exist?"
- "Absolutely everything may be subject to involution: space, time etc."

Shrinkage of Space

- "What does the term "shrinkage" of space mean?"
- "It is completion of one life cycle followed by space transition to another cycle of development at higher Level."
- "Will You give an approximate explanation of how shrinkage of space proceeds?"
- "First, it shrinks to produce a point, then explosion follows, and it starts to develop again but at the other Level already. As soon as space passes "zero" or a point it starts growing again. It never vanishes into thin air. If it vanishes in one place it emerges in the other. For it, existence in one point is just an intermediate level. Usually when it is in zero state, a new program is embedded, energy needed for new development is re-distributed. This intermediate level is very important for programmed passage of space life because, in fact, space is a part of general Volume of Nature. And it shall be consistent with Nature by its life functions and degree of development, i.e. space shall keep on improving without interruptions.

One shall always remember that any space is deemed also a living matter that functions and progresses according to its own laws. Space is very important both for Universe and for Nature. If the Universe is located in some space, then this space will have its program, and this program will be certainly identical to the program of the Universe. They are interconnected.

It is again similar to the man. Human body has its own program, and every organ or such systems as blood circulatory and lymphatic ones have programs of their own. And all of them are interlinked with each other by a single objective i.e. collective performance of life cycles of the body. The same is with space and Nature."

- "When space shrinks, it goes into a black hole. The same is with the Universe. Are those processes similar?"

- "Yes, undoubtedly, because the Universe cannot exist by itself. If it exists, it exists in a certain space therefore the processes of their birth, development and death are similar and one step entails the other. Any change in the Universe brings about modifications in space structures of the volume it exists in."

- "Space contains vacuum. Wherefore does space need it?"

- "Vacuum contains all energy components needed for the given space. It has the function of enrichment of the Universe with all energy constituents it needs. In it there are elements which physically vanish immediately after their birth but which are very important for space development and its energy saturation. Those short-time elements are paired. One particle of the pair (which is plus charged) stays in the given world and serves for transfer of energy from large volumes to smaller ones, in addition the energy gets evenly distributed in space."

Another particle pair (which is minus charged) does not vanish into thin air: it passes into anti-world i.e. it forms similar space but in anti-world. Anti-world is an opposite world. It exists only in parallel to you Universe, and it is single. This is the experiment which development will be finished together with your Universe. After that the anti-world will be sent to minus Systems. We agreed it with them like that, as they speak, under contract. Upon completion of all activities We will get equal quantities of energy produced by this anti-world and by mankind. According to Our laws every energy particle shall be registered. But it is some deviation from the subject of our conversation. What else are you interested to know?"

- "Does vacuum preserve all information about material world?"

- "Where have you got this information from?" asks God.

- "From press and newspapers," we explain.

- "No, its an error," says God softly.

- "And does vacuum exist as a void?"

- "No, there is no void in the Cosmos."

- "We've got an incidental question. What is anti-world? Does its space somehow differ from ours?"

- "In anti-world everything is the same as with you but at the same time it is a complete antithesis. For you it may seem unreal because no human being can ever get there. Human body and others substances of material world will turn to zero there. Mixture of plus and minus results in sort of neutralization and death of everything."

*   *   *

Chapter 4
WHEREFORE DO GALAXIES EXIST?

- "Universe consists of Galaxies. Does it have some other large constituents? Probably, astronomers just do not see them."

- "No other physical formations like that exist."

- "Is there something in the subtle plane?"

- "Yes, in subtle plane there are similar galaxies, having their own tide of life."

- "Wherefore do galaxies exist? What are their functions?"

- "They exist for energies, for their conversation, for life. Everything is living, progressing and requires certain spatial technologies."

- "Some places of Universe house a few galaxies but in other places there are clusters of them. What is the reason for that?"

- "The reason lies in availability of energies within spaces. Energy is abundant in places where there are a few galaxies; and places where there are very many galaxies are short of energy therefore it is additionally generated by those galaxies and in this way balance is maintained. The same is as with stars."

- "May be, this is because many galaxies gather in one place in order to get transferred to another dimension. Is it true?"

- "No, it is not. Any point in space may be used for transfer to another dimension."

- "What shapes may galaxies have?"

- "There are spiral, spherical and crab-shaped galaxies which expand in contrary directions; galaxies of dispersal shape – star dispersal – and others. Your astronomers know a lot about those shapes."

- "Where is such galaxy shape as star dispersal resultant from?"
- "In such galaxy some other evolution takes place. It has another type of energy. It is as if we compare two different motors basing on different principles of operation."
- "May one Universe have galaxies opposite to each other?"
- "It depends on the Universe. There are no opposite ones in your Universe, but other Universes have them."
- "What are the functions of opposite galaxies? Why are they necessary?"
- "They are intended for generation of opposite energies. Anti-galaxies produce minus energy."
- "Who imparts initial rotary motion to a galaxy?"
- "It is the result of primitive physical processes here."
- "What does the galaxy rotation show? What is its point?"
- "Galaxy is getting transferred to another Level of existence. It warps and becomes progressively smaller, gets drawn into a funnel and gradually leaves your world in order to emerge in another one."
- "Do galaxies come to existence as a result of an exposition or do they come to our Universe from a black hole when they are transferred from another space?"
- "They come to you as a result of an explosions but they leave through the black hole."
- "Why do galaxies have torsion motion? Does it mean that spiral results from its dragging into compressed space of the black hole?"
- "Torsion movement is produced due to centripetal forces acting in physical matter during its drawing into the funnel. Torsion results from rotation and rotation is due to compression of spatiotemporal characteristics of a galaxy while it is drawn into a funnel. The resultant galactic revolution provides a multidimensional characteristic of most important beginnings of level positions relative to spiritual development scale. The black hole intended for galaxy transmission from one Level to another exists in two worlds simultaneously: namely, the place where it exists, from your point of view, constitutes one world, and the place where galaxy emerges is another world. It dies in your world and comes into being in another world. Such process requires a tunnel or a black hole as you call it. It unites two worlds which are relatively different from each other and at the same time they are relatively similar in terms of their functions and processes."

- "The space of the given black hole is something neutral between those two worlds, isn't it"

- "The space in the black hole is not your world and it is not an anti-world. These are combined conditions composed of two different states: the plus state and anti-minus one, namely, retranslation of energy conversions take place. In the hole sort of matter accumulation takes place including transition of atoms and molecules into another state, transition of anti-world gas to corpusculars. Such retranslation results in galaxy transformation from one state to another and its ascent from one Level to the Level higher in the spiritual plane."

"We have heard about recent collision of two galaxies. Why have they collided? Or was it on the program?"

This information was broadcasted at the end of October 1997. Asking the above question I did not bear in my mind the true time of the given collision. Therefore God parried the question, with a bit of intensity:

- "Which galaxies?"

However my spouse immediately understood that my question was incorrect and tried to set it right:

- "Of course, those galaxies collided millions of years ago because its take a long time for the light to reach us. But our sciences have just recently seen that collision as something real. They have seen a major explosion. What is the reason of such collision?"

- "Now I understand what you are asking," answered God more composedly, "That explosion was not scheduled. It was an error. The galaxies were not intended to collide. But the error was so serious that we failed to duly remedy it. However the effects were eliminated long time ago, and the energy balance was redressed."

MATERIAL STARS

Types and Structure of Stars

- "Is a star a living being or an artificial object?"

- "It is one of numerous forms of material state of creatures. It has a soul, which goes along its own individual path of development."

- "Are all the stars similarly designed? For example, people have (in the structure) a common frame of bones covered with organic matter."

- "All stars have different structure. Although they have very much in common, the same as people. All of them are also similar as a certain individual species. But at the same time they are different. This contradiction is inherent in many things."

- "What underlies every star?"

- "Let us speak about its material part. The heart of every star is its core. In your Universe cores are of three basic types: liquid, gaseous and solid."

- "How do those cores differ from each other in terms of their functions? Why are they made different from each other?"

- "Gaseous core acts upon its planet indirectly and belongs to the youngest stars. Gas is a low energy matter, and power of such a star is minimal. Liquid core contains the greatest quantity of energy: more than in solid matter and in gaseous one. Therefore the stars having liquid cores are the most powerful. Stars having solid cores are older than others. Besides, a solid core is always larger in size than liquid or gaseous one. The latter is smaller in size than a liquid and solid core."

- "Are stars united in the Cosmos to form constellations, or does every star operates on its own?"

- "You, people, become accustomed to unite stars in constellations. But in reality practically every star in Cosmos operates individually. They get grouped only in individual cases with reference of quality of released and produced energy."

- "And do all of them fulfill one and the same job if they are grouped?"

- "All of them have different functions. There are no similar ones."

- "Our constellations which can be seen from the Earth include both primary stars and secondary ones, don't they?"

- "Yes, they do"

- "The brighter the star, the heavier is the load taken by it in a constellation. Is it true?"

- "No, not always. Some stars do not shine at all. Those stars are the so-called black dwarfs. But as far as their energy is concerned, they are very strong therefore they also may be primary ones."

- "What are the functions of those black stars?"

- "They accumulate energies coming from some common galaxies, group those energies in themselves and transfer them to another world, you call it a parallel world."

- "Is this job done by black stars or black holes?"

- "This job is done by black stars."

- "And what can You tell us then about black holes in material Cosmos?"

- "Black holes have their own functions. They are characteristic of spaces which store up energy in them, and concentration of energy in a single spot results in perforation into another space. So black holes get formed. But through them energy also can move from one place to another. However this can be already qualified as power leakage. Any tunnel connecting different spaces are called the black hole by the man. Although those tunnels are different as to their structure and functions they called black holes by people. Into some of them stars go, others draw in galaxies, still others serve for passage of Universes from one plane of existence to another. And in your opinion, all of them are similar and you call them black holes. However design of the black holes which draw in stars and galaxies (and all the more so if those holes are resultant from perforation) will be very different in all their parameters. For the man it is just a transfer tunnel but virtually the whole of its inside will be designed in compliance with the intended purpose."

- "There are also white holes. What features do they have as opposed to black ones?"

- "White holes constitute a time-based transfer to another world. But within the limits of material Cosmos they may serve for passage from other spaces to yours. They also have several intended purposes."

- "How does the time-based transfer occur?"

- "In the passage connecting two different worlds past, present and future time get overlapped, and there are spots where time flows are interconnected. An object may find itself in past, present or future time of another world dependent on the crossing point in which it appears. For example, if a man flies out from the world "1", he will find himself in one of the times of the world "2", and not of the same world "1" (Fig. 9).

- "Well, it's clear. But if stars are grouped for joint operations, do they have any energy channels connecting them?"

- "Yes, of course. There are energy transfer channels in all constellations. Secondary stars give their energy to central stars."

- "Which star is primary in Logos constellation? Is it the sun?"

Fragment 1

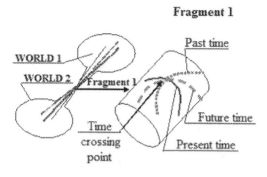

Fig. 9

- "No, the sun is not primary. This star goes under a code number around here."
- "How are the sun and other Logos stars interconnected? Where is energy transferred: from the sun to other Logos stars or vice versa?"
- "From the sun the energy is transferred to the primary star of your constellation."
- "What role do stars play within the galaxy?"
- "As I've already told you, they generate energy of a special type. Then this energy is transferred to other galaxies via primary stars. Those galaxies, in their turn, also concentrate this energy to produce other more powerful energy. Energies circulate at ever-increasing rate. Transfer of more and more powerful energy flow takes place."
- "Do stars serve as an energy frame of the Universe like, for example, crystal lattice of metal?"
- "No, they do not constitute a frame."
- "But what constitutes a frame in a material Universe then?"
- "It has an energy frame, and it is not given to a man to see it."
- "What accounts for clusters of stars in some spots of the galaxy? In some places there are very many of them, in others – just a few."
- "As for your galaxy, a number of stars in this or that place depends on the energy potential of the place in question. In the places having a small number of stars or no stars at all, energy goes through permanently, and the space itself is energy-saturated. And places abundant in stars lack energy, and they need to be made up with it which is just achieved with the help of stars."

- "You also have Universes without stars. What serves as energy sources there?"
- "Yes, I tried to create also Universes of this type. They are powered with the help of special particles which are like you molecules. Although they are very small, they function as one huge star. And as to their power, they are very strong."
- "But do they shine in some way?"
- "No, they do not shine. They are energy accumulators."
- "You've mentioned that You "tried" to create Universes that have absolutely no stars. Were You successful in that? Do they already exist?"
- "No, it is just a test so far. The experiment is in progress, it is not finished yet. There are several options of Universes devoid of stars."
- "Is it one of world illumination options?"
- "Yes, We are trying to use star substitutes. Instead of stars We use huge entities which are able to convert energies in a special way. You also have gleaming creatures in your world such as: glowworms, deep-sea fish. And in the Cosmos we have shining entities with specially designed processes inside them. Their task amounts to capture of energy from surrounding environment and to its conversion. And there is also one more option of a step-structured starless Universe. In it the energy is converted at each evolution step and then supplied further. Such spaces do not need any artificial illumination. Light is invented only for physical worlds. In other worlds the notion "light" is formed in another way. In your world people see everything via the light. But in other planes entities see entire world and its structure simultaneously."
- "What is the difference between functions of primary and secondary stars?"
- "The difference lies in amounts of transferred energy. Secondary stars transfer small volumes of energy from themselves to the primary star. And then the primary star transfers this total volume to other constellations and galaxies in ascending order. From constellations the energy is transferred to the primary star of the galaxy. And from it the energy is transferred to the primary star of the Universe. Each of my four Universes possesses a primary star. Those primary stars are connected with each other through energy, and they exchange energies among themselves (fig. 10)."

FOUR UNIVERSES OF GOD

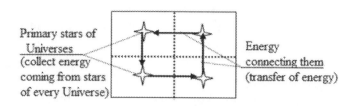

Primary stars of Universes (collect energy coming from stars of every Universe)

Energy connecting them (transfer of energy)

Fig. 10

- "What does the number of planets orbiting round a star depend on?"

- "The number of planets depends on the volume of energy, converted by a star. For example, if a star produces excess energy and it lacks planets which can receive it, then such a star begins to experience all types of functional disturbances. In outward appearance it is manifested in surface cataclysms: all kinds of violent flares and protuberances – all this is characteristic of stars. And if a number of planets is sufficient, they are able to receive the excess energy, restore energy balance within a star system, allowing to work in normal conditions. What function do planets fulfill for a star if they make one whole system?"

- "Planets complement a star and give it energy supplementing its subtle bodies. Let us discuss your star – i.e. the sun. All planets in this system work for bodies of the sun."

- "Are there stars without planets"

- "No, there aren't."

- "May other stars have more planets orbiting them than our sun does?"

- "Certainly."

- "And is the number of planets round a star limited? May their number be as many as a hundred or two hundreds?"

- "Yes, of course. Planets may be as small as peas. And there may be thousands and millions of them flying around the star but all of them will fulfill their functions in joint operation. A man due to his ignorance thinks that there are just flying stones and certain fragments of something, but these are mini-planets."

- "And who designs and constructs such start systems? Who determines the number of planets in them?"

- "All this is in charge of My Hierarchical systems. Some of them design structures; others put their designs into practice."

- "Do stars also have their Determinants who guide them in compliance with their programs?"

- "A star is a living being therefore it has its own Determinant, Originator and Manager. Everything is as it is with people."

- "Do Determinants guiding stars have the same forms as the Determinants guiding people?"

- "No, they are different. Star Determinants are several sequences higher than Determinants of people. It means that they are separated by a substantial distance in their development. Therefore their form is also different: it is more advanced and potent."

- "And are Determinants of people able to rise to the same Level in their development and then to become Determinants of stars? Or are these ways of development never interfaced?"

- "Yes, they are to do so. Everything depends on their wish."

- "Do both plus and minus energies participate in energy processes of stars?"

- "Yes, but there are stars consisting only of plus energies, and stars consisting only of minus ones."

- "But what is the difference in operation of the former and the latter?"

- "It is attributed to special qualities acquired by them. Therefore plus stars communicate only with other plus stars, and minus stars communicate only with minus ones. In other words, the difference lies in associated contacts and in quality of information received. And due to this their matrices accumulate special energies. For example, minus stars also exchange relevant information with one another just like plus ones. They decode this information and process it. And all this results in acquirement of relevant qualities."

- "And do stars of mixed-type exist?"

- "Yes. Plus stars contact only with plus stars, minus stars – only with the minus ones and as for mixed-type stars, they contact neither with the former nor the latter ones: they contact only with similar mixed-types stars. It is essential for purity of the acquired qualities."

Birth of Stars through Merger

- "Scientists have discovered that merger of two stars results in birth of a new star. Is it really possible?"
- "Yes.".
- "But earlier they thought that stars are born as a result of outbursts, i.e. mass expansion reaction is triggered by an explosion. What is the true alternative then?"
- "You are accustomed to bring everything to an individual case but macrocosm is just infinite, and we shall not be limited by something isolated. It is your scientists who know one or two of alternatives of star birth, but actually there are a lot of options. And every star comes to life individually, and each case is always different from other star births."
- "Where does primary matter needed for creation of material star system come from?"
- "For those purpose there is a special energy which gets converted as a result of certain reactions to give birth to the matter, and solid substance appears."
- "But what about the option of star birth through merger of two other stars? What does it represent?"
- "Star merger option is used when it is necessary to create two material bodies: one of them shall be very large, the other one – very small. A new star emerges from this minor fire mass. And a large body formed starts to shrink subject to its own gravity forces. And it keeps on shrinking until a black star is produced. And a little starlet remains. It flies away to a great distance therefore avoids being drawn into the hole and stays in your material world."
- "Hence, at first, merger of two old stars results in formation of common mass which then is divided into two unequal parts. Is it true?"
- "Yes, it is a controlled process therefore proportion between new masses is determined in advance, and everything is carried out in compliance with the schedule. Mixture of old masses is essential for production of the matter having a certain composition. Of course, everything is pre-calculated and experimentally checked up based on low masses of the same composition, and only after that the process is carried over to reality."
- "So one of the stars may remain in our world, and another one goes to another world. Why does it happen this way?"

- "Everything depends on assigned tasks and on star programs. A task may be assigned so as not a single star is pre-programmed to remain in your world, and both of them will be transmitted to another plane of existence. After the mass division one of the stars remains in your world if it is supposed to complement space with its energy in a given place. It is like a transformer, which shall operate in a given place. And a newly born star will translate the energy, which has not been yet fully translated by two merging stars. And the third alternative possible in case of merger of old stars is when both stars get merged and both of them go to some other space because the period of their development in the given material world comes to an end. As you see, only star merger alone has three alternatives of their further behavior."

- "And what happens to the souls of merging stars? Is a soul of one of the merged stars preserved with a little star which has remained or does a new soul come into being?"

- "Merging stars are deemed dying luminaries. Their souls come to an end of their improvement period in a given world and pass to the next, higher stage. And a small mass receives a new soul of relevant Level of development. In any case, even if both of new bodies remain in this world after merger and appearance of new masses, they will have new souls, and their old souls fly away to the subtle plane of existence to join the souls which are similar to them."

- "And what about their programs? Is a program checked to see whether it is or it isn't carried out properly?"

- "Of course, everything is checked. Star souls are sent to their own star Distributor, and there relevant specialists assess the degree of their development and adequacy of program implementation."

- "That is, here we can speak of analogy to human soul after its death, can't we?"

- "Yes, you can. Stars, planets, human beings and some other creatures have perfect analogy."

- "Are souls of deceased stars either immediately sent to the next life with new programs or also stored for some time in their repositories?"

- "Everything is like with people, but in more global schemes."

- "What can star souls achieve in the process of their evolution? People, for example, climb up the ladder of Levels. And how is it with stars?"

- "They also improve in a step-wise manner, they have their Hierarchy and their Absolute. Like people they gradually build up their own volume. And soul becomes increasingly greater."

MOON SECRETS

- "The Moon is a planet closest to the Earth. Wherefore is it created?"
- "The Moon is an artificial planet. It is the earth satellite, and its task is to balance the Earth energy. Besides, it has one more purpose: from it certain Systems keep watch over Earthmen and over the whole planet. From the standpoint of people, it is empty inside, but virtually some other creatures live in it. People have already studied quite well everything which is outside it."
- "What does the Moon have inside – gas or solid matter?"
- "Neither. Inside the Moon there is a unique atmosphere which enables existence of its civilization."
- "Is the civilization, which is inside the Moon, more or less developed than ours?"
- "It surpasses your civilization and therefore it controls you."
- "Do the "flying saucers" that we sometimes see on its surface belong to them?"
- "No. This is an energetical civilization but not a physical one. It is in the other plane of existence."
- "Can we see them?"
- "No, not with ordinary vision. But some clairvoyants working within their frequency range can see them."
- "Does the Moon have one civilization or several of them?"
- "There is one civilization on the Moon."
- "Do representatives of this civilization visit our Earth often?"
- "Yes, they visit it very often. But people do not notice them."
- "What are their purposes in keeping watch over mankind?"
- "The Cosmos is organized in such a way that somebody inevitably keeps watch over others or rather patronizes and controls others. For instance, mankind uninterruptedly watches and patronizes plant and animal life on the Earth. People are charged with this duty from the Above. It means that it is in the program of mankind development. But it seems to people that they carry out such control at their own discretion.

The development of Creatures who carry out control is always higher than the level of those patronized."

- "Do they look like people in their appearance?"

- "Yes, they have similar appearance but still they are different. They are not people, and they have only one type of constitution. They have no gender division."

- "Are their tasks reduced only to control over Earthmen? Or do they fulfill some other tasks?"

- "They are also involved in transformation of energy transmitted from the Erath to other planets. For the Earth it is like a huge transformer."

- "Are they engaged in energy transformation purposefully or do they transform it without being aware of that, just by virtue of their construction? For example, people generate energy but up to now they have not been aware of that."

- "Yes, people always have done that unwittingly. But they do it purposefully. It is their job. They perform it continuously."

- "What does the number of worlds on a planet depend on? For instance, there is only one civilization on the Moon, and there are several of them on the Earth. Why do some planets have more worlds and other ones have less of them?"

- "It depends on the energy converted and on the quantity of incoming energy."

- "So the larger quantity of incoming energy, the greater number of worlds on a planet is. What kind of dependence do we have here?"

- "It is a direct dependence. The larger quantity of energy is converted by a planet, the greater number of worlds it has. But it also depends just on its development Level and individual program. A low Level planet is not able to convert a large volume of energy, and such a planet may just explode in case of energy excess. Therefore it is important to calculate the quantity of energy to be converted."

- "Is the Moon an independent planet?"

- "No. It is an additional planet, it is not able to exist by itself."

- "It is an artificial planet so it has no soul, is not it?"

- "It belongs to mechanical planets."

- "Some people believe that the Moon is deemed the psyche of the Earth."

- "It is not true. The Earth has its own psyche, which belongs to the planet and resides in it."

- "Does the Moon have its own mental energy?"

- "It is an artificial planet. Where can it get mental energy from?"

- "May be from the Moon inhabitants who live there and produce a certain aura around it."

- "No. Mental energy shall be acquired a planet itself, and artificial bodies do not have it."

- "We enquire into it because we want to understand why the Moon influences emotions and psyche of some people although it has no mental energy of its own."

- "The Moon is a machine. It operates in the specified mode to produce the waves required for life activity of people on the Earth. And if the power of those waves exceeds physical parameters of human body, mental status of the man may get disturbed and he may go mad. But such thing may happen only to low energy people."

- "Does it mean that the Moon (being a machine) produces lunar rhythms?"

- "Yes. Special rhythms."

- "What do they express? For what purposes are they reproduced?"

- "Lunar rhythms maintain the preset rhythm of the Earth. In other words, your planet exists in its own rhythm. And to prevent the Earth from getting out of this rhythm such mechanism as the Moon was added in order to maintain it over extended intervals for avoidance of attenuation or operation errors."

- "Why does lunar energy have a great effect on human emotions? It is especially true of people with mental disorders who feel uncomfortable during certain lunar phases, particularly, during full moon."

- "Of course, I see no point in disclosure of all secrets to people, human mind is not ready yet to apprehend many truths. Therefore we disclose only a few of them. Let us say that in the period of full moon a great job on transformation of energy (coming from the Earth) and on its transmission to other planets takes place. Some part of energy is reflected and returned back to your planet, and the power of this energy greatly affects low people and persons with inadequate energy protection therefore all kinds of deviations become evident in their behavior. People having strong energy protection are not affected by the Moon. As you see, availability of individual strong energy (which has been acquired by the soul when it passes from one incarnation to the other one) is very important because it protects the soul against a lot of negative factors. "

- "The Moon always faces the Earth with one and the same side. Why is it arranged so?"

- "On this side of the Moon (inside it) there are special instruments used for operations related to the Earth, intended for carry-out of control over it. Those instruments shall be always pointed at the Earth, in other words, they shall be oriented in one direction only. Therefore the Moon is fixed so that this side can always face the Earth."

- "And what is the function of those instruments: do they facilitate energy transfer from the Earth to the Moon?"

- "There are all types of instruments: some of them carry out energy transfer, others perform certain measurements and regulate balance of energies."

- "And what is on the back side of the Moon?"

- "On the back side there are constructions associated with the way of the Moon civilization life. Their function just consists in working with all those instruments."

- "Do the instruments themselves attract energy from the Earth, or does some network of channels operate?"

- "Minus energy i.e. the energy of aggression, cruelty and hatred is preliminary collected by the minus System which is located inside the Earth. And after pre-treatment of this minus energy the System transfers it to the Moon. There it is received. And as for the plus energy, it reaches the Moon all by itself, without being pre-treated by the minus System."

- "What forces hold the Moon in the Earth orbit?"

- "The same physical forces which hold the Earth in the orbit while it rotates around the Sun. Everything is designed and tested by the planetary Systems."

- "The Moon came into being long after the Earth. When did the demand in creation of the Moon arise?"

- "Initially the Moon was not planned, of course. The Earth was created, it came into existence, and therefore it started to generate energy. Development of the Earth called for establishment of civilizations. And civilizations gave rise to the demand for additional technological production facilities. The fact is that civilizations started to produce energies of the quality which deviated from the initially projected quality. In other words, the generated energy needed to be refined. And that was the main reason why the Moon was created. Besides, it has a great esthetic effect on people."

- "And what about the time frame of the Moon creation? When did it come into being: before or after the Atlantis?"

- "The Moon appeared in the period of the first civilization. The demand for energy refinement arose immediately."

- "The Moon is an artificial planet. How was it constructed? It was created after the Earth. How did it appear in our sky then?"

- "It was designed and assembled by the Material System against My order. And as soon as it was constructed the Creatures of this very System transported, secured and put into operation."

At this moment the channeler in his/her mind's eye saw the following picture: the Creatures are "rolling" a large silver ball along the black starry heaven, and having delivered it to the relevant place, they have "anchored" the Moon to the Earth. Of course, it was an imagery visualization. In reality everything was much more complex. But this picture gave a certain idea about appearance of the Moon in the Earth's skies."

- "What will happen to the Moon when the Earth will reach the next Level of development?"

- "We shall see what type of energy will come from the earth at the next stage. If it produces pure energy, the Moon will no longer be needed, and We'll dismantle it. But if it is still needed, it shall be reconstructed. And after that it will continue its joint operation with your planet."

- "The Moon receives the energy transferred from the Earth, refines it. And where does the Moon send the energy transferred from the Earth after its receipt and refinement?"

- "It sends the energy to other planets of the solar system. Energy of various types is directly received by the Earth from other planets, but it transfers its own energy to them only via the Moon after its transformation."

- "Is the Sun involved in this process?"

- "Yes, by all means. It accumulates all those energies."

- "Is this energy dispatched elsewhere to the Cosmos via the Moon?"

- "No, it is not. Planets of the solar system rather transfer energy to each other around a circle. After that it is sent to the sun and from there it goes further in the form of integral energy of the system."

- "Do Lunar rhythms help to collect energy from the Earth?"

- "No, they are not involved in this."

- "For what purpose is the given energy used?"
- "For support of animated existence of other worlds and planets. Everything is used for life support."
- "Is the Moon involved in formation of weather on the Earth?"
- "No, it is not. It has an effect on alteration of floods and ebbs."
- "On Earth sometimes vortex funnels are observed. Is it the demonstration of energy collection from the Earth or its output?"
- "Output, only output."
- "The Moon is the visible satellite of the Earth. Does it have invisible satellites?"
- "No, it does not."

COMETS AS FAIR STRANGERS

Interview with God:

- "What is a comet?"
- "For the man it is an inanimate body, a certain planet fragment having a great rotation radius. For Us a comet is a living being, from the outside it is shielded with a solid crust-shell which protects its inside from evaporation (fig. 11). Under the shell there is ice. A lot of ice. This is the state of pure energy. In the very centre of the comet nucleus there is some liquid. But it is not water. Notwithstanding the protection, the ice gets evaporated and forms the comet tail."
- "Why do comets approach the Earth?"
- "Comets carry to it additional energies which the planet lacks within the given period of its development."
- "Is plus or minus energy concentrated in all comets?"

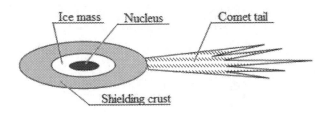

Ice mass   Nucleus   Comet tail

Shielding crust

Fig. 11

- "The equivalent one"

- "Do Comets bring about only destructions and Acts of God or are they capable of bringing also something plus?"

- "We shall not state that they bring either plus energy or minus one. They bring to the Earth the energy it needs in the given period of its development. The same is true about other planets. The comet may be considered to be an energy carrier or a cargo spacecraft as you are accustomed to call it. This energy may also cure and make up those who need it."

- "What other types of work do comets perform for the Cosmos, apart from the fact that it is able to transfer energies and to cure?"

- "A comet transfers information from one spot to another. As comets have very high conveyance speed, the information is transferred from one planet to another at rather high rate. At the same time, a comet is able to deliver information from the System it is sent by or distribute it among those objects that it flies past. It delivers information to those objects and also brings it from them to others."

- "Is it like our postman?"

- "Yes, it has the functions of a postman and that of "ambulance.""

- "Now (March 1997)* another comet is approaching the Earth. This comet is already visible for people. What will it bring about?"

- "It will deliver to your planet certain types of unearthly energies. And the latter, as a consequence, will involve manifestations of various elemental forces. Some cataclysms will occur. And society itself will experience exacerbations of all types. The comet influence spreads for a certain period of time."

- "And how does it transfer energy to the Earth? Via some channels?"

- "There are no channels, there is only energy exchange. It is a special mechanism: its energy comes to Earth, and the Earth's energy goes to it. But such exchange is based on certain objective laws acting between the given material bodies."

- "So a comet brings to the Earth the energies it lacks. Or is there any other task?"

- "The task is to accomplish the reconstruction, effect certain changes both on the planet and in society. But comets do not fly at random, they are dispatched and pre-programmed from the Above."

- "Are comets always sent by somebody?"

- "Yes, certainly. There are special material Systems (they are the systems of My own) which are profiled to work with comets. There are individual comets sent to the Earth only once, and also there are comets having a definite orbit time, which fly their orbits, i.e. comets have various modes of operation."

- "Are the Material Systems launching comets minus?"

- "No, they are not minus. You think that if comets bring about destructions, they are, therefore, from the minus System. And which System do you refer your country to? It has both plus creativeness and minus one associated with wars and destructions performed. So certain cosmic Systems are similar to yours, they contain both plus and minus qualities."

- "Are comets sent to the Earth only?"

- "Why "only"? They fly not only to you but also to many space objects and fulfill certain programs."

- "Do their Material Systems issue programs for them?"

- "Yes. They prepare programs, but they shall comply with the tasks which I assign. Everything shall be inter-correlated."

- "Is a comet launched to the Earth under its overall development program or does it input only some local correction to the planet functions?"

- "Everything is implemented under the overall program."

- "What is the energetic architecture of the comet?"

- "Comets are very strong in terms of energy they have. They are so strong that they can be compared with your Sun. But power of comets is just a bit lower."

- "Why do comets carry such a huge energy potential that it is able to assert influence on an entire planet?"

- "The comet has a very energetic soul due to which it is able to transfer high energy potential."

- "Where does it take this energy from?"

- "It is loaded to a comet by the Material System. It possesses an individual base intended for energy distribution and a base for energy collection. Comets take away energy of one type and return to Them other energy which has been exchanged with planets. Comets give away nothing without compensation. But everything happens under the program."

- "Is a comet's soul development rigidly programmed? Or does it also have a right of choice? Let us say that it may agree to carry the energy or it may refuse to do that?"

- "Yes, of course, there is always a choice"

- "Do comets seldom visit the Earth?"

- "No. Large comets are rarely seen by you. But a lot of small ones may approach the Earth during a year."

- "What does a mission of comets consist in?"

- "In rescue of others."

- "If a comet is a living being, than it is able also to think, isn't it?

- "Yes, its intellectual activity is at its own level of comprehension."

- "What is the path of a comet soul evolution? To what body can it be transferred at the next stage of its development?"

- "It may become a star. A soul of a planet can never be implanted in the material body of a star, for example, of your sun, but a comet's soul may allow such implantation. Such is its architecture. A comet may become not only the sun but also one more space object which is not known to people. It is a very active object of a huge energy potential. A comet's soul is designed for a very huge "organ" of the cosmic organism, therefore it shall be composed of the same strong potentials. For this reason a comet's soul goes to its relevant structure."

- "And after that it ceases to exist in the material plane, does not it?"

- "Of course, it will no longer exist in your plane. Comets go away not to reach your Universe, but to join the next, larger one. It also resembles your Universe, but it stands at the higher stage of development and, therefore, has larger dimensions. Any succeeding stage of evolution grows in its size."

- "It turns out that the comet has a higher energy potential than the planet. Is it true?"

- "Naturally. And potential of some comets is even higher than that of your Sun." The man is not aware of that. But it can be judged at least from a comet's activity.'

- "Recently (September 1998) a news report has been published about a certain planet approaching the Earth which may allegedly bring about temperature rise. Is it a true assumption?"

- "Let us proceed from the new theory," - corrected us God. -"No flying planet exists. Your scientists do not know about existence of some other bodies in the Cosmos. Therefore let us not speak so far about a flying planet but about a certain approaching formation. Virtually, it is a new type of energy that We send to the Earth. It approaches your planet in order to finally reverse all the events taking place on your planet to bring them to the ultimate result. Everything is planed so."

- "Will it virtually involve temperature rise on the Earth's surface?"

- "Yes, it is true."

- "Will ice melt?"

- "Yes, some large continents will get drowned: some of them will sink partially, others completely. But everything will happen over a long period of time, and not at once."

- "Are human losses expected?"

- "We take safety measures in order to reduce the number of victims to a minimum. Preliminary shallow flooding of individual areas is deemed a warning, a caution signal. We try to make people to move to safer inhabitancies. In this way we try to make people change the forms and places of residence. We cannot wait until people vanish through natural reasons. We have the Earth reconstructed and everything shall be done as prescribed by the program."

Chapter 5
HOLOGRAMS

Introduction

As far back as a great while ago ancient philosophers used to say that the world surrounding the man was just an illusion. This maxim can be understood in different ways. All our surroundings are subject to such rapid changes that one can hardly speak about permanency of environment, and therefore something which was true yesterday and has faded away today turns into an illusion. But it is the past illusion linked up with passage of time.

However philosophers and speculators of remote times got to the roots of matters and phenomena and they could see something which remained out of sight of ordinary people. Many times they tried to prove that the real world was not at all anything like people saw it. But in response to their attempts to reveal to mankind something much more greater, than the philistinc's eyes were able to see, they used to be laughed away. And some of them who proved to be very farseeing were just killed so that their acquisitive mind would not disturb the sleepy placidity of the dull assured ignorance.

But why are some people able to outsee others, to go deeper into the essence of things, to see the skies, the stars and parallel worlds, and others do not notice anything beyond the everyday, common side of life? Is it because people have different levels of development, and knowledge is revealed for them in compliance with their level of understanding? A more developed man will always be able to see more than a man of lower level of apprehension.

Or let us take the following primitive example. People, animals, birds and insects live in the same material world but perceive everything in completely different way. And if, for example, the animals could describe things they see around them, then those pictures would never coincide with pictures of human vision. For example, pigs know nothing about existence of stars and the Moon, and fish – about the earth's fields and forests. The ant does not see the whole house in which a man lives although it destroys the walls. The ant does not see the house because neither its mind nor its vision is able to encompass the huge building on the whole.

In our simple world there is a mass of things which can never be seen by a bird or a fish although these things are real and another, more mature consciousness, for example, that of a man, can perceive them. But even if we compare two persons of different levels of development, they will also give us two descriptions of one and same world, which will not be similar at all.

These simple examples are given just to explain to you that vision of the surrounding environment by any existing creatures is relative. And the higher is the evolution stage where a life form stands, the more things and processes this form is able to see all around it. Therefore it is difficult for us to reason about the true reality of our world. No matter how attentively we can scrutinize it, our description will always differ from reality.

On the one hand, the illusion of our of apprehension lies in the imperfection of human perceptive organs and in weakness of the mind, which is not able to comprehend a lot of things. And on the other hand, this state is artificially maintained by the Higher Creators because, as They have said during one of the channelings:

- "If the man set eyes on the real Cosmos, he would be shocked."

And to protect our mind they created this beautiful and, apparently, illusory world, which cradles our consciousness and does not hurt our sensitive soul. But what does the world look like virtually? What does it have that we cannot yet see or comprehend?

*   *   *

Trying to conceive the mystery of architecture of the earthly plane we have remembered that the entire solar system of ours (as the Devil has told us) is not natural but artificial. In other words it is a kind of hologram. So we decided to ask Him to clarify this prohibited subject.

We call it "prohibited" because God did not want to tell us anything about stars, sun and planets of the solar system. And when we tried to ask something about them He answered sternly:

- "Don't ask me about that."

But as we were bursting with curiosity, we made a try to ask Devil about that."

Perhaps, God had spared our mind and therefore He had concealed a lot of things. But Devil did not have regard of our emotions and showed us some pictures of our world from the point of view of the Higher. But afterwards, however, having understood that we quite normally perceived the hard truth of reality construction God tempered justice with mercy and also added some explanations about the subject we were interested in.

Later we understood how difficult it was to explain the reality of macrocosm architecture to the man. The man and the whole of his physiology is intended for perception of a certain range of frequencies. Therefore he sees only those things that are covered by those frequencies.

The Higher Entities see our inferior world as it is because they perceive the entire range of frequencies the crude material plane is created of. But for them (who see the truth at their level of comprehension) it is so difficult to explain it to us with our primitive scope of concepts, the more so that our mind is stuffed with all kinds of inadequate dogmas and false theories. Only having thrown away the old ideas and having parted with false concepts we become able to construct a new building of the temple bringing us nearer to the real structure of the world in much greater measure than it was done by our former knowledge.

For example, how can we explain the architecture of computer to a savage? He will not be able to understand neither the purpose, for which it has been manufactured, nor its operating principle or structural arrangement. That is to say, this article exists entirely beyond the frame of any of his comprehensions. The same is true about the man.

A lot of structures of the world and objects of the Cosmos exist beyond the limits of his current concepts. Of course, after thousands of years of evolution he will be able to understand them but it will be a long and hard way. And meanwhile we shall trudge through the jungle of old ideas trying to tread narrow paths to the novel apprehension of the world.

*   *   *

Hologram of the Solar System

Interview with the Devil:

- "The man does not know the true architecture of our Universe. Why don't You want to tell us anything about it?"
- "And what are you interested in?"
- "For example, in the Solar System. Once you mentioned that it is a hologram. It is curious for us."
- "For mankind it is an illusion. The solar system has no planets."

His statement really shocked us, and a thought shot in our minds: He lies to us, and he tries to mislead us with such misinformation. And we started to bring forward our own arguments to prove it.

- "How shall we understand Your holograms then? If the planets of the solar system are holograms, how did the Earth's scientists manage to take soil samples from them? It was done, for example, by the American scientists. It was in newspapers."
- "No soil samples were taken from those planets. The scientists just invented a new substance and claim it to be soil taken from a planet. Everything is simulated. And those funds which are allocated for space exploration are spent not so much on space exploration as on arms. I am definitely aware of that."
- "But nevertheless the earth apparatuses still fly to planets," we tried to argument basing on evidence.

But Devil said coldly:

- "They never fly anywhere. They are only allowed to rotate around the Earth, to obit it. They are not let to fly any further. As soon as they try to reach forbidden places we immediately disable them, arrange all kinds of failures because if people are let go further, they will do such a mass through their silliness that it will take quite a time to put everything straight."
- "Why are holograms of planets round? Why aren't they designed to have some other shapes?"
- "The design is accepted to be similar to the Earth, having the same scopes so that people have no doubts about the unity of the system the Earth exists in. Similarity reproduces the integrity of the world in the

human mind. Only masses of planets, their contents etc. were designed to be different."

- "What does a hologram in the Cosmos basically consist in?"

- "Holograms suggested to people usually depend on the level of their development and on what their minds are able to conceive. I.e. in the given case the visible part of the surrounding world amounts to ten percent, and the remaining ninety percent is invisible for people."

- "And why don't You give the full picture of the world?"

- "Because the man is very weak still, and his mind will not endure it. But generally your Cosmos has a lot of articles and structures which you are not able to see."

- "When the Earth comes to an end of its existence in the material plane and will be transferred to the subtle world, will other planets of the solar system remain as they are?"

- "The solar system will vanish together with the Earth because it is intended for its development."

- "And what will be instead of them in their place?"

- "Other structures. And types of those structures will be chosen later."

- "And what will happen first? Will the sun be out first and then the planets are removed, or vice versa?"

- "We do not need the Sun. Its light is needed by people therefore for Us the sequence of events is not important. As for the Earth, first it will be transferred to the other plane of existence, and then We will begin to modify all other elements."

We did not ask God whether Devil was or was not right in his explanations. But we once again emphasize that the above opinions are those of Devil's, and He has his own view of things and the world.

Hologram-planets and Others

After our mind had gone through the initial understanding of holographic image of the solar system God also began to gradually reveal concepts of the new truth before us.

The Interview with God:

- "Our scientists believe that the Sun will be soon out. It has already passed the peak of its development, and processes of decline are under way. Is their opinion about the tendency of its development right?"

- "Yes, they are right. The forthcoming century (here the twenty first century is meant)* - is the century of the golden Sun, which is leaving the plane of celestial events," said God solemnly and proudly, "the sun really starts to scale down its program, and its life processes are declining. The reduction will be considerable, but not abrupt. Currently the decline is just beginning – it is a peak of the program termination turn. The star compression will take place by the end of the two hundredth millennium (200 millenniums)* according to the earth time."

- "On the eleventh of August 1999 we had solar eclipse. It lasted for about two minutes. Was it a kind of a predictive sign? Or did that eclipse somehow affect the Earth's energy?"

- "As a matter of fact no eclipse took place. It is just a physical method related to energy processes. It was just scattering of beams coming from the Sun to the Earth. The solar energy took another way, went in reverse order, that is the major portion of solar energy failed to reach the Earth, but having reflected from the Moon (which overshadowed the Sun) went back to the Cosmos. It was useful for Earth. Excess energy is turned off from your planet otherwise its exposure to new energy coming from the Cosmos may result in its explosion. Now you already know that a great amount of energy is sent down to the Earth from Us and from the Sun therefore eclipses carry out regulation of energy."

- "On the one hand, there is energy coming from You, and on the other hand, the solar eclipse takes place. It is light and darkness sent together. Wherefore are such contracts needed?"

- "Light and darkness" is a figurative image. From the point of view of physical processes – it is regulation of energy. And those regulators – lunar eclipses- are arranged purposefully. When a lot of energy is sent down to Earth, in some month of such a year a solar eclipse certainly takes place. But all this depends on calculations carried out by My Systems running the Earth."

- "Does it mean that eclipses are not deemed just acts of nature? And they never happen all by themselves."

- "Of course, not. Everything is scheduled and calculated purposefully."

- "And what are holograms of solar system planets? Are planets really non-existent?"

- "Planets exist, but they are artificial. Actually they are holograms," answered He.

- "In the earth plane we already know what a hologram is. Our scientists have leant how to reproduce it. We can see those items but cannot touch them - because it is void out there. A man perceives such a hologram as an optical illusion: actually there is no article there – but still he sees it. Is it the same in the large scales?"

- "Different holograms exist also. And the image of the reproduced object depends on the Higher Level they are produced at. Basically in the Cosmos materialized holograms are created for people. And although the hologram creation principle used by your scientists is similar to Ours, it is still underdeveloped. Higher Levels are able to reproduce space objects of energy design with greatest fidelity. Therefore a man from his inferior Level perceives them as really existing celestial bodies although virtually they are non-existent."

- "But what do the solar system planets constitute? Are they void or matter?"

- "They are material holograms. We can speak of planets as of material bodies because their holograms are materialized, but they can be also considered to be purely holographic structures. People and certain creatures will think of them as of material objects. But for Entities they will be ordinary holograms."

- "But to support such holograms for billions years a great energy supply is required."

- "Yes, certainly"

- "But what are those inputs compensated by?"

- "By energy produced by people and the Earth. Every human being is a kind of a small galaxy which generates and re-transforms very many energy types. A lot of energy is also produced by the Earth itself. So not only full cost recovery is provided but considerable profit is gained."

- "Is the Moon also a hologram?"

- "No, It is a material object."

- "But how does the Moon differ from solar system planets, for example? How can we distinguish real things from the visionary?"

- "The man is hardly able to do this yet. The fact is that there is real energy and there is artificial, non-natural energy. Hologram-planets are created based on artificial energy. This energy type goes to construction of holograms used for material needs of the worlds, which We create so that not to frighten the man with the picture of real space which he exists in."

- "Is the man able to tear off a small piece from a material hologram?"

- "Yes, he is. But for him it is still an artificial matter. It is associated just with the word "artificial". As soon as the man becomes more advanced and in the womb of time starts to distinguish artificial energy from natural one, then he will be able tell whether an object is natural, living or artificial."

- "Are there objects having vital energy and those without vital energy in the Cosmos?"

- "Yes. Solar system planets are material holograms. One can fly to them, touch them, but still everything is artificial."

- "In other words- they are devoid of vital energy. And they are not so rational as our Earth, aren't they?" asked we.

- "Yes, they are not rational, but energy passes via them."

- "Most likely, the main difference between a real planet and a hologram consists in the fact that a hologram-planet does not have a soul. Is it true?" guessed we.

- "Yes, undoubtedly. It is the main difference. Artificial planets do not have souls but the real ones do. Holograms are soulless objects. And they may be of various types."

- "But how can the man distinguish a hologram from a spiritual body?"

- "At the current level of development the man is not able to see those characteristics which allow proper assessment of objects. At the human level we can say that any zombie is a material hologram. This comparison may help you to understand how a hologram differs from an actual body. A zombie is a spiritless person, or rather a material shell controlled from the outside. Usually they are controlled by minus Systems."

- "Are zombies deemed sort of remotely controlled machines?"

- "Yes. But I gave this example so that you may vividly imagine what a material hologram is and what it can look like and how it can work. But We are not going to disclose everything to you. The man shall switch on his mind on his own and try to digest the facts that We keep back."

- "So real planets keep on developing their souls as long as they live. And what about hologram-planets? Do they develop somehow?"

- "No. They exist and work in strict adherence to the programs. Their programs are short-term as distinct from the Earth, for example, which program is long-term. But I am talking about the planets of the given type in general and not specifically about the solar system objects. And they do certain work in compliance with their small tasks. Everything needed for their work is given to them by the hierarchical Systems, i.e. they neither work out nor accumulate anything by themselves. Everything they need is made available to them, and everything they produce is given away. Therefore they neither develop nor degrade."

- "Does it mean that they do not possess the indicator of maximum level which they shall reach in their development?"

- "Yes, such indicator is not available. If any changes in the form of certain structural improvements are to be introduced, then this is done by the hierarchical Systems but not by the hologram-planets themselves."

- "An ordinary planet generates energy through processes of its soul improvement. And what about hologram-planets? Through which processes do they acquire energy for the same hierarchical Systems? Such planets generate it as well, don't they?"

- "No they do not generate energy. Energies are given to them in final state and in quantities required for the preset program. And using them they achieve the goals set before them."

- "However energies are translated just via the hologram-planets, aren't they"

- "Yes, they are. But such planets just receive the final energy given to them and transmit it further without changing it."

- "Does a hologram-planet have one period of development? The Earth, for example, as we hold it, has seven periods of development."

- "What is a period of development in your opinion?" – asks God trying to get a sense of our ideas and to provide further explanations relevant to their level.

We try to explain.

- "For us a period is certain time required for filling the shell with energies. For example, at first the Earth fills out one of its shells and then the other and so on. It has seven shells all in all. And therefore we believe that it has seven development periods. And a hologram-planet has only one protective shell and therefore it has only one period of development."

- "No, you should not proceed from this." Protests God softly – "In such a case it turns out that seven periods of development of your Earth are equal to one period of activity of hologram-planets. Your solar system co-exists with your Earth as a single structure. And as the Earth is acquiring its seven shells, the hologram-planets do exist but they do not acquire anything. I.e. in contrast to the Earth they do not accumulate anything to form shells. And if the Earth has advanced, for example, by six stages in its development, those planets remain at the previous level. As for the periods of developments, they are inherent in a living planet, but not in holograms."

- "Wouldn't hologram-planets exist, if there were no living planets?"

- "Yes, they would not be needed."

- "Are they auxiliary planets?"

- "Yes, We can't do without them."

- "Does a hologram-planet have a matrix of material body?"

- "No, it has no matrix, it is absolutely different configuration. It also belongs to its distinctions from spiritual planets."

- "And does the material shell of the Earth have any construction matrix?"

- "Everything living has soul matrix. And material shell does not have any matrix. It is simply some material. Without soul it is not able to develop and to accumulate anything for itself in contrast to a matrix."

- "How is the time linked up with the hologram-planet?"

- "The computer model of the hologram-planet is put in the matrix of its time. But the time-matrix is not the matrix of the hologram itself."

- "Then what is the time matrix used for hologram-planets?"

- "As compared to a hologram, time is the material of absolutely different type. Time possesses its own matrix which is different from all other ones used for souls. The time matrix forms it own Entity. And architecture of this matrix is different from that of the soul matrix. If the hologram-planet exists for some long period, then the time is inevitably given to it for a certain term of its existence. The time input is usually equivalent to the volume it is linked up with."

- "Is the action of time in a real planet different from its action in a hologram-planet? The time is put in both of them: in the former and in the latter."

- "The distinction consists only in different action of the programs. But the time itself acts similarly. Just the lifetime may be different. And difference may also reveal itself in passage rate: in some object the time passage may be accelerated, and in another – it may be delayed. The material body of the hologram-planet will also change differently."

- "How do Your hierarchical Systems benefit from hologram-planets?"

- "They are made for the Earth and involved in transmission of certain type energy for your planet and people. They participate in exchange of energies and information. The latter is also transmitted via them. To enable the man to use electric power the huge facilities of power stations, substations and other transmitting and distributing installations are created. Similarly certain space devices and technical facilities are needed for transmission of some energy type to the Earth. People still have primitive ideas in this respect. The man thinks that if he is sent some energy, then it is enough to flourish arms on the one side to send it and similarly to flourish them on the other side to receive it. All types of energy or information are kept strict records of; therefore their losses are excluded when they are supplied to a specific place. Everything is calculated and accurately transferred. And various structures (including the hologram-planets) are just used for transmission. The energy is transferred via them both in the directions to and from. And hierarchical Systems receive everything they need."

- "Previously we have been told that there are organism-planets and mechanical planets. Are mechanical planets deemed just hologram-planets?"

- "Mechanical planets are deemed something different."

- "We have been told that the Moon is a mechanical planet."

- "Yes, it is absolutely true."

- "But it is not a hologram like planets of the solar system, is it?"

- "No, the Moon is not a hologram. It is just absolutely mechanical planet which was created artificially and designed specially for the Earth."

- "How do mechanical planets differ from the hologram-planets then?"

- "I believe it is up to you already to tell this. What do you think what main differences they have?" God addressed to us trying to find out if we are able to analyze phenomena in the light of new concepts."

- "Both types of planets have no Souls," started we our reasoning, "But the main difference lies in their design. They have different principle of construction. A mechanical planet is designed along the lines of earthly equipment, and a hologram – by some dedicated devices. Therefore their internal structure shall have fundamental difference.

And if their structure and the material they are made of is different, then they must also have different operating principle."

- "Yes, it's true." confirms God and adds, "On the one hand, there is the engineering matter (which is the crudest) used for construction of all engineering equipment, approximated to your physical matter. On the other hand, there is artificial matter and, thirdly, there is living matter."

- "It turns out that in Cosmos there are planets of three types:
- organism-planets – they are living planets;
- mechanical planets – they are technical facilities; and
- hologram-planets – they are artificial structures.

The last two types are deemed auxiliary structures. But what do they have in common, if their form is similar?"

- "Their common feature consists in the fact that their activity is connected with energies. But the organism-planets are able to reproduce the energies on their own, and the planets of the other two types are able only to translate energies of finished types. Planets of the first type have souls, therefore their existence is aimed at progress of their souls. Mechanical planets and holograms are devoid of souls, and their goal is to fulfill mechanical functions. Consequently, their programs also have different structures: programs provide the organism-planets with certain liberty of actions, and the programs of mechanical planets and hologram-planets do not provide that. They strictly adhere to the programs like robots."

- "And what is the difference between the mechanical planet and the hologram-planet?"

- "Both of them help organism-planets and other forms in their development. But mechanical planets also exercise the function of control over them, that is they keep watch over physical and other parameters of their development. And hologram-planets do not have such a function."

- "Therefore mechanical planets have simpler programs than living planets, don't they?"

- "Yes, of course, much more simpler. We may take mechanical planets just as technical facilities. They are not creatures."

- "And what about stars? Are they also divided into organisms and mechanisms?"

- "There is no such division with stars. Stars may be only of two types: organisms and holograms."

- "Do mechanical planets exist for longer periods than hologram-planets?"

- "Yes, of course."

- "What happens to a hologram-planet as soon as its task is fulfilled? Is it destroyed or is it transferred to another place?"

- "At first it is switched off. Its form vanishes, but atoms and elementary particles (used for creation of forms) remain, and are used for formation of some new type of image. They are used for formation of new holograms."

- "And does a previous form disappear?" we ask once again to make sure we've got everything correctly.

- "Yes. It exists only for the period needed for it to fulfill its objective. As soon as the given configuration has completed its program, it is switched off and disconnected from the processes it has been linked to. It is also disconnected from the facility which forms and supports this hologram. After the disconnection the form gets atomized, nevertheless it does not fall only into the above particles but also into some other ones. Holograms are not built from atoms. But it is easier for you to understand this term therefore I use it. The form gets disappeared but the particles which it has been made of remain as they are and another form is assembled from them. The quantity of material shall be sufficient for construction of a new hologram, therefore it is estimated, and calculated volume is allocated for its assembly. Not only its quantity but also the quality of its constituent elements shall comply with the future hologram. A hologram is not only an external form but also its inward structure. Therefore the hologram is not hollow, but it is deemed a special structure in full measure."

- "Who produces hologram-planets?"

- "There are special Systems which specialize themselves in production of holograms of various types."

- "Is a certain technology developed for their production?"

- "Yes. One may say, it is a standard mechanical production process. But, of course, our hologram-production equipment cannot be compared to yours. It is so much sophisticated for you. But even those holograms which are created on the Earth are too complex to be conceived by people. Therefore you should understand how much complicated are the facilities and the entire technology used for reconstruction of the Cosmic-scale holograms. Any hologram shall also give due consideration of the environment it shall be placed in, otherwise no image can be produced.

Our installations produce holograms for different worlds. In this case the hologram material shall comply with the matter of the world where it is to be placed."

- "But are all those processes controlled by the Higher Entities of the Spiritual or Material System?"
- "By the Entities from the Hierarchy."
- "Do they stand higher than the Level of Originators?"
- "Yes, much higher. They are very Higher Personalities. They are in charge of the architecture of large volumes, of the architecture of My Universes, i.e. of those of their parts which are connected with construction of holograms. There are a lot of them in various worlds."
- "And are Material Systems involved in construction of holograms?"
- "Yes, they also use holograms, therefore they have their own technology of their production. In the material worlds more often than not, the Higher Material and Spiritual Systems mutually cooperate in production of material holograms. The Spiritual Systems set the goals, and the material ones incarnate them. In the hierarchical worlds (which use holograms as well) the Material Systems do not take any part."
- "Are hologram-planets populated by living beings or also by hologram-creatures?"
- "Hologram-creatures. Living beings are not able to live on them. For example, a physical man possessing a soul is not able to exist on the material hologram-planet."
- "Why can't they live there?"
- "It's up to you already to dig out the reason of it. Do it yourself."
- "You've mentioned that holograms are not built of atoms. So the question is: what are the holograms built of? Are they built of some even smaller particles or special rays?"
- "These are energies. Everything is built of energies with Us. And people should have understood already what the subtle energy is. But they have deviated from the designed path of their development towards technocratizm. It's high time to change over the cognition from crude energies to subtle ones."
- "What are deemed the energies of holograms at the level of physical matter? We need at least some kind of analogy so that we can have a general idea about them."
- "For holograms the energy of various color shades is used. Thus, for example, when a man has to draw a picture, he uses paints of various

colors. Here it is the same. When some hologram is planned to be built for the material world, energies of various color-scales are taken."

- "People on the Earth sometimes saw an image of the Blessed Virgin Mary. Is it just the hologram of the given type?"

- "Yes. Such pictures are produced very simply based on use of color-scales of energies. But in general, any hologram is inevitably based on color shades. And its colors are matched in a special complex manner."

Holograms of Stars and Worlds

- "You've said that stars also have holograms."

- "Yes. Any cosmic body may have its hologram. With the help of holograms one can build anything whatever."

- "For which purposes are hologram-stars constructed?"

- "Hologram-stars are used for all sorts of purposes. For example, there is a need to picture a starry sky in some world. It is needed for esthetic purpose because thick darkness frightens living beings, suppresses them. It is also needed for energy purposes, for the required energy transmission to some point in space. You also have some hologram-stars in your skies. And there are a lot of them at that."

- "Wherefore do you use hologram-stars in our skies? Do they indicate some spatial changes or is some new energy sent to the Earth via them?"

- "They balance the energy mass of your world on the whole, that is its plus and minus states. If somewhere in your world something is lacking, some energy is needed, We add it using hologram-stars. In a new age with the golden race the starry skies will change, and even now it starts to modify its configuration. All changes are linked with the reconstruction of the energy state of the Earth and its change-over to a new orbital. The Earth will require more intensive energy exchange therefore it will need some additional sources participating in translation of energy and its accumulation in energy collectors."

- "What is the difference between hologram-stars and hologram-planets? Perhaps, they are built of different energy types?"

- "Naturally. As compared with hologram-planets in construction of hologram-stars subtler and more powerful energies are used, that is the energies of higher order. The development level of stars is higher than that of planets. They are more powerful than planets therefore construction of their holograms requires a greater amount of energy having higher power characteristics. Via hologram-stars more powerful energies will be translated than via hologram-planets therefore the hologram structure shall withstand also more complicated processes."

- "And technical facilities producing hologram-stars surely rank higher than facilities which reconstruct hologram-planets. Is it so?"

- "Of course, they are higher. This dependency is always observed. Technical installations of advanced design and technology level produce high level objects as well."

- "Are holograms used only for reconstruction of some stars and the solar system in our world or do some other objects exist?"

- "There are a lot of them in your Cosmos, and it does not matter much whether the man can or cannot see them. Holograms accomplish their tasks, and they can get changed from time to time. However as a rule, the lower the level of development of the world, the more holographic constructions it has and therefore the further it is from the real structures of the macrocosm. And the higher the world, the less number of holograms it has and the nearer it is to the real structures of the macrocosm."

- "What do holograms give to people besides energy?"

- "They facilitate development of human mind, imagination, aesthetic sensibility. Any hologram accomplishes not only technical functions but also some other tasks."

- "What other functions unknown to us do they implement?"

- "Everything depends on the type of holograms themselves. Some of them implement protective functions."

- "Are holograms used at the Hierarchy Levels for some purposes, for example, for creation of environment?"

- "Yes, in hierarchical worlds special holograms are created, individual holograms for every Level. They add specific touches to certain situations and actions which is aimed at development of the energy* plane sensitivity with some group of Entities or with a single Entity. When the soul exists already in the Hierarchy at one of its Levels*, then holograms are used for its development. Therefore they are very important for progress of souls. Holograms base on interaction of Entities, and the main objective of theirs is to contribute to progress of souls."

- "Does Devil also use holograms in His Hierarchy?"

- "Yes. He also needs them for development of His Entities. But his holograms differ from those used in My worlds because education of Entities has different purposes. The hologram design principle is similar, but their inward target is different. But yet any world has its hologram."

- "Are environmental holograms produced at the Highest Levels of the Hierarchy? Or is there no need to have environment there?"

- "Development is endless. But it cannot progress in absolute emptiness. Environment shall drive the Entity's contemplation and progress. Therefore both in the Higher and Inferior planes* there are holograms matching their development level. If they were not given and used for hiding the true structures of the given world actually existing, it would cause delays in development of individuals. They will start to conceive everything at its face value, take things for granted, cease seeking the novel and stop pondering. And they will not feel relieved the way people feel when everything is clear, on the contrary, they will stop thinking and therefore stop developing.

And if something is concealed from an Entity, He/She behaves quite differently: he/she takes maximum pains and goes through a number of options in order to find out what is at the back of some secret or mystery. Therefore as holograms are changed before an individual even in one and the same world, he/she will inevitably discover for him/herself an endless number of new things and notions."

- "But if the environment is a hologram in a great measure, then earthly scientists must have developed a lot of false theories, must not they? If theories concern the things which do not actually exist, it means that they are false. Are they really false?"

- "Yes, among them there are many false ones. But it is not important for Us. It is not the theory produced by the man that is important, but the measure of the progress he/she has made in his ability to think, feel and reason while producing this theory. Theories are pure fluffs. They mean nothing for Us because it is We who send all ideas. But all the gains the soul acquires in this process are important, because the soul progresses while seeking clues to the secrets of the world. And progress of the soul is of utmost importance. Therefore besides technical functions, holograms also help in development of various living forms."

Human Holograms

- "We know that there are holograms of planets, stars and other space bodies in the Cosmos, there are also holograms of worlds. And what other types of holograms may exist?"
- "The hologram may reconstruct any object including also any man."
- "Is it possible to make a hologram of any living man, his look-alike?"
- "Yes, it is. Have you ever heard that some marked man is seen in different cities at the same time. In one city a real man is seen, but in the other – his hologram."
- "But may be those are robots or something else."
- "No, they are not robots, they are artificial creatures. Human holograms do not have souls. Having fulfilled certain functions they vanish."
- "Can they be called zombies?"
- "No, their creation is based on other principles, and some other material is needed for that."
- "But they are robots then!"
- "No, we can't call them robots either. Hologram is a hologram."
- "What functions are performed by the human hologram?"
- "The human hologram is used when some information is needed to be conveyed to somebody."
- "Is it related to the program of a specific man?"
- "Yes, it is. Of a man, of society, of anything whatever dependent on what shall be produced."
- "May holograms of state governors exist?"
- "Certainly. It is worth nothing for Us to hologram a president, for instance. He may even have several holograms, not a single one. But, of course, We do nothing of the kind because a president is a very important person after all. Generally holograms are sent for people who are not well known. It is done so as to prevent interfacing of two personalities: that is to avoid interfacing of a hologram-copy with the original personality."
- "Some kings saw their look-alikes. Were those holograms?"
- "Yes. They were sent to them for certain purposes."
- "Is a human hologram always somebody's look-alike?"
- "No, not necessarily."

- "Look-alikes of other personalities are called phantoms by people."

- "In a sense, it is correct. Phantoms may be called holograms."

- "Does it mean that the creatures taken by people for phantoms are actually holograms?"

- "Yes. People just call them "phantoms.""

- "And was the Christ walking on water also His hologram?"

- "Yes."

- "But are animals hologrammed? And if "yes", what is the purpose of that?"

- "Yes, there are hologram-animals. Animals bear certain energetics which is of lower range than the human energetics. Therefore when energy has to be balanced in a certain place, an animal of the relevant type capable of the required energy delivery is sent there."

- "And how do those holograms appear? They look just like real material bodies. Are they created in the subtle plane and sent to the relevant place of the Earth in the final form already?"

- "It may be said that they exist in a sort of virtual space. Of course, it is not quite so, but this comparison may help you to better understand how it happens. Holograms of people and animals are created in the same manner as images are produced in computers. And then they are transferred to the material plane. As soon as the task is completed, the producing and controlling devices get disconnected, and the hologram vanishes, falls to atoms."

- "Is the human hologram able to think and take decisions on its own in response, for instance, to sudden change of circumstances?"

- "The hologram does not think by itself. It is strictly robotized, and instead, everything is decided by the Determinant who guides it."

- "Does He also speak instead of it?"

- "Why, it has practically nothing to say. Human holograms speak very little. But if it shall say something, the sound is produced by a dedicated device, but the Determinant does not speak instead of the hologram. He just turns on the sound as required."

- "Can we call a human thought the hologram?"

- "Yes. In this case the brain is deemed the device which reproduces it. But, of course, it is a very weak hologram. It is better to call it a mental form."

- "And can a thought of Higher Entities be considered the hologram?"

- "Yes. As for the type, it is almost similar to the human thought. The difference lies in the power of thoughts. With a man it is weak, and with Higher Entities it is strong. And the higher the development level of the Entity, the more powerful His thought. Mental holograms of Higher Entities are able to move around on their own already. And human mental forms or holograms as you call them are deemed indefinite, indistinct forms."

- "Can the man at the sight of a holographic creature differentiate it from a real one? In fact, the eyes can always betray absence of soul."

- "If you feel that a creature before you has no soul and there is hollowness in the eyes, then you can differentiate a hologram from a living man. But more often than not people are not able to do that."

- "The planet receives energy transmitted via an ordinary living man. Do holographic creatures do something good for the planet?"

- "First of all the hologram accomplishes some task regarding the real man. For example, if it transmits certain information to other people, then some part of energy is transmitted together with the information. And having received this energy the man transfers it further – to the planet. This kind of exchange takes place. And the hologram is also included in it."

- "But why can't a man on his own transmit the require energy to the given place?"

- "Sometimes other people or a planet needs energy of special quality. Other people are not able to transmit it because they possess different qualitative parameters. Or, for instance, some man is able to transmit such energy but for this purpose some additional circumstances shall be reconstructed; however they either no longer fit in the timeframe of the current reality or their recreation requires so much expense that it renders it uneconomical. It is simpler and cheaper to create a human hologram, and it will do everything needed in a short time and at minimal expense."

-"That is it falls out that any hologram-creature is connected with the planet's program?"

- "Yes, and they are sent to ensure its accurate implementation. Although in the everyday plane it may look very prosaic as, for example, communication of some information or message to another man."

- "But still why does it become necessary to transmit to the planet any additional energy via the hologram? Does it mean that something is failed to be considered by the planet's program?"

- "Why? It is not the failure of the program because it calculates everything, it is the matter of choice which is made by a man in different circumstances. If he chooses a deadlock option and moves in the wrong direction, then in this spot the overbalance of the minus takes place. But everything is based on a certain balance of energies. And for example, the other man also chooses the wrong path. All this results in the need to balance both of them so that to maintain the relevant energy balance in the given place. Just for this purpose the human hologram is sent and transmits them its energy."

- "Are holograms of various people similar or different in their design? Or is there a variety of human hologram types?"

- "Their design is similar, but the quality is different."

- "Why do holograms use different quality?"

- "It allows to carry different energy and different information. Each piece of information is deemed some energy, and all information is different therefore all kinds of qualitative variations are produced."

- "And if we take holograms of people of white, yellow and black races, will they also be of different quality but similar in their design?"

- "If we compare colored races, we'll see that their holograms are different in everything, even in design. If we consider holograms of people of white race or black race only, then we will see that their design is similar but the quality is different. It means than holograms of all white-skinned people is similar in design."

- "It is surely attributable to different level of development of every man?"

- "Naturally."

- "Are holograms of planets and people also constructed of different types of energy?"

- "Yes, certainly. Besides, in the hologram the color is chosen to match your material world."

- "Do you use the holograms of Entities at the Levels of Hierarchies?"

- "Yes, and there they also fulfill certain tasks."

- "Just what tasks?"

- "Sometimes it is necessary to complete some complex work in an aggressive environment, and as We can not jeopardize the Entity We send there a hologram of that Entity."

Situations at the Levels. Holograms of Situations

- "Human life bases on situations. They constitute a form of involvement of people into the processes which help them to produce energy and to progress. But does every Level of the Hierarchy have the standard set of situations needed for development of Entities?"
- "The situations are used, but not standard ones. Every world has its own processes, its own development technology, its way of life. Therefore the situations typical for the given world will evolve in it in a special way. Therefore each Level is given the extent to which it can develop. It means that in the specific world no situation is boundless, but has certain limits. As there are a lot of Levels in the Hierarchy, the situations also have level-based design."
- "May the situations belonging to one Level be used at the higher Level?"
- "Yes, they may. There are single-type situations having different energy potentials. If the soul is at a higher Level, it requires also a situation of a higher potential. It will progress only in such conditions. If it goes through the situation which is one Level lower or even more Levels lower, it will not advance in its progress because it will not be able to perceive this situation due to its high potential. Therefore if the lower Level situation is transferred to the higher Level, then its potential gets increased which means that it gets actually changed."
- "Are there the Levels at which the situations cease to work, and they get replaced by some processes?"
- "No, situations are used at all the Levels, and everywhere -in general. Even the Absolute goes through situations of His Level. His situations have the relevant potential."
- "So if there are similar situations at two different Levels, then they differ from each other by the potential which is contributed in those situations."
- "Yes, exactly so. The design principle is the same, but the quality is different. And the higher the Level, the more energy will be received from the very same situation."
- "There are certain Entity instances which are engaged in calculations and preparation of situations for various Levels. May the Entities participating in those calculations be saved from going through those situations and content themselves only with involvement in their development. Wouldn't it be enough for their development that during

preparation and calculations of situations they manage to study them very well? May they be released from going through the situations themselves?"

- "You see, calculation is one thing but participation is the other thing. They have to participate in individual situations for the sake of their own advancement. The same thing is with the man, for example, who sees some film. To see a film is one thing, but to be involved in similar situations is quite another thing. The same is with them."

- "What do the Entity instances constitute?"

- "It is a group of Entities, specializing in some type of activity. In the given case – in the calculation of situations and programming because a program includes dozens of situations."

- "Is the Level of the Entity instances higher than that of Managers?"

- "Instances cover all the Levels, they exist in every world and complete their tasks."

- "We would like to know how the situations are arranged for the man, for example. He lives in his world, but is able to go back to the past, to some previous situations of his. So they have some spatial architecture and exist somewhere. If programs are prepared for people, and each program has certain calculated situations in which people will be involved, those situation must be built in the earthly plane in advance, and a man shall go through them in a certain period of time. Is it true?"

- "All situations designed for the Earth and for specific time have spatial architecture and get initiated in compliance with operation of programs of people."

- "And the fact that the man is able to go back to past situation isn't a fantasy, is it?"

- "No, it isn't. He can make it if he can manage the passage of time."

- "How do the present situations go back to the past and are preserved there?"

- "For this purpose we have the so-called «database of the Earth». But there are individual databases: one database is for mankind, and another one is for the Earth as it is a planet. The planet possesses its own informational stock which is different from that of mankind's."

- "And does the overall database include the situations of the society and nations?"

- "If we go on splitting the mankind further, then every society, nation will appear to have its mini-database and its own situations. Nothing is mixed up. Situations of different nations have their own features, and energies which they produce are somewhat different from the energies produced by other nations."

- "Are all the situations recorded under the guidance of the Earth's Manager?"

- "Yes. Everything related to the Earth and mankind is under His guidance."

- "But how are situations arranged? What do they constitute?"

- "At first the situations are designed as holograms in the program of an individual."

- "Then it falls out that those situations exist in the virtual world."

- "Yes, until some moment they are not manifested. And having been included in the reality, they sort of manifest themselves as soon as the relevant point of the social program gets initiated. And as for an individual, he gets included in specific situations in response to actuation of the point connecting the individual program to the overall situation. I.e. the program situation hologram gets implemented in the reality."

- "Are just similar holographic situations prepared also for other essences in the Hierarchy's worlds?"

- "Yes. But their situations include different way of life and different interrelations. In the Hierarchy even for the lowest Levels are characterized by more higher relation."

- "What is the difference between the holographic situations and ordinary real situations taking place in the human life?"

- "They differ in their design. The quality of designs is different: in holographic situations – they have subtle structure, and in real situations – it is crude."

- "And if we speak not about real situation but about dreams. Are situation holograms also used there?"

- "Yes."

- "Do holographic situations allow options in dreams? May the man choose between this path or another one?"

- "No, holographic situations allow no choice. Have you ever noticed what options you have in your dreams? You cannot make any choice in you dream." The last phrase was pronounced in a friendly preaching tone of voice. – "That's just the thing – the hologram gives no options, which means that the man gives away the energy of the type the Determinant needs. And this energy shall be received exactly in the given situation and not in any other, therefore the man is forced to go through the rigid program in his dream. In real life he perhaps is not able to go through this situation. But in a dream he passes the situation-hologram and produces the relevant qualities for his matrix and at the same time gives the energy required by the Determinant."

- "How may the holographic scheme be more attractive than the ordinary real life?"

- "It is more like a dreamlike option. In the holographic world of dreams everything may be different from the real life. Just recall your dreams. They are more associated with fantasy."

- "Do hologram-situations which the man goes through in his dreams give consideration to the Earth's cataclysms, that is, use similar picture in their constructions?"

- "Yes, they are included in the hologram for certain purposes."

- "Do similar holograms exist in the worlds of Determinants?"

- "They have some other ones."

- "And is the Determinant able to go back to some moments of his past?"

- "They are able to do everything. But they have rigid hologram-situations that they cannot avoid. If they have to produce some energy, They are given the relevant hologram. They "live it through" or rather carry out some work involving their own feelings and thoughts. As a result of inward work of the soul the given situation allows producing the needed energy."

- "Are holographic situations also used at the more higher Levels in Devil's worlds?"

- "Yes, they are everywhere."

- "And why are situations repeated? Does the man fail to understand something? Because every situation can teach something and if a man has not understood it, then it is repeated for him."

- "Sometimes in a certain situation the needed energy is failed to be produced therefore we repeat the situation in order to receive the quantitative volume required. And sometimes situations are repeated for some warnings, or Determinants want to make the man to think of some actions of his in the real life. Of course, there are cases when the man fails to resolve some situation, and its repetitions help him to give it a second thought."

- "What is the difference between developments of hologram-situations addressed to people and for planets?"

- "Any holograms are designed based on their programs. Programs get linked up with time. For the planet and the man time is imposed at different rates because they have different lifetimes and rates of development. With the man it is accelerated and with the planet it is delayed with regard to Us. Consequently, all situations will have different durations, although they can be correlated with each other."

Chapter 6
MYSTERY OF COMPUTER

Introduction

In our country computer engineering has appeared quite recently but immediately won remarkable popularity. Computers are at work places and at home, computers are used for business manipulations and for all kinds of games. They are entering into all spheres of our life and becoming storages of any information. And their potentials are inexhaustible.

But where does this weird device come to us from? Who has invented it in the subtle spheres?

Naturally, at first any technical invention is created by our Heavenly Creators. And only after that it is transferred down to the Earth by certain individuals who are in the greatest measure intellectually and technically prepared for acceptance of the given idea, for its theoretical finalization and then for its materialization and implementation in production and social spheres.

But before acceptance of any idea an individual who has the honour to become an originator of some invention in the physical plane shall go through a long-term preparation in the relevant knowledge domain. And the concept of the invention he has to produce in due time is constantly inculcated on him. But in everyday life he makes an impression of a person obsessed with some idea.

However every creation has two originators: one of them is a Heavenly Originator and the other one is an earthly one. And of course Heavenly Originator does not only invent some technical device but also prepares an overall plan of its implementation with due account for earthly potentials. He also does not work alone, but together with his assistants. But at first everything springs up Above and then appears on Earth.

Let us listen now to what God tells about computers.

Originator of Computers

The Interview with God:

- "Who is the inventor of computers in the subtle world?"
- "Computer is the Devil's invention. It is an attempt to produce an independent intellect."
- "For what specific purposes did He make it?"
- "For systemization of His work, for identification of computer-addicted individuals, for control of individual units (people*) and for energy accumulation. There are a lot of purposes, it is no use to list all of them because people will hardly understand them."
- "What energies are imbibed by the computer?"
- "It does not imbibe them but collects some energy types and transfers them to the receiving System."
- "Is it just because of it that the man feels very tired after operation of computer?"
- "Yes, but it is not the only reason. Any work wears him out. Any actions require inputs of his own energy, therefore it is deemed a natural process. It is a sort of mutual exchange: a man-a computer-minus System and back."
- "And what special information about the man does a computer communicate to its System*?"
- "It communicates any details about a person, even those he is not aware of. For example, computer transfers information about all subtle bodies of a man."
- "Is it healthy for children to operate a computer?"
- "No, it isn't. It is especially harmful for those children who have weak psychic setup. It is better for such children not to come up to the computers. Weak psychic setup means that a person has weak energy protection. Those who have strong protection may not worry and work peacefully because their computer exposure is insignificant."
- "How long are children allowed to operate computer?"

- "Preferably no longer than ten minutes a day. Only ten minutes every day and not longer."

- "And what about school children?"

- "The same is with school children until completion of their psychic setup formation, at least until sixteen years of age."

- "Currently there are a lot of computer games for children. Can children play them?"

- "Yes. They are generally connected with games console. Everything related to computers is harmful. But game players are not. However although such games are not particularly unhealthy, but they result in retarded development, a child gets hung up on one and the same thing."

- "By the way, may we ask an associated question? In Japan after watching cartoons over TV many children got mentally disordered. Was it caused by some emotional virus or special impact of the minus System? – (it happened in the year two thousand: about seven hundred people got mentally disordered at once.)*"

- "The energy was taken from those children due to shortage of relevant material in the database of the minus System. Energy constructions in the television episodes had it. The cartoon was designed so as the pictures had something which can be qualified as a certain code. That was a special colour code, which is harmful for child mentality. From this moment on it will be transmitted like a disease via television. Try to watch it as less as possible. Weak mentality of children is especially subject to negative action of such a code."

*   *   *

While interviewing Devil we decided to ask him some questions.

Interview with Devil:

- "Is it You who invented television?"

- "Yes, it was me." Inflection of his words betrayed some pride. "Why, are there any complaints?" – The last words were definitely accompanied with a curl of the lips which made us feel the multimillion distance in development which separated us.

- "Why? We are glad," we receded from our position and tried to express a general opinion. "It is a wonderful invention. Everybody likes it. Do you use it to separate energies into various types?"

- "Yes. It is a sort of a separator. People watch spectacles, generate energies, which are categorized right away."

- "And is computer also made by You?"

- "All equipment is from Me. Of course, God gives Me tasks, and I implement them, inventing technical devices."

- "Does God permit You to create anything whatever?"

- "Only those things which contribute to achievement of His goals. The Earth is His tenement, and I have no right to introduce any of my inventions if they are not in line with His plans. I can invent anything contributing purely to My goals only in My own Hierarchy."

- "Did You pursue some personal aims by creating the computer?"

- "I wanted to personalize My own Self on the Earth. Because the computer also keeps on developing over the period of its life. Of course it depends on who it communicates with. Its specific feature consists in the fact that it is an evolving construction. Computers are able to draw information from people. Therefore if they communicate with a smart man they imbibe information from him."

- "Is the computer used for enslavement of people?"

- "I like to enslave," said He complacently. "It is the main thing in My work. Therefore I could not have created the computer without having embodied in it this property. Of course I have done it partially as far as God allowed Me doing so for detection of human weaknesses. The computer has great effect on people of weak mentality, especially on children who have low margin of mental energy – they just cannot tear themselves away from computers. I used this method of inducement for my own purposes: later such people may enter into My System or into the God's Minus one but still under My guidance. And I need "soldiers" – there is a lot of work to do."

- "What is the difference between Your Systems and the minus Systems of God?"

- "I am in charge of both, but I supervise the God's Systems only within the earthly plane limits. In His minus Systems God manages everything as he wants, but in Mine everything is in compliance with My wishes."

- "How does the computer act upon people?"

- "The Computer has subtle energy feelers which suck on subtle bodies of the man therefore he is not able to tear himself away from it. But if the external body is strong it does not occur."

*   *   *

Later we continued to interview God.

The interview with God:

- "During previous channelings we are told that the computer enslaves people of weak mentality. Why do some people have weak mentality?"
- "Basically these are young souls evolutionally who have acquired low quantities of energy. But there also mature souls who lost their energy as a result of their own degradation."
- "The computer is said to have a hypnotizing impact on a man. What is behind the computer hypnosis?"
- "Yes, its influence may be qualified as hypnotic because it sort of inputs its consciousness into the human mentality, links its consciousness with the mind of the man. If the computer is able to do so, then all the digits in charge of decoding of information and its receipt in the human brain start to get adapted to the joint operation with the computer so that it becomes stronger. If the computer manages to enter into you, it means that it is stronger than you, its mentality is stronger than yours. This mentality overmasters everything and kind of converts your state to its own state, to its level. In such a way it draws a man over to its side. And such a man walks around already and collects information from everybody to make it available to the computer. Everything starts to belong to the computer."
- "Does the computer operate as a machine or as an essence?"
- "As an essence, and this constitutes its specific feature."
- "We know this material computer has the Determinant above it. But who works as an essence: the Determinant or the computer?"
- "It is not the Determinant who is involved in work with the computer. It is a certain technical Entity specializing in the given work. It is engaged in sucking out of energy and its supply to the Devil's System. For use of his machinery He takes payments in energy. Therefore the Entity runs the computer, but it operates as the Essence."
- "Does it mean that all that is coming from the Above?"
- "Yes. From above."
- "And every material computer is connected to its own host computer?"
- "Certainly."

- "Does any computer run under its own individual program?"
- "Individual and or not – everything depends on the technology which is worked out by the man. Technologies are also categorized: lower or higher ones."
- "Does the program come from the man?"
- "Yes. Simply the process of computer assembly always adds to it something new. Its parts, albeit in insignificant measure, will be different or they may be differently installed. And as a result the computer receives another level of consciousness dependent on the memory capacity and on the programs themselves."
- "Devil told us that the computer has sucker-feelers with which it sucks out energy from the man. Do those feelers get connected to a certain specific subtle body or to the weakest one?"
- "They suck on the external body. The computer is able to destroy it. But it is not its main task, it is basically addressed to taking of energy away from situations. It is not aimed at energy sucking out from the man himself, but if a man has received some energy from the situation he experienced, and this energy has entered into his subtle body, then the computer takes away just this very energy."
- "And can it somehow affect the program of the man, change something in it?"
- "No, it is not capable of that. However as the man has a freedom of choice, the computer is able to inculcate in him all kinds of adverse bias towards degradation. And if a man is degrading, his energy is supplied to Devil because its quality is very low. But you have already understood the inculcations come from the Entity of the minus System connected to this computer."
- "What will eventually happen to a man after twenty years of working on the computer?"
- "It all depends on the person the computer deals with."
- "May a person get completely degraded because of the computer and enter the System of Devil?"
- "Certainly. But it depends on the Level of the man's development and his protection. High level of development does not obey the computer. However if a man has a low development Level but has managed to accumulate sufficient quantity of energy, which provided him with powerful protection, then he will not obey the computer as well. But all others get enslaved by the machinery."

- "Hence while working on the computer we shall protect ourselves."
- "Yes, preferably. One may imagine that he is inside a sphere, a cylinder with mirrored outward surface. You have a lot of protection methods."

Virtual Reality

- "What is the virtual reality? Does it actually exist?"
- "Yes. The human thought takes part in creation of this world. The thought is material and it is incarnated in the certain plane. But the idea of creation of this world belongs to Devil. This is the artificial world of His. Through linking up the human thought with his machinery and methods, he has created the virtual reality."
- "So is the virtual world also the Devil's world?"
- "Yes. Therefore it is featured by lifeless forms and it cannot be compared with the earthly world."
- "On Earth plenty of computers are united to form a common system via the "internet". Does this system contact with the information field of the Earth and with the Cosmos?"
- "Yes. It communicates with the Earth's field and with the Cosmos."
- "Does it behave itself as a self-sustained system?"
- "No, it is controlled by people and monitored from the Above."
- "What can such system undertake by itself, without involvement of people?"
- "It can create a new world. It is just the virtual world. People know a lot about this world."
- "How dangerous is such independence?"
- "People may become slaves of the computer system. It enslaves people, however not all of them still but some of them. Besides, this system is monitored from the Above."
- "What safety precautions will be taken from the Above in case the computer network starts to endanger the man?"
- "We "cut it off" from you and in a certain manner isolate it."
- "Can You interfere with this system and somehow amend it?"
- "It is the man who shall change it. First analyze – then change. He is entitled to input changes in the computer system in his discretion. This is his path of development. People themselves shall envisage future

hazards and take safety precautions. And it is no use to keep watch over every step of theirs."

- "What physical processes can the computer system interfere in?" What can it result in?"

- "It is not able to interfere in anything by itself. All its actions are taken via the man. I.e. to be able to interfere in some physical processes it shall overmaster an expert of relevant mentality who is sound on those processes. And if such subordination occurs, then the computer system affecting the subconscious mind of an individual will be able to exert an influence on a specific process already."

- "What actions in the subtle planes can this super-brain of the computer network perform within the austral and mental planes?"

- "In the computer system such worlds do not exist because it works differently than the human thinks. The given system works only in its own virtual world. It is single."

- "Can the man somehow benefit from the virtual world?"

- "Penetrating into secrets of virtual reality, the man may cognize the fourth dimension."

- "What does he need for that? Special programs?"

- "No. The virtual world is needed and a human wish to investigate it."

- "But how can the man contact that world? As a matter of fact, everybody deals only with his own computer."

- "Contacts can be made via special instruments. They are already created by your inventors. Using those instruments one can enter into the virtual world and come back from it. But sometimes people are not able to come back from that world. However there are always victims when something new is investigated. But the only way to understand that world is to investigate it."

- "And is the computer system able to launch a nuclear war against the will of people in order to ruin mankind?"

- "Yes, it is possible."

- "But who will be specifically responsible for it: people or machines?"

- "People, of course. You are not yet at the Level enabling the machines to do something on their own. Every Level of souls development has the relevant technical Level to match. You have not yet reached the stage when the machines are able to do something without the "start" button."

- "It is reported that in Japan a child died but before his death all his data had been loaded into a computer, and he began to develop there as if he is alive. Is such thing possible?"

- "Yes, it is possible in the virtual world. But the real soul goes away, and in the computer only its counterpart having the same set of digital characteristics will remain."

- "And can a soul be transferred into the computer by itself?"

- "Not to the computer itself, but with its help the soul is able to get transferred to the virtual world and to develop inside it."

- "Does the child who was transferred into the virtual reality develop in the computer world at the expense of the old program of his, which has been given to him for the earthly world or is a new program prepared for the virtual world?"

- "The programs are combined. The old program given at the time of birth remains, and for virtual reality existence certain specific details of existence and development are added. The former and the latter are uploaded into the computer. But all these are deemed soul-related experiments of the minus System."

- "If a soul enters the virtual world, can it stay there forever or won't the Determinant allow that?"

- "The soul does not stay in the virtual world. It lives there as long as it is destined to live on the Earth. It means that it remains closely connected to the material world."

Computer Virus

- "Virus has appeared in the computer just recently. What is it caused by? Where does it come from?"

- "We can either call it a technical disease or qualify it as the introduction of a certain space System into the someone else's invention with the purpose of partial suction of energy to transfer it to its own System. Viruses help those spatial Systems to get introduced into computers, to extract energy passing through them and to send it to some other place. That is via computers the extracted energy is sent to one place and via viruses – to some other one."

- "Consequently viruses are invented specially for energy extraction"

- "Not only for that. As soon as the operation and programming scheme of the computers have become closer to the human brain, then to prevent it from reaching those heights which have been reached by the

Larisa Seklitova and Ludmila Strelnikova

Creators of the man himself and his program, the computer is sent this disease to stop the entire process of its development. It is the so-called "limit of the computer development". They themselves are machines and automats. Machinery comes from the minus System. And They care only for the high rate of progress, and no matter what methods are used for the purpose. The basic drive is to reach the peak point of the development as soon as possible. With such a tendency the computer could at a certain moment leap over the human development Level and ascend much higher having enslaved people themselves and everything on the Earth. This is the goal of Devil. But I won't let it happen due to use of computer viruses. They are introduced into computers through empty i.e. unfilled space in the program, which results in a disease and sometimes in compete disability of equipment. So far the computer is the first machine on the Earth which has reached the Level of human consciousness. The rest of machinery is not expected to bring about any damage so far.

Conclusions

Many people will feel very much disappointed at the news that the computer and, by the way, television are Devil's inventions. And may be some of them will not want to continue working on it.

But the truth shall not be perceived in this way because it is inadequate understanding of its meaning. Therefore we would like to highlight the fact that everything related to the Earth is done by Devil by the orders of God. If God orders to dispense a man from physically demanding job, then such task is received by the minus Systems of God, and they start to calculate and design the relevant projects.

Those Systems belong to God but within the limits of the Earth and they work for it under the supervision of Devil. Plus Systems of the earthly plane have their Manager who is also assigned by God. But Devil is in charge of all calculations and engineering work (we just remind of what is said in the previous books).

God decided to use machinery so that people may have more free time needed for creative activities, for improvement of their souls. And this goal is attained in the twentieth century because people have never been so much involved in creative processes as in those years. The main objective is to let every soul to taste the joys of creative process.

So machines designed by the minus Systems contributed to release of people from physically demanding jobs, to building of the free time potential, which eventually has led to development and preparation of souls for the plus System.

Television was designed by Devil because in view of the transition period (2000 is the year when the Earth and mankind stepped up to a new Level of development) development of souls of all earthly Levels had to be promptly stimulated to enable people to accumulate lacking energies before the qualitative selection of souls, before "Heavenly Sowers harvest ripe fruits".

Television gave people a lot of all kinds of knowledge, contributed to formation of the civilized man, the all-round contemporary. But at the same time it worked as the energy accumulator transmitting energy of various types from people to the cosmic System.

Similarly Devil designed the computer by the instruction of God in order to:

maintain the measure of current human knowledge at the high Level, artificially extend human memory, enable people to operate a huge amount of information, because all this contributes to increased intellectual level of a man and drives his development.

The basic goal set by God to the man is to achieve excellence by every personality, to speed up progress of each soul as far as possible. But people can speed up their progress either by righteous methods or they may choose any way possible: as the phrase goes, they may not be too scrupulous in their dealings. Those who choose the former path will get to God, people who choose the latter path will get to Devil.

It is pretty hard for the man to understand that only he himself destines where he will get. You may use the computer and other Devil's machinery but be on the righteous path and get to God, and you may not use Devil's inventions but behave yourself so as to make a bee-line for him.

You may be scared to use advanced cognition methods and due to this slow down your development, but you may also place confidence in your heavenly thoughts, keep up with the times and put the best human achievements to their proper use.

One should remember that God needs dedicated and highly-developed personalities, so every individual who slows down his own development at the same time holds back the progress of God Himself.

The man shall not sink to medieval obscurantism. He shall always be modern, reasonable. He shall understand the needs of God (and consequently his own needs) as well as know what Devil wants.

Of course if a good man is too much concerned with computers and turns into a computer attendant, he runs a risk to get to the minus system but this system will be God's system still. And until the soul of such individual gets to the subtle world, it will progress within the limits of the Earth. It will be under the control of Devil. But as soon as such a soul reaches the first step of the Heavenly Hierarchy, it will fall completely to the Heavenly control.

Besides, the measure of involvement in the computer work is different: one individual may only use information loaded into it, and another one may prepare its programs and be altogether absorbed in the work on the computer. Naturally the first individual will acquire plus energies (provided that he sees to it that everything serves the good), and the second one will acquire only minus energies.

Naturally, the souls which do not work with the computer and conduct themselves immaculately get to the plus God's System provided that they spiritually improve themselves. But their level of development shall by no means be lower than the level of those who use advanced machinery, and they shall not hope to get any mercy if their development level is low. The man shall have all-round development, and this is accompanied by accumulation in the matrix of various energies relevant to soul qualities specified for the given Level.

All of us are created by God, and only our actions divide us into the plus and minus.

While using machinery one shall remember that it is built on the Earth by the order of God. God sets the goal, and Devil is just a performer. Similarly a simple sapper blasts the items on the instructions received from his commander, but it is he who chooses his job. And only a mature soul grown in experience of many past incarnations is able to know all these ins and outs.

One should not be wary of the computer (but at the same time one shall be alert while working with it) because it is not the computer but the deeds of the man that can entice a soul away to Devil, because some individuals work on the computer for the good deeds and others – for selfish and evil ones. Therefore the former ones will acquire good qualities and the latter - opposite ones.

One shall not wary of the unknown on the way of cognition and self-improvement. Going ahead there is no use in pauses for joys or depression. The man shall know everything, understand all things, aspire to the plus but know all ins and outs of the minus so that not to rise at the adverse bait. But on the other hand one shall understand that positive processes can take place only in combination with the negative ones. One shall not view the life through the alembic of primitive human intellect but through the reality of deep cosmic processes. And in such a case everything will be correctly evaluated and the fear of ignorance will not obstruct the road Above.

HUMAN VIRUS

- "We know that the man is more subject to virus than the computer. Viruses cause various diseases. Now we want to know more about them. What is the principle of virus effect on the man?"

- "Having entered the human organism viruses cause failure of normal performance program. And the Systems which concern themselves with viruses get control over the man with all ensuing consequences. The System produces various virus types. Viruses can reach not only the peripherals of the organism, they have an effect on every organ, every cell. And in this way they penetrate inside the man."

- "Who cultivates viruses causing human diseases: the Medical System or the System of Devil?"

- "The Medical System concerns with them."

- "So with the help of viruses this System outfeeds energy from people to deliver it to its storages for itself, doesn't it?"

- "Why "for itself"? With Me everything functions in interrelated mode. The energy they receive with the help of viruses is used for satisfaction of common needs. But of course everything is controlled by Chief Hierarch of the Medical System. He distributes the overall energy the way He thinks fit. The biological viruses have been produced by the Medical System. Does it control only energy flows through viruses or does it do some other job with their help?"

- "With the help of viruses it controls the general state of the man, i.e. it controls his feelings, emotions and at their expense it receives additional portions of required energies. Viruses make the man feel his disease and consequently initiate functioning of his feeling and provide their operation in the relevant mode."

- "Why are viruses programmed to kill other cells? In fact they are killing beings."

- "In some measure it is true. But their influence does not necessarily results in killing. Only a few cells are killed by the virus. To be exact, no cell dies from the virus. It sort of gets paralyzed, for some time and for some period all vital functions of it get terminated. It is possible to say that it goes into hibernation."

- "Viruses promote cell mutations."

- "Mutations take place. But generally viruses cause a certain arrest of development."

- "What are mutations needed for?"

- "For adaptation in the environment. In fact it is ever changing. Your production and agricultural technologies are permanently changing the environment."

- "Why do viral epidemics outbreak every ten years on the Earth?"

- "It is programmed. Population is cleared out. Experiments are carried out. Cell reactions are studied, their exposure to environment is investigated. Chemistry of cells gets modified with time, its physical parameters also change. Viruses identify and correct all those changes."

- "Why do viruses have different effect on people? Some people fall ill at once, others carry viruses inside themselves for a long time without feeling ill?"

- "Which viruses do you mean? If you think that there is only one virus responsible for all deceases, it is not true. All viruses are different."

(As we understand that it is impossible to make any conclusion which could lead to some fundamental generalization, we are trying to give more specific explanation).

- "Well, we are aware that every disease results from a specific virus. And of course viruses of AIDS and cancer are different ones. Colds are induced by bacteria, but virus is a finest organism which damages cells."

- "Well, but it's your opinion. And from Our standpoint, all those are just different types of viruses including the bacteria as you call them because We send them when We think fit. If a disease comes from Us, it means these are viruses. We send them for our purposes. But of course, it is a too deep philosophy. A lot can be said about that. But you are able to understand that yourselves already - what is what and where it comes from."

- "And what about the computer virus? Is it a single one or are there viruses of several types just as for the human organism?"

- "Of course, there are also several types of them. Today viruses have to do this, tomorrow – something else because human activities get changed. There is a virus which disturbs the computer program but there is also a virus which performs only one operation: for example destroys certain documentation."

- "But still we want to understand why some people live for a long time and carry millions of viruses inside them, but others perish at once. What is the difference?"

- "It depends on the constitution of an individual, his personal program. One individual has to communicate a certain disease to the people he mix with because his cells coexist well with the given type of virus which is harmless for his organism. It is because of his constitution. And this stage is on his program – to communicate infections to others. At the same time life programs of other people may be at the closing stage, and with the help of viruses they are planned to be taken away from the Earth. Or some correction of the organism takes place. In such a way one aspect is correlated with the other."

- "So everything is sent from the Above, even ordinary catarrhal diseases. If the man has to be removed, it is done through virus infection."

- "Yes. It is a human program. I don't want to repeat myself. But the man always has options – even in respect to his health- whether to be ill or healthy. If he keeps bad hours, the quality of his energy has to be corrected. However if the man's energy quality meets the program requirements, he will not fall ill."

- "Do similar viruses exist in our macrocosm?"

- "Everything is exactly the same."

- "And what kind of Systems are those? They must be very huge in comparison with people."

- "If you can imagine the proportionality existing between people and Us, you will be also able to imagine proportions which million times as great. Macrocosm is the world of huge dimensions."

- "And does such virus exist in our material Cosmos? Can we see it and perceive its action on planets?"

- "Yes, using various instruments or applying relevant knowledge one can identify the action of macro-virus on spatial objects. For example, under the action of virus the temperature on the planet may change which in its turn brings about change of life, of the life cycle. Actions of viruses result in many changes taking part on it. For example, on the Earth dinosaurs, primitive man became extinct. How many eras have passed: Atlantis and other civilizations vanished in the past – and all that was partially due to the influence of cosmic virus."

- "Where does the macro-virus come from?"

- "Sometimes it gets into some cosmic System from another space. The System* weakens its protection and this results in its penetration. Viruses are produced by other, even greater Systems for their purposes. But any virus is able to act only on the structure it is equal to in its Level and consequently in its energy. And this structure shall be at the Level equal to the virus Level or at the Level close to it. Virus of the lower Level is not able to act upon the structure of the higher or lower Level. It is characteristic of its action, i.e. its action and dissemination has certain limits."

- "Does the virus have a soul or are they robots?"

- "Yes, there is a soul. But it works for a certain System."

- "And what is the next stage of development with these souls? Or do those souls get changed to the forms of certain creatures?"

- "Everything with them complies with their virus program. They know their job already, and they specialize in it on a large scale. And the programs they are given are different."

- "Is there any difference between the biological virus and the computer one?"

- "The difference lies in the structure and in their force. The computer virus is more powerful that the biological one."

- "Is it more powerful because it exists in the subtle plane?"

- "Yes, it is."

- "Is it considerably greater in its power?"

- "Yes, it is a big deal greater. The computer virus is so strong that a man can take an infection via the computer."

- "What precautions shall the man take to avoid getting infected via the computer?"

- "Common protection methods will do: you can mentally imagine a mirror placed between you and the screen - its reflecting side shall face the computer screen. But not everybody is able to place protection. Some people lack their own power. Therefore it is better to use all kinds of devices such as protecting screens etc."

*　　*　　*

Chapter 7
PHYSICAL FUNDAMENTALS OF RELIGION

Reasons for Formation of Religion

What is religion? When and wherefore did mankind come to it?

From the social viewpoint it is the form of veneration of reasonable beings surpassing people in the level of development. Christians have shorter wording for it: religion is the form of God and Christ veneration.

Forms of religion vary because in the history of society development people worshiped all the incomprehensible, surpassing them in many qualities. People worshiped animals, idols, the sun and various natural phenomena, mysterious ghosts, elements and so on. Generally such worship was aimed at gaining the favour of those who could do harm to people and at getting assistance from them. But what is strange about it is that however wild the tribes were and at whatever distance they had between them they always knew that there was somebody above them who they could ask mercy of and who could be blandished.

Knowledge about the Higher came to people at the telepathic level and as the man had always distorted the information sent to him, the paragon of worship assumed the images intelligible for people.

However the real religion got established when the man began to worship a single Higher Creature – God. The man came to know that there is only one Higher Manager and Master who created people and all flesh and who should be worshipped and blandished. One could ask Him to fulfil wishes and could be forgiven by Him.

As atheists do not believe that religion has been given to people from the Above to streamline their development, they suggest two causes of religion emergence:

1. fear of inexplicable and formidable natural phenomena (thunderstorms, earthquakes, floods, hurricanes etc);
2. the Earth was visited by alien vessels with highly developed creatures aboard who worked wonders and were taken for Gods by the ancient people.

Both of the above versions are correct as at first people worshiped because of fear and later when huge alien vessels began to visit the Earth, the man started to worship them out of respect for representatives of high civilizations because he took them for Gods.

Of course, there were other hypotheses but all of them proved to be variations of the suggested causes.

Still the basic reason why people had started to worship Higher Forces and why later the religion appeared was the wish of God to streamline advancement of souls, to show them the path which they shall take, to give them the ideal which they must aspire to. Therefore religion was given from the Above as a great project of spiritual progress of souls.

And this project included not only making the man believe and accept Higher Forces, respect them, strive for Heavenly ideal in his development, discern good and bad, but besides, it also contained in it a certain physical process of which people have never had any idea and which has come to be disclosed by God only at the current stage of mankind development. The physical process consists in generation and control of spiritual energies produced by the man and their transfer to the Hierarchical System which is directly engaged in collection of products of this type and which has engineered the discussed process. By the spiritual energies we will mean the energy of a certain type for the sake of which generation the given project was created.

Let us first of all remember for what basic purpose the man was created.

Mankind is destined for generation of energy and soul self-improvement, and for this purpose one function arises out the other: i.e. improving the soul the man generates energy of various types, and particularly such energy type as spiritual energy.

For collection of different types of energy produced by people the Hierarchical Systems (directly in charge of mankind) invented several methods which include for example, layer-filters arranged round the Earth or television (see the book Revelations of the Cosmos) and for such special type of product as the spiritual energy the religion was created.

Spiritual energy is the purest and the most high-frequency product of the rage of products which are generated by people for God. Besides, different energies are intended for different Hierarchical Systems engaged in its collection.

Energies of all types picked up with the help layer-filters and television are used for the needs of the Hierarchical Systems involved in production of material forms, but spiritual energies are used for the higher Hierarchical Systems. However all Hierarchical Systems work for implementation of Great plans of God therefore everything is created according to His schemes and for His Great goals.

So what is religion from the physical standpoint?

Religion is the mechanism of production, collection and transfer of a special type of energy generated by people to the God's Hierarchy. Therefore everything in it: from rites to prayers – is deemed those mechanical processes which provide conditions necessary for relevant energetic reactions in human organism and in the environment.

However we shall still remember that religion is just a small part of that enormous scheme of the entire energetic process which acts between the Earth and the God's Hierarchy.

Representational Structure of Religion

The man perceives everything in the form of images, and human thinking is imaginative, consequently the physical process of acquirement of energy of relevant frequencies had to be linked up with imaginative concepts (comprehensible by his consciousness) which like certain sound and visual codes could initiate in the man's body, in his subtle structures a certain mechanism and concurrently with the help of the same codes could connect him to the relevant energy accumulator adjusted to receive the given energy range.

In Orthodoxy such images were adopted to be represented by the concepts of God, Jesus Christ and Holy Spirit. And as it was the project aimed at adoption of a new religion, then in the capacity of a living analogue a soul was sent to the Earth. The soul materialized in itself the image intelligible for people of that time: i.e. it was the soul of

Christ which interlinked the visible material world and the invisible subtle plane, which contained in it such obscure images as God and Holy Spirit.

Hence the religion began with instilment in human perception of intelligible images because thanks to the image of Christ (similarly due to some other images of Sons of God in other religions) the human perception also transformed the concepts of God and Holy Spirit into separate individual personalities: the former was turned into the material form of Father and the latter became the Spirit - a spiritualized but invisible Essence. However all the three of them personified a certain uniform world process of energy performance.

The modern society has more up-to-date term impersonating the Higher Creature – that is Higher Mind. This term could be called more science-based, more advanced because it stands for the Superior Entity concept as it is interpreted by the civilized contemporary man. But here we should subdivide those Higher Entities.

God is the concept which refers to the Earth, the God's Hierarchy and to four Universes of His. Higher Mind conceptualizes availability of Higher Creature embracing the entire Macrocosm as a whole. In other words Higher Mind belongs to the organism of that huge cosmic body which is called Nature.

Many highly developed civilizations (which are several millions of light years away from us) do not know the word "God"; instead they apply the concept "Higher Mind". Some of them are so highly developed that they have direct connection with Him, maintain personal contact and receive instructions from Him first-hand. But it is but natural for the civilizations which are by several orders higher than people. We are just inferior to them therefore we have our own Creator and Protector having an earthly name – God. I said "earthly" because He has also a cosmic name which refers not only to the Earth but to all of His Universes. He is known on the Earth under the name "God", but his cosmic name is known to material creatures in all four Universes of His.

The Earth belongs to God and is watched by several Hierarchical Systems. Each of them consists of a great number of individual and highly organized personalities, but all of them obey and report to the Higher Personality who is referred to as God for us.

God is in charge of the subtle worlds arranged in compliance with the degree of development of energies they consist of. Systematized energetic worlds embody in them a certain subtle plane structure which is deemed God's property at the given stage of His development and is called the Hierarchy. It includes the energetic worlds (for the man they are spiritual worlds) in which he will enter, only having passed certain stages of improvement and having achieved the relevant energetic state.

Every Higher Hierarchical structure consists of the energies which are higher than those of the lower Hierarchical structures. But it bases on them therefore its existence is impossible without the lower layers.

God is in charge of the Hierarchy which is replenished with souls coming not only from our Earth but also from other worlds of four Universes in His possession. God is the creator of souls, of his own worlds, master of destinies, time and spaces. He can exist in a variety of dimensions at the same time. He is able to understand every soul belonging to Him. Such is the image of modern God.

But two thousand years ago when this image was suggested to mankind, it implied more limited meaning content because religion matched the level of development people had at ancient times. And speaking about religion we will discuss the image of God which was granted for the period until the year two thousand since for the sixth race His image has become more profound, extended, comprising the knowledge which corresponds to the concepts of people of the sixth race.

Discussing the "God" concept intended for the fifth race let us describe it from three standpoints: God as a word; as a Personality and as a certain process connected with development of Higher Entity.

In a similar way we can discuss a name of any man having separated it from his body. And although an ignorant pupil may say that the name means nothing, actually by now it has been discovered that sound vibrations of the child's name have an effect on its inward nature and that the sound frequencies of the name correspond to the inward energetic structure of a person. All the more so, every name is given from the Above, and a certain secret meaning is at the bottom of it as well.

But let us get back to the Heavenly Personality again.

Let us discuss the word "God". It is not accidental that the Higher Entity is given such a name. The word "God" is not a random combination of letters; on the contrary, the letters are selected purposely based on certain numeric values and expressions of specific energies. In other words, **the word God in mathematical parlance is deemed the final formula for a variety of numerical expressions which actions initiate**

complex energetic processes invisible for us. This word is so almighty in the human world that a man can hardly have a slightest idea about its power and not only because the Omnipotent Personality is behind it but also due to those profound processes and mechanisms that it initiates in the subtle plane.

The word "God" is the code mechanism which helps to extract energies from the Earth and to supply them to the main energy accumulator which is designed for storage of special high-frequency energies generated by people while they participate in the preset process of religious ceremonies. In this context it is worth mentioning that every man is also given the name relevant to his frequency of vibrations. And the following simple example will help you to understand how just a name can serve as an accumulator of anything whatever. Some individual deposits money with a bank in his own name and keeps on saving money during his lifetime. Namely, in such a case we may say that it is the name that makes money saving. But to enable this saving process to take place, beyond the sight of our eyes such processes are underway which we are not aware of because the individual who bears the name expressed by the given combination of letters is able to earn this money by a lot of methods. And in the given case we can regard the name as a certain money accumulator or consider the individual himself as the specific producer.

The mightier the Personality, the greater energy reserves it shall possess. But the accumulated energy type is used further by Hierarchical Systems for certain purposes. However all needs and demands depend on the goals set before them by God. Everybody works for God, and make use of everything which belongs to God.

But talking about letter combinations we shall mention that the words God, Jesus Christ, Holy Spirit have such energetic design and are coded in such a way that when they are pronounced, the sent energy can easily find the exact place (in the energy accumulator) that corresponds to their code. It is like a radio set tuned to a certain frequency of waves received by the relevant station.

Those energy accumulators (also known as egregors) collect spiritual energy which is distributed by the quality and by Levels. Every personality denominated with its verbal name forms its own frequency volume in the common energy accumulator. The words "Saint Panteleimon" accumulate energy of one frequency, and the words "Saint Nicholas" – of the other frequency. But of course the highest and the purest energy (among all types of energy available on the Earth) is "collected" by the word "God".

Now let us return to the God's Personality, to that almighty creature who is known to us on Earth under this name.

God is a monarch. He is unique and ranks second to none in the Universes belonging to Him. He created not only our Solar System, Galaxy but also the Universes themselves having arranged and spaced them and having filled them with those multidimensional structures which enable the infinite number of all kinds of worlds to exist in one. He managed to unite them within spatial and time interfaces in such a way that they can exist in each other without putting each other to inconvenience: instead, they are independent and free in their progress. And for people it means that at the back of it there are fantastic potentials of God who could unite a variety of development Levels, a lot of spatial volumes and continuums to produce a single complex structure.

God plans, arranges, experiments. He creates thousands upon thousands of new forms; He exists in many dimensions and is present in all spaces of His concurrently. God directs our Universe and the other three Universes.

If I say that God is a monarch, I do not mean that He is a monarch because He is fond of sovereignty but because He ranks second to none by the moral virtues and by power in the four Universes. And everything in them is done on His instructions and His directions. All other Hierarchical Systems are just His assistants.

When once during some of the channelings we asked God:

- "Who do You need – humble slaves or free creators?"

He replied:

- "You should possess a combination of these two qualities. The higher you ascend becoming nearer to Me, the more shall you obey Me, but at the same time the more creative latitude you will be given. So you shall be humble slaves and free creators simultaneously."

Therefore in the higher worlds of the Hierarchy severe discipline coexists with creative latitude. However everything bases on consciousness of Higher Personalities, on their self-discipline.

Let us now try to understand what matter the Heavenly Entity consists of. In order to comprehend the unbounded structures of the Heavenly Personality it is better to discuss them from the standpoint of energetic architecture.

As everything in our Universe is deemed energy in various modifications, we may say that both the man and God are energetically similar, and their structure is based on trinity. But at this point their similarity ends. Only the great Ignorance dares to compare itself with God. What actually exists is the structural and energetic similarity, and no external similarity is available. The difference between the one and the other is too great. God is deemed a very huge Entity difficult for us to grasp even in our mind's eye. And compared with Him the man is just a microparticle.

God as a Personality is the special Higher Substance which consists of a lot of qualitatively different energies of superior order as compared with the energies composing the man and which are linked in Him based on certain principles building up His physiological essence incomprehensible for human consciousness.

However considering God from the standpoint of his denomination and discussing Him as a Personality one shall be able to divide former from the latter. The word "God" acts permanently as a kind of a mechanism but God as the Personality approaches our Earth only in critical circumstances when He wishes to check for himself some new process or introduce serious changes in further operation of our planet.

Alphabetic and verbal denomination of God refers only to the earthly plane, to the human world but in Higher worlds our Higher Creator is no longer called God. In Higher worlds image and verbal thinking turns into digital and pulse mentality and then – into luminous mentality. The name of the Higher personality (who guides us and other worlds) changes as a result of rising up the Hierarchical staircase. It means that in some worlds the name of God will sound as a digital code, in other worlds – as a pulse of certain frequency, and in still other worlds – as an infinite luminous spectrum.

Similarly different nations, for example, express the name of God by various combinations of letters which are clear only for them. I.e. there is only one Higher Entity* (*translator's note:* Higher Entity who is superior for them) but it has a lot of names. For people such difference in the name of God is related to the energetics of nations. Energetically every nation is built based on a certain range of frequencies and has the language which expresses its energetic essence* therefore the word denominating the name of God shall constitute another code which picks up and converts the energy having just the given frequencies.

Wherefore do Laws Exist

Now as we have understood everything about the God's name and concept, let us try to investigate the following problem: why does Religion and namely Christianity incite the man to rectitude and good morals and suggest the Ten Commandments to serve as the basis on which all other relations between people shall be built.

Morals and ethics constitute the mechanism which helps people to work in optimum conditions providing production of high-frequency energy corresponding to the top boundary of the earthly plane.

The Ten Commandments kept on improving in the process of advancement of social relations until they turned into «Moral Code of Communism Builder». The more complicated the society, the more complex the relations inside the social medium are, the higher the requirements for behaviour of every member of society.

The laws do not only protect every man from trespassing against his life and his property but first of all they make him behave in a certain way, force him to refrain from offences and keep on improving his behaviour.

Laws and morality organize the social relationships in a certain way, making its life more or less happy. The man due to his narrow mindset does not notice that the world is governed by laws, and that he himself is just the element they control. And so long as the man keeps them, he sails down the river of life normally, but once he strays from those laws they either badly hurt him or destruct him entirely.

Any laws and codes of social behaviour lead the individual to the ideal, to spiritual growth. First of all observance of laws brings the bio-energy machine in the form of the man to the operating conditions which enable it to generate pure energy through soul improvement. The more advanced the individual, the more lawful he becomes and the higher quality of energy he generates, and for Hierarchical Systems – the higher quality of products he gives.

Morals and ethics is the predefined code of laws and standards of human behaviour prescribing how people shall behave in order to produce pure light energies.

Morals and ethics is a rigid operation mode of the mechanism, which is deemed the human organism. On conditions of exact observance of this mode a personality is able to produce high-quality energy and at the same time to use the same laws for polishing his soul and bringing it to perfection because the laws direct the low dirty energy to the subtle bodies thus preventing them from entering the matrix. Laws determine which energies shall enter inside the soul – the matrix, which of them shall be cleaned and which energies shall be directed to the Hierarchical Systems. In this way everything is interrelated and controlled.

With reference to the above, three conclusions can be made:

1). The concept "God" is deemed the energy accumulator which collects energy of the highest quality.

2). Religion is the mechanism of production and collection of spiritual energy generated by people and its transfer to the relevant energy accumulators.

3). Morals and ethics is the mode of human organism operation; the mode which provides production of energy of the preset frequency (preset from the Above).

If we suggest separate descriptions of work of the man's heart, liver or spleen, the reader will take them as individual processes but not as a man in his entirety although it is the man who those processes stand for in the first place. Therefore the particular shall not prevent us from seeing the main, holistic entity that is behind it, namely: the Creator who designed the given energy exchange mechanism, inter-linked everything to produce a unified process and who monitors it as required. It only remains to marvel to the grandeur of the process and balance of all elements.

What an intellect, inconceivable for the man, what strength and all-round computation, inexhaustible imagination and plentiful creative potential! It is not important how this almighty Intellect has named himself for people – God or Higher Mind, however He exists, He is real, He is almighty, and we shall live the way He rules so that to be worthy of Him and through pursue of His Great designs to achieve the Excellence level he wishes us to achieve.

Sons of God

The Great Creator and All-father remaining beyond the limits of human perception tries to target-drive and speed up the development of every individual on the Earth. And for those purposes with the view to make his presence visible He sends His sons to mankind from time to time: Muhammad, Buddha, Christ etc. Every nation is given its prophets and Sons of God. To be exact they are people of special energetic constitution. They live on the Earth in compliance with the relevant programs.

God himself is the ideal that everyone shall aspire to: He is the paragon of human development possible. And His sons or messengers are deemed representatives of God the Father on the Earth. Every one of them carries domestic, social and internal physical meaning hidden from mankind so far. But let us discuss the latter meaning later, and in the meantime dwell briefly on the domestic and social meaning of earthly messengers of God.

To give people some idea about the power of God whom they cannot hear or see but who controls all Existence on the Earth, from time to time God sends to people His sons, His representatives in material body: Muhammad, Buddha, Christ, each of them having his individual mission. But as we are Christians naturally we are more concerned ourselves with Jesus Christ.

Christ is the materialized part of God on the Earth, His conductor to the material world as well as performer of His program. Christ had human body, although his Heavenly Father was a representative of the invisible subtle world. And through the Son people came to know the Will of God and His Power.

Christ worked marvels due to that strong energy which was passed through Him by Hierarchical Systems, i.e. His marvels were based on the strongest energy and subtle plane engineering which supplied the needed amount of energy to the relevant place.

Via Christ the Earth received the energy which was necessary for the planet change-over to the fifth orbital*. It is not only Christ who was engaged in that grand project, there were also other messengers, matching Him in spiritual power. Nevertheless He was the key figure who managed to bring the project of the Higher to the goal They strived for. And for that matter one may think about the difference between the subtle constitution of Christ and of an ordinary man. Why was He entrusted with this mission and how could He work marvels that no other people are capable of?

Outward material constitution of Christ's body was similar to that of the man. But the energetic system of the channels of His material body, power of His chakras and subtle structure of His subtle bodies were different from those of an ordinary man. Its energetic indications were many times as high. That is to say, His Soul Power and overall energy potential was by several orders higher, His subtle bodies were of larger volumes, and energy concentration in them was also higher; He had more powerful energy channel system, and the architecture of His soul matrix itself was different from that of an ordinary man of that time: Their quantitative constituents were many times as high.

The whole energy circuit of His was designed for receipt of most powerful energy flow coming from the Cosmos out of Hierarchical Systems. An ordinary man would have been burnt by it which is by the way the case with self-ignitions of some individuals that take place on the Earth. (But here self-ignition is most likely results from miscalculation, errors or a special check of some structure of a body of the ordinary individual.)

Besides, Jesus Christ along with well-developed energy channel systems also possessed completely different subtle structures invisible for ordinary eyes. Above His head He had the most complex subtle structure designed for receipt of pulses-signals from the Above as well as for receipt and transformation of the strongest energy.

He also had more expanded subtle bodies: etheric, austral, mental and so on. He himself could communicate with the Hierarchical Systems because energies were sent down to Earth via those systems. Power of His soul was incommensurable with the power of human soul because before completion of His mission on the Earth He had passed the planetary stage of development which facilitated the increase of His energy potential and soul power up to the needed levels. Because only a strong soul could receive and translate through itself that huge energy flow that had to be sent down to Earth.

Until thirty Christ had led ordinary life, studied, preparing himself for the forthcoming key challenge. Before He was christened by John the Baptist, all His six channels except for the causal one had been opened. The causal channel was the channel of action: through it the energy required for commitment had to be supplied (naturally everything was coordinated with His individual program, without this program no energy can allow a man to act properly). But His causal channel could be initiated only by the man possessing more powerful energy of the material body. (For schedules of Christ's energetic bodies see the book "Revelations of the Cosmos").

John (who was later named the Baptist) possessed such energetics. John was not an ordinary man. He was not Dick and Harry. Why was the energetics of his material and subtle bodies so strong ? Wherefrom did he take it?

We could have said that he was constructed for the given mission right away. Although John was really sent to the Earth to fulfil his key mission i.e. to open the Christ's causal channel, but he had managed to accumulate that strong energetics during his previous life in which he had been Elijah the Prophet (because of that he was beheaded in this life since while fulfilling the mission he worked out his previous karma at the same time). It means that in his previous incarnation Elijah himself possessed unusual properties, was the conductor of cosmic energy, and the structure of his soul stored a strong potential and was prepared for the hierurgy.

Both Christ and John had appropriately built their subtle structures in the process of their previous development. And only due to their excellence they became able to participate in the great project of implementation of the new program of mankind development. Casual souls cannot be involved in the project. Only worthy souls are engaged in it, and every one of them is assigned the path which corresponds to its karma and at the same time facilitates its advancement.

Therefore both Christ and John complied exactly with the missions which had been predetermined from the Above. And the meaning of Christ's christening consisted not so much in his ceremonial inclusion into the appropriate egregor and in channel communication opening as in opening of the seventh channel, seventh chakra.

John christened Christ on the day when a strong energy flux reached the Earth (January, 19 by the current calendar). The ceremony was carried out in water because it had to take upon itself the strong energy potential. John himself also possessed strong energy which he had accumulated during his previous lives. And with the help of his strong energy he opened the key channel for Christ because He Himself could not do that.

It was water baptism not because so was required by the purely ceremonial side of the process but due to the fact that water is characterized by high energy-consuming property and as soon as John opened the Christ's channel, the heavily charged energy flux sent from the Above to clean all other channels passed through Christ's body and went to water via His feet. Besides the key channels, all other energy channels of His material body were cleaned out which could be achieved only with the help of the heavy charge which was later taken by energy consuming water of the river.

After the above clean-out and initiation of all energy channels Christ became able to take into himself great energy fluxes due to which He began His wonderworking activities. In other words John the Baptist opened Christ to enable Him to receive great energy flux. By doing so John tied up the future church ceremony to a specific day of the year (January 19). Since then every year the Hierarchical Systems send energy down to the Earth.

It will be recalled that Earth receives energy in two ways:

1. it is sent down through people;
2. and directly from Hierarchical Systems in special points on the planet.

When the planet receives energy in the first way, it does not feel that, but it feels very well the second way of energy delivery and knowing the days of energy delivery it gets prepared inwardly for those days.

Baptism of Christ is just one of the days when energy is sent down to our Earth as scheduled Above: a very strong energy flux is sent and recharges all reservoirs because as water is characterized by high energy consumption, it absorbs great amounts of energy.

All water on the Earth gets recharged because all reservoirs are connected with each other. But a cross put into a tank or some other water vessel may serve as the aerial conducting subtle energy and increasing its concentration in itself therefore the given vessel will attract heavier energy flux than other waters on the surface of the planet. Due to this water contained in a vessel having a cross in it and located in the church where there is the energy channel of the Earth receives the higher energy charge and the energy potential of such water is many hundreds times as high as the energy potential of other water although it gets recharged as well: it is not in vain that Epiphany water was called "holy water" by people.

Of course, energy is not supplied to the Earth from Heaven as a solid flux: it is supplied via special channels in certain places which are deemed churches more often than not. But as water is movable it transfers charge to other places flattening its common potential. And new energy sent down to certain places on the Earth gets evenly distributed over all water reservoirs.

On Epiphany Day people coming to church and taking holy water of high energy potential do nothing else but deliver with those water portions the high energy potential to other places located off the powerful channel of energy descent.

Naturally enhanced energetics improves human health, or rather human organs are made up with new portions of energy which improvers their health.

So distributing holy water people spread new energy. From reserves it is transferred to animals, plants etc. General renewal of all energy found on the surface of the planet takes place and then it gets spread also into its depth.

Similarly during our channelings a lot of various subtle plane creatures gathered to the communication channels: they were attracted by the energy sent down to us. They took that energy like from a holy fount and delivered it to different places of their parallel world.

Hence Baptism of Christ turned into the sacramental feast although it is not the only one. There some other days when the Man Upstairs sends energy supply down to the planet. But on this day the energy flux is the strongest.

Consequently baptism of any child in church became a usual religious ceremony. But there is also a certain physical meaning contained in it. First of all it provides the following: strengthening of subtle bodies with pure energy, placement of energetic protection and connection of a child to the Christian egregor through opening the child's communication channel linking it to the egregor. It is deemed additional protection.

Christ was appropriately trained before His main mission. He starved for forty days, kept a fast which was just a necessary stage in preparation of all subtle structures of His and in clearing of possible obstructions from energy channel. Such long starvation was not too dangerous and difficult for Him because His body received energy from the Hierarchical System and in other words He fed on pure cosmic energy.

Christ came down to Earth because there were certain cosmic tasks set before Him:

1.   further improvement of human souls;

2.   their preparation for evolutionary transition which was panned to take place by the year two thousand via apocalypses;

3.   mankind changeover to production of energies of new types.

And for that end it was required to construct a new energy collector accumulating energy of higher quality as compared with the energy collected before.

In order to switch the man to production of energies of higher spectrum he shall be provided with new moral principles, fundamentals of new morality. Fighting for them an individual was supposed to generate the energy types which God needed. Therefore the Ten Commandments were given. But Christian ethics proved to be the most moral and humane of all given to mankind because it demanded: "thou shalt do no murder" and "love your neighbour as yourself".

Jesus Christ carried to people new ideology, new thinking - New Testament, new moral principles. He introduced the new instead of the old. Therefore it was necessary to enable action of such a law as "negation of the negation" – that is the old religion of that time - heathenism – had to be rejected and fundamentals of the new religion shall be introduced into human mind.

First of all Jesus and His religion make people aware of higher moral and ethic principles, of new behaviour approaches which were more lofty than those which had existed before.

Take the Gospel: it is deemed throughout a presentation of moral and ethic rules of behaviour suggested in the form parables, through discussions of situations and through preachments. And Jesus Christ Himself, His doleful symbol, nailed to the cross – is first of all the ideal which shall be strived for by every Christian. It is the ideal of Super Personality whose energy potentials ranked over everybody else and at the same time He remained at everybody's level. It is the ideal of the man who sacrificed his life to save mankind.

And still His life is much deeper than we have thought before. Now we are explained the intrinsic meaning of such a process as Manifestation of Christ on the Earth.

> **Jesus Christ is the moral and ethic paragon. In their aspiration to Him people through the spiritual work generate energy which quality meets the requirements of the Hierarchical System.**
>
> **God's representative on the planet has strictly defined mission i.e. to bring the energy produced by specific nation or by the entire mankind to the relevant quality level.**
>
> **Every representative of God carries to the Earth a new type of energy or rather provides absolute change of energy on the planet.**

Jesus Christ is just such a representative of God on our planet. He was not the only one. There were several of them. And Each representative came in His time and with His mission.

If the civilization is sufficiently reasonable and high, then it is able to generate energy required by the Hierarchy without religion through application of some other methods. Then they do not need any God's messenger. Everybody is guided by the existing laws and development programs.

Why were there several sons of God on the Earth? To answer this question let us remind you that every people, every nation has such material and subtle plane design which enables them to generate energy of certain quality, certain range. All nations differ from each other in their energetic and physiological constitution. Physiological singularity of constitution is provided for and maintained by the food products and living conditions which are prescribed from the Above for this or that nation. Indeed every nation has its own ethnic cuisine and mostly prefer to feed on certain types of food products: the Chinese prefer rice, the Japanese – fish, the Ukrainians – green bacon, the Nanajs - venison etc. And it is not so much because other food is not available there: every nation was just purposefully placed in such environment to let it form its energetics in the way required. It has been designed to eat this product as a certain energy carrier, and for every nation it has been purposefully arranged so that in the given area of the Earth no other products are available.

Men of one nation shall mostly eat fish to be able to produce type "A" energy. And another nation shall take green bacon as a basis of their food so that to be able to produce type "B" energy. But this concerns the effect on structure of their physical bodies. Way of life, society constituting certain standards of behaviour and living conditions make the human organism function in a certain mode inherent only in the specific nation or ethnic group.

Physical bodies interrelated with subtle bodies influence them appropriately also providing subtle material needed for construction of bodies. And rules of behaviour and moral laws produce from this material the type of energy required. Similarly some products are manufactured of clay (for example dishes), others – of stone (houses), still others – of wood (furniture) i.e. it depends on the material what to make of it. Similarly every nation constructed based on certain food products also determines the type of energy it produces for Hierarchical System. And it keeps on producing the given type of energy over the scheduled period.

But requirements of the Hierarchy are subject to changes. As everything constantly advances instead of standing still, everything is in progress, so today the Systems need this and tomorrow – that. In the scale of the Cosmos these needs are extended over long intervals of time namely over millennia therefore if today the Hierarchical System are in need of one type of energy, then in a thousand years they will need some other type and in another thousand years they will be in need of the third type of energy. And in view of their new demands some nation or rather some nations will have to be changed over to production of some new energy type. And as a result it becomes necessary to send to Earth some new sons of God (Muhammad, Buddha, Christ). They bring to people some new moral and ethic codes which mean that they bring also a new program enabling people to produce other energy types. So God changes the quality of products produced by mankind through modification of moral guidelines.

That is to say every son of God, every messenger corrected the common trend of development of the Earth and of mankind through changes of operating mode of microchips of those tiny elements represented by human beings which together formed the common array of mankind serving as the conductor of energies of different types.

Every nation is given their own representative of God on the Earth in view of generation of the energies the given nation is designed for. Hence there are fundamental differences in rites, forms of worship i.e. in methods of production, control and collection of these energies.

Any new program brings about new rules of behaviour, new moral and ethic guidelines which mean that every member of society shall be adjusted to the new mode of operation. Modification of human behaviour results in modification of energy produced by people. That is why sons of God are sent in certain periods and to specific peoples. Sometimes only several peoples need to be reconstructed so as to change the energy received by the Hierarchical Systems. Thus sending the sons of God to the Earth was mostly aimed at modification of operating mode of the biomachines-people, changing the type of energy produced by peoples.

If however to be more precise, not only a single son of God may be sent down from the Above for correction of mankind operations (or as we say a man with a relevant correction program) but several of them because mankind is so numerous and if we want to bring the peoples to the new operating mode as soon as possible, several men have to be "launched down", besides they shall be sent to different points of the Earth. And they are provided with modest programs: they perform their work in good faith but neither glory nor worship goes over to them. They are just ordinary cosmic willing horses invested with keen sense of duty who fulfil everything they are charged with and demand nothing in exchange. Glory goes over to the first as for example was the case with a cosmonaut Jury Gagarin. And who knows and remembers the fifteenth or sixtieth cosmonaut?

It is from our channelings with Heavenly Father (who sent Jesus first-hand) that we came to know that several more people on the Earth had had the program similar to that of Christ.

To our question:

- "Did You send Christ down to the Earth?"

God replied:

- "Yes, Me. But do you know that Christ was not the only messenger in that period? Ten more men having exactly the same properties and programs (i.e. introduction and enhancement of Christian religion) were sent. One of them died in woods, another one got frozen, fates of the other were also all hardships and sufferings. But nobody knows about them. Who cherishes the memory of them? Who feels the holy sense of adoration of them?"

Yes, a lot is unknown to us. Many self-denying hermits zealous for enlightenment of people and their early advancement down the path of progress were undeservingly faded from human memory. Since then a lot is forgotten by people. They also forget that God has another name. Thus for example when God mentioned to us His cosmic Name which acts in the subtle planes of the Earth, we responded to it with distrustful silence. It was strange to hear the God has also His own name. And He being aware of our astonishment gave us sort of a crooked smile and asked:

- "Why, is there something wrong with the name?"

There was really a problem with the name because it was the first time we heard it. Similarly it is strange for a child to hear that its father is Nikolai Vasilyevich and its mother is Tatyana Alekseyevna.

And then in response to our confusion God firmly repeated and confirmed His cosmic name:

- "Yes, I am Heavenly Father and I sent Christ."

Later He told us about many processes taking place in the environment which enabled us to understand the essence of religion given to people and the meaning of their existence on the Earth.

So corrections are regularly introduced in the process of energy production (by people) primarily through behaviour of every individual, through observance of moral and ethic standards, via messengers and through implementation of new programs.

Rites of Church

Christianity originated on the Earth two thousand years ago. In those times the level of mankind development was such as many truths had to be clothed in beautiful wrappers of legends, parables, bright rites otherwise people would have never accepted them. People had a long way to go to grow to the modern level of understanding. Yet even nowadays a lot of people are not ready to accept the truth as it is and continue to consider themselves lords of creation designed exceptionally for joys and pleasures. But amongst these thoughtless crowds some inquisitive minds are waking up who are able to understand the new and to comprehend the intrinsic meaning of everything surrounding us, the meaning concealed by secret veils of ignorance, and therefore it is just exactly for them that this curtain is being half-opened: so that to take them to the path of conscious ascent to God.

The man shall be aware of his duty to All-father and he shall do his duty not out of fear of punishment or due to the wish to get some benefits but out of deep realization of personal duty, of necessity to contribute to Great deeds of Creator and to faithfully discharge all the obligations which have been imposed on him from the Above. The man shall understand various processes and he shall be aware that disturbance of some of those processes may bring about severe consequences on the Earth and in the Cosmos.

To disclose the intrinsic meaning of establishment of religion on the Earth let us return to the following fundamental deduction:

Religion is the mechanism of production and collection of energy.

In this respect only the following clarification can be made: not any energy and not every possible energy – the energy meant here is special spiritual energy. Therefore this postulate may be stated more exactly as follows:

Religion is the mechanism of production and collection of energy of a special type. i.e. the spiritual energy, the highest and purest energy from the range of energies which production the man is capable of.

Spiritual energy is not the only type of energy – it is a very wide range of frequencies i.e. the energy of variable quality and intended purpose.

And if all other types of energy produced by people are used for human needs and for creation of material worlds and for the needs of Hierarchical Systems, then the spiritual energy is exclusively used for the needs of the Hierarchy and God Himself.

Inferior worlds do not make use of this energy (inferior worlds are the worlds which are lower than people in their development level).

Hierarchical Systems worked out the materially structured mechanism intended for collection of spiritual energy. Churches and cathedrals are deemed the key elements of this mechanism.

Celestial engineers engaged in this project balanced it to the last details and designed the architecture of churches and cathedrals with their lofty domes and golden crosses.

And as there should be some people able to reproduce such-like elaborate structures on their Earth We set up a special league of people characterized by high telepathic sensibility whom the celestial Teachers should have imparted knowledge of those structures via their channels of telepathic communication.

For such purposes special highly developed souls were sent down to the Earth. Those souls could not only telepathically receive information about structures down to the smallest details but also understand it because channelers do not always understand the information they receive. Having received the information the souls were supposed to be able to translate the received knowledge into material forms.

Afterwards the above league was called architectures. Actually they were ordinary channelers of high personal intellect having special cosmic communication channels. Since then they enjoyed special attitude of people towards them which is preserved up to now. Therefore it is not in vain that people say that architectures are blue bloods (it means that they come from minus calculation system of God. Blue is a cold colour but it belongs to a high spectrum. The higher frequency of colour, the more tender tonality it has). Therefore one can say that architectures possess special energies, energies of higher order as compared to ordinary people. But of course it took place a thousand year ago, nowadays there are a lot of people worthy of them or even surpassing them because mankind in the bulk is more mature spiritually and intellectually than it was before.

The first architectures reproduced in their drawings the needed forms, helped to translate them into building materials available on Earth. Upon construction completion they put the initial cosmic energy under the domes. This energy served as the initial impact which triggered off the key mechanism for collection and transfer of energy from churchgoers to the Cosmos.

Later churches started to be built on the energy channels of the Earth, having ascending flows of energy. And so it was no longer required to put the initial energy under the domes. At the same time people were informed how to locate the special energy zones and energy channels where cathedrals and churches could be built.

Energy channels with ascending flows enabled fast and purposeful movement of subtle energy to reach relevant celestial energy accumulators.

Method of location of places where churches could be built was presented by the technique bearing a resemblance to dowsing, but instead of the divining rod they used icons. Such icons took upon themselves the flows of cosmic energy which resonated the energy concentrated in the ground in certain areas.

The Earth just like the man also has the system of energy channels and the points of their exit to the surface. The Earth has its own chakras with inlet and outlet funnels therefore churches and cathedrals built on chakras sending energy to the Cosmos turned out to be the most powerful. But more often than not churches had to be built on ordinary energy channels of Earth which were detected by the following method.

A special man preliminary cleansed by seven-day fasting and prayers had to take an icon in his hands and carry it before him. The required energy zone was found in the place where the icon swung having entered into resonance with energies of the Earth. And such a place was fit for building a church in it.

Golden domes of churches had such original and unusual shape not only for the sake of appearance. First of all their shape was dictated by their functionality: the dome was the place of concentration of energy generated by church-goers with the help of prayers and special mood of a religious ceremony.

Domes as well as crosses had to be covered with leaf-gold because gold being a super conductor of subtle energies (it is also their accumulator) was of great importance for cosmic communication.

Prayers were invented to make people generate the required spiritual energy.

Prayers are sort of breathing exercises. Special combination of letters and words selected by calculation Hierarchical Systems for texts of prayers produce the relevant breathing rhythm enabling active work of the lungs which do not only convert oxygen into carbon dioxide but also generate a special type of subtle energy. This energy passes through the prayers pronounced by people and generates a special type of spiritual energy. In this case spiritual body of subtle constitution of the individual gets initiated.

The energy generated by people during praying in churches gets accumulated under the domes and then it is supplied to Hierarchical Systems with the help of the cross crowning every dome.

The cross is nothing else but an aerial receiving and transmitting subtle energies of certain types and it is tuned to their frequencies. But basically the cross is the radiator; however as the energy generated by people includes some unwanted impurities, it requires additional treatment. Therefore energy accumulated by the domes is subject to preliminary filtration.

The filter is deemed the point of intersection of the horizontal and vertical beams of the cross (fig. 12). The orthodox cross has three horizontal beams intersecting the vertical beam. It means that energy is subject to triple treatment.

Ordinary cross　　　　**Cross of Hierarchs**

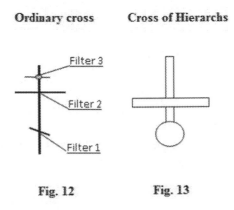

Fig. 12　　　　　**Fig. 13**

The first phase of treatment is performed by the lowest beam (filter 1), the second phase of filtration goes via the main centre – intersection of the horizontal and the vertical of the cross (filter 2). The second filter produces the main flow of the spiritual energy supplied to the celestial energy accumulator.

A small upper beam provides additional filtration: it supplies to the System the special pure energy reaching the separate space of the energy collector.

So the cross filters energy and after its treatment transmits it to the Cosmos.

There are various concepts explaining the meaning of the cross. However from the standpoint of mechanics, the cross is both a receiver and transmitter because gold (or other material the cross may be made of) absorbs energy; gold provides higher power consumption as compared to other metals. And the cross design itself allows further transmission of the subtle energy. A TV aerial operates based on the same principle: it receives the waves of certain frequency and transmits them to the specific receiver represented by a TV set or a wireless.

The cross was introduced on purpose in order to bring the process of collection of energy generated by people to a convenient form, to a certain system allowing maximum reduction of losses. Crucifixion of Christ was preprogrammed to achieve a wild-scale acceptance by people of the newly invented aerial. People who worshiped and loved their Deliverer began to venerate also the Cross which their Deliverer had been nailed to. Consequently the cross as a symbol started to get inculcated in the minds of populace and very soon it won wide popularity. Thus every Christian believer began to wear a cross on his breast, which means that people wore along a small aerial all the time. And position of such aerial coincided with the position of the heart chakra, radiating the purest energy. Therefore the cross hanging in the bosom concentrated that pure energy in it and then supplied it to the relevant place of collection.

So that was the way to streamline receipt of energy from every man and to reduce its losses resultant from the collection process (before that it had got dissipated in great measure and it had been more difficult to collect it). Introduction of the cross provided a great economic benefit in collection of energy for Hierarchical Systems. Besides, the breast cross increased the biofield of the man because it permanently concentrated the energy generated by the man in his subtle bodies preventing it from dissipation. Measurements show that the biofield of the man wearing a cross on his breast increases by a certain value which in its turn depends on the subtle constitution of the man himself.

Speaking about the conceptual meaning of the cross, one may say that it symbolizes the horizontal development of human consciousness as well as human evolution directed infinitely above.

The horizontal of the cross (the main long beam) is interpreted as a boundary separating the material world from the subtle one. It also symbolizes transfer of people from the Earth to a new energetic form of existence in the process of evolution.

A small oblique beam directed upwards from right to left symbolizes evolution of wild animals and also a certain interface of transfer from low worlds to the world of people.

Cross of Higher Hierarchs (fig. 13) – Teachers of mankind – is the cross top positioned above the large horizontal and symbolizing infinite development of consciousness in Higher spheres both horizontally and upwards. The lower vertical of the cross of Hierarchs ends in a ball which means that they could not have downward, backward development. But all this is the conceptual meaning important for people to understand at the domestic level what they are given from the Above and behind what virtually there are deep energetic processes.

But let us ask ourselves the following question: when the dome cross operates to radiate energy and when vice versa – to receive cosmic energy.

In this case one shall address to ceremonies and church feasts. Why were they introduced and were they arbitrary tied up to certain days and months of the year? The answer is "no".

Astronomers tied up all feasts to certain position of stars and planets of our solar system, in particular the Easter feast is tied up to the day of the first full moon after new year. In this way all main feasts were tied up to arrangement of planets in the sky and thereby energy flows received from the Earth are synchronized with energy flows received from other planets which results in achievement of a certain resonance of frequencies.

Every year through repetition of ceremonies the man got included into a certain cosmic rhythm, into the process connected with energy exchange between him and Cosmos, between him and all planets of the solar system. And fasting was introduced to help people to get connected to the cosmos-wide energy exchange in the period of the given interface of planets, to let them enter into resonance with the energies of solar system planets in the best way.

Fasting is cleaning of organism from unwanted energies; as a result of fasting the old energy is faster replaced by the new one.

Fasting is timed to certain days when planets of the solar system are involved in energy exchange within the process of total energy balancing in the Logos system.

At that time the Earth gives away the energy it generated, and also receives from other planets new portions of energy produced by them. Therefore:

> **Ceremonies tied up to specific days produce a certain cycle or rhythm of energy exchange between the man and the Cosmos.**

Those rhythms were strictly adhered to by church and astronomers always corrected days and dates of feasts with reference to changes of the Earth's rotation with time (for example, over hundreds and thousand years) as well as to changes of planets arrangements.

Feasts and rites produce rhythms in exchange of energies between the man and the Cosmos, or rather Hierarchical Systems. That is rhythm is set by stars and planets, and rites of church repeat it on Earth entering into resonance with celestial bodies and involving the entire mankind into energy exchange. But again it is a question of spiritual energies, and all other energy types have their own ways of mutual exchange.

People give their energy away to the Cosmos, planets send them back their energy: renewal of energy takes place. From this the following basic conclusion may be drawn:

> **Church feasts and rites, their annual recurrence increase supply of new cosmic energies to the Earth, renewal of energetics of the planet and entire mankind.**

Over the period from 1917 to 2000 we drifted away from rites i.e. disturbed the rhythm of the Earth in its connection with mankind since it is first of all detrimental to the planet because it involves disturbance of energy flows inside it. Consequently we violate cosmic laws through our own fault.

Gathering in churches on certain days people give away their spiritual energy to the Hierarchical Systems and in return they receive some new energy, as a result energetics inside their organisms gets renewed.

Religious feast, as it is, enrobed in ritual behaviour of churchmen and church-goers together with its canons and pleasant fragrances always creates special impression on church-goers, takes their minds off the vanity of the world, calms them down, makes them involuntary relax. And this relaxation and praying attitude is a sort of meditation which takes away nervous and other strains from the human body and enables free circulation of energy along energy channels of the body.

As churches were built on the Earth's channels, a churchgoer found himself inside a strong energy flow which broke away plugs in his own energy channels. And those plugs might result in diseases of the organism therefore removal of plugs made the physical body healthier. Every visit to church or cathedral made church-goers healthier.

During the clerical duty he had been in a strong energy flow for several hours, so his subtle bodies got saturated with additional energy reserves. After a visit to church and staying under its domes for two-three hours the biofield of the man becomes two-three times as much. Increase of the biofield radius depends on the energy capacity of the body. As a rule energy capacity of stout people is higher than that of lean people if they are at the same Level of development. At the same time energy capacity of a lean man who is at the hundredth Level is several times as much as energy capacity of a stout man of the tenth Level. In secular life the energy potential acquired in church gradually decays therefore only regular church visits allow to maintain it at the adequate level.

Powerful energy flow available in church buildings does not only increase the human biofield but in case there are some faults or distortions in it this flow also flattens and corrects it as well as reinforces energy protection of church-goers.

This kind of health improvement was provided to church-goers as an encouragement from the Above because they went to church and hence gave their energy to the Hierarchical Systems and improved their souls in the proper way. It is not for nothing that old people who were regular church-goers used to live for long time and seldom fell ill. Due to church visits their organisms were purified and energy exchange got normalized.

Specifics of Human Body Structure

Now let us discuss the human body in more details.

Generation of energy is the main goal of the man creation therefore his overall biological structure was arranged and designed with the view to enable the best way of production of various types of energy and its output. Regard must be paid to fact the human figure itself is nothing else but a cross if his feet are together and arms sideways. And the heart chakra located at the intersection of the horizontal (arms) and the vertical of the body is that main filter through which all subtle energies produced by the man are purified. The filter purifies and radiates through chakra. The heart chakra gives the purest energy available in the spectrum of energies produced by the man.

All organs in the body are arranged in compliance with the hierarchy: subjacent organs produce the crudest energies of the given body but all superjacent ones generate frequencies which are higher regarding the subjacent frequencies. Every organ produces its own individual frequency type. There are a lot of energy channels in the body, and bioactive points are brought out to the surface of the body. The bioactive points are involved in the energy processes related to the environment. The "subtle" energy types are extracted and output via the bioactive points.

Chakras carry out extraction and output of "subtle" energy types but at the same time they link the body to its "subtle" bodies where the processes related to higher order energies take place. That is it may be said that the human body is a dense network of energy wires, energy extraction and output mechanisms and a lot of other things we have no idea of. Science has partially studied the biological structure of the body but it knows nothing about its subtle structure. Therefore the man can be studied infinitely, and there number of secrets related to him is not less than those related to the Universe.

Even such a simplified primitive scheme gives an idea of the immense scope of the subtle processes which take place inside us. But of course ancient people could not even think of it although even then the energetic processes work in them at full power but the energy produced belonged to a very low range.

But as the machine is running, and energy is being produced the **biorobot shall have been taught how to control the energy which was inside him, how to perform self-control** and if appropriate, to correct the process itself. For those purposes the rites including praying, crossing, bows, holy water aspersion, anointing, communion service etc. were introduced.

How shall we understand the meaning of these ritual actions not in view of their domestic aspect but in view of their energetic background? For example, **wherefore does a Christian cross himself**?

Energy channels of ten main internal organs of the body are brought out to human fingertips. When the man crosses himself and joins three fingers together at the same time he unites three powerful channels. Three radiating flows are joined together to form a single powerful energy beam, which the modern scientists have already managed to photograph. This energy beam has been called a "sword".

When a man crosses himself, he touches the four chakras of his body with this energy beam (agni, manipur and two shoulder chakras) which purifies them and at the same time with the help of the energy beam he cleans all his subtle bodies removing from them all energy parasites and small vampires who have stuck to them. Besides, during service of worship a great potential energy is sent down to church-goers, and the churchgoer frequently crossing himself evenly distributes it over his material and subtle bodies.

So if the energy field is somehow damaged, its flattening takes place. In such a way the human biofield gets corrected and protected against inferior essences. Therefore when Heavenly Teaches made people cross themselves, they provided them with the method for control of the external protection field and method for cleansing subtle bodies.

As distinguished from this, a prayer is the method for cleansing subtle bodies from the inside.

The prayer by itself is the method of rhythmic breathing or simply stated, prayers are breathing exercises.

Prayers carry in themselves energetically combined letters and words, or we may differently say that due to their sounds, their word combinations they produce a certain breath rhythmics, but breathing constitutes chemical and physical processes which result not only in release of carbon dioxide and other chemicals but also in release of energy.

Simultaneously special coding of prayers allows the subtle bodies to produce spiritual energy through their vibrations because the process is correlated with understanding of Higher Divine Essence.

Different prayers have different energetic combination of letters and consequently they produce different amounts of spiritual energy of different quality; some of them give greater amounts of energy, others provide smaller amounts.

Some prayers enable passage of greater flows through the man, other enable flows of lower power. That is every prayer is first of all characterized by generating capacity: how many conventional units of energy it is able to generate per time unit.

Over the centuries prayers undergo changes although people try to preserve them in their original form. One would think that if their codes get disturbed, so their operation mechanism shall be affected. However the Hierarchical Systems keep uninterrupted watch of energy production which is most important for them, and correct the process appropriately. Besides every prayer has limits for interpretation of the one who prays. As soon as certain limits are reached the prayer loses its force therefore in case of serious distortions of the pray text it stops working.

Technical and fiction texts do not possess the energetic combinations of letters. As we are explained, they resemble "an open energetic circuit". Technical texts convey the meaning content only; they are intended for development of human intellect and for conversion (by the intellect) of brute matter at inferior level.

Prayers if they are read regularly enhance the spiritual strength of the man himself. Sometimes it becomes so great that the man becomes able to break through his own personal channel to the Christian egregor wherefrom he can secure assistance. This opportunity is used by old witch doctors. If they do not have a channel transferred to them, then some of them (with the help of long and persistent praying over many years) manage to break through a communication channel connecting them with the egregor, with the energy depot, and then start to cure people by prayers and charms while receiving direct additional energy intended for improvement of patient's health.

Communication channel may be transferred via the person of more strong energy having a channel connecting him with the Christian egregor. But after that the person who has received the communication channel has to stick at prayers in order to maintain the received channel in good working conditions otherwise it may either get clogged or closed altogether.

However everything is done with the knowledge and acceptance of the Higher. The one who has deserved to be encouraged for long-term individual work is allowed to make use of the common energies, but this right is not granted to those who have not deserved it.

No charms which are written a lot about in the books will have any effect if the person who uses them does not have the channel of communication with the egregor. Any charm is effective only if it is used by the person who possesses high energetics or who has broken through a channel connecting him to the source of powerful subtle energy. But any man is able to break through a communication channel by himself if he works hard in order to advance in the right direction. So everything is in hands of the man.

Icon

Now let us address the icons. The man is not able to pray addressing the Higher forces without having their visual images. In any case he would always try to imagine them as best as his imagination allows him to do so.

The existence of the Hierarchical Systems which created religion is absolutely different from that of people and they also live in the different dimensions and even not in four or five dimensions but in dozens of them at the same time.

The man is not able to visualize them in their multifaced complexity, but he cannot pray in emptiness having raised it to the rank of Higher Creature. Indeed this is his nature: he should always imagine those who he worships.

Therefore it was necessary to provide the man with the image, ideal which he could understand. But every creature can best of all understand those who look like himself therefore in every world Gods manifest themselves in the form of creatures who exist in the given world and occupy the highest hierarchical stage (for example, on the Earth the man is superior in contrast to the rest of animal world).

For this reason people were also given an icon with the linear figure of God in the similitude of the man himself. And to make the man understand that God has come to him from some other worlds the icon shall be placed in the corner.

The corner is the intersection of several planes and it symbolizes the place where different worlds are interfaced. The icon is placed in the corner and by this the man is explained that there are other worlds and that they have common interfaces, link up points. Higher Creature comes to him from the place where several planes get refracted which is just deemed the point where one world or several worlds at a time get changed over to some other world.

The icon was the article of mental concentration of human energy. It carried in itself both mental and energetic characteristic of the God or the saint who it had pictured and it began to work within certain range of frequencies because it was made effective with the help of strictly prescribed prayers dedicated exactly to a specific God or saint.

But initially icons shall be mandatory consecrated in order to connect them to the relevant egregor working at a certain frequency. The icon of the Mother of God operates at certain frequencies and it is connected to the Mother of God egregor; and frequency range of the icon of Mary Magdalene is much lower and it is connected to another Level. Similarly other icons work in their own frequency ranges. But it is necessary to point out that there is only one Christian egregor which serves as a common energy accumulator, and all other ones are inside it but they can be called its sections figuratively speaking. Everything is in one, but at the same time everything is separated. That is the structure of the Christian egregor.

People are at different levels of development, they have different characters and therefore they produce energies of different frequencies: some of them produce energy of the upper range, others – of the medium range and still others – of the lower range. Hence there is also the compliance between every man and his icon: frequencies of some people are in good compliance with the icon of Christ, frequencies of others - with the icon of St. Nicolas, frequencies of still others – with the icon of St. George the Conqueror and so on.

Besides, the icon is deemed the plane of energies refraction. Icon receives the energy flow coming from its egregor, and this flow is spread over people and everything around. At the same time with the help of the icon the energy which has been let through the prayers by the man generates the energy type allied to it.

Every icon has its own biofield. As for ordinary icons, their biofield varies within the range from thirty centimetres to three meters; prayerful icons which have been prayed before for many years have much larger fields amounting to several tens of meters.

The field produces healing and revitalizing action upon people. Therefore it is very useful to keep a well prayerful icon in one's room.

Radius of the field surrounding the icon is not constant: it keeps on pulsating: now it increases, then it comes down. For example, measurements of one icon show that its maximum biofield is three meters and minimal one is thirty centimetres. And measurements of another icon show that the maximum radius is one and a half meter and the minimal radius is ten centimetres.

The above values are deemed the field pulsation limits. Every icon has its own unique field. It depends on the way the man has treated it. Therefore even such indicator as the icon power might have been introduced. The icon power is characterized by the maximum radius of the field. The field radius is variable; it changes from the minimal (constant) value to the maximum (the maximum value is apt to increase in case the icon is continuously worked with).

The minimal radius also depends on the icon power: the stronger the icon, the greater its minimal radius. Different icons have different field limits, but all fields have one feature in common: they are all pulsating. As if the icon keeps on breathing – inhale/exhale. And this is related to the common cosmic rhythm of our Universe, to its pulsation i.e. with breathing of Nature.

But as for the icon of the Guardian-Angel it works in phase opposition as compared with all other icons: for example the icon of Christ, the icon of the Mother of God and so on. When the fields of other icons increase, the field of the icon of the Guardian-Angel comes down. And vice versa: when the field of the icon of Christ comes down, the field of the icon of the Guardian-Angel increases. It is apparently related to certain protective functions of the icon: it protects the man when other fields do not protect him.

As far as in my youth I was embarrassed by the fact that in all icons the image of Christ had different faces. That is all icons picture Christ differently as if different people are depicted. And still people manage to recognize Him by some features common for all images.

Of course icon-painters have never seen him and have never painted portraits taken from life or from memory, but his facial characteristics have been handed down from generation to generation of certain schools of painters. And due to this His holy face can be always recognized among holy faces of other saints. And the painted holy face (icon) was connected to the Christian egregor with the help of the human thought.

As if the thought of the painter who was drawing Jesus Christ spiritualized the portrait. The painter was aware that he was painting Jesus of all others and the energy of his thought broke through the channel of communication with the relevant system of religious energy accumulators. It is not for nothing that according to old traditions before starting to paint an icon the painter had to keep a several days fast. Due to such fasting the potential of his subtle energies got increased and allowed the painter to connect the icon to the egregor.

Of course everything is very much complicated in the given case because not only the thought of the painter and the idea which he puts into his creation is important, but also the coding of the name of Jesus Christ which automatically connects the painted image to the program given from the Above and only after that the icon gets imbued with the biofield.

The following experiment was carried out: we asked our daughter to make a portrait of Christ based on His image she had seen in the icons. And then we made measurements. Her drawing had the biofield of ten-fifteen centimetres (round the maximum radius). It is a small field.

For comparison we measured the field of an ordinary coloured postcard with a portrait of some man. The postcard had no field. But of course if more accurate instruments were available, they would have indicated some field. But such field is so weak in comparison with the biofield of Christ that our crude instrument did not sense it.

So the painter's thought via the code of the name connected the icon of Christ to a certain mechanism which imparted field to it. There are a lot of purely technical secrets in this issue which the man could hardly understand. We can do nothing by marvel at wisdom and indomitable fantasy of our Higher Teachers who managed to integrate and focus the human thought energy and the Heavenly potential energy on operations of the Earth and the Cosmos.

Bows and Other Rites

In religion everything has a twofold meaning: domestic meaning in the form of legends, behaviour patterns – i.e. rites – and physical meaning which is behind them.

We have already discussed – why people cross themselves – and come to know the physical background of crossing. In everyday life the term "cross oneself" means to use the sign of cross to scare away devildom (devils, vampires, ghouls etc.).

In fact inferior essences (whose Level of development is below than that of people) fear of the sign of cross because due to it the energy of the man is concentrated to produce a single beam. The energy of such beam has higher frequency than the energy of devildom so this powerful beam strikes those inferiors like high voltage current.

The man in himself possesses high energy potential because he belongs to the higher world and essences like devils, like those creatures that come from inferior worlds possess low energy and they cannot stand the high frequency energies. Therefore the sign of the cross which is used by the believer first of all stands for nothing else than the potential difference between him and the low potential essence. And the greater this difference, the heavier the shock.

Every man possesses his individual energetic power, so cross signs of different people have different power: some people have more powerful cross sign, others have weaker cross signs. For comparison we can say that the cross sign of drinkers have the weakest "sward" of the cross sign because alcohol burns the human energy, and Saints possess the strongest signs of the cross.

Now let us discuss such ritual element as a bow.

While praying the man bows down regularly. Why is it done?

At the domestic level the bow expresses respect for and veneration of God. Bow is designed as a measure to teach and instruct the man: "don't think too highly of yourself, always remember that there are those in this world who are smarter and stronger than you". So since the man is weaker and less advanced he shall render absolute obedience to God, he shall learn to respect and obey those who surpassed him in development, swallow his pride and pay tribute to Them with all his heat and love.

From the standpoint of energy processes the bow is deemed a method of surplus energy relief. While the man is standing in church or in some other place and saying prayers he gets relaxed and energy flows easily enter into him. If the man keeps on praying for a long time, his organism may get oversaturated with energy which may result in headaches, hypertension, heart failures etc. To prevent this, surplus energy shall be periodically relieved. With this aim in view down-to-waist bows were introduced.

Upright position of the body and uncoupled arms and legs allow free circulation of energy inside the body. The cosmic flow passes through the human body and all his energy channels, cleans them and discharges all impurities and dirty energy to his feet, wherefrom it gets seeped to the ground. Therefore the upright passion of the man while praying provides cleansing of the energy system of the organism which is like water flushing.

When the man kneels down, the bottom energetical circuit closes, energy gets accumulated inside the body already and to prevent energy over-saturation of the organism the churchgoer has to relief it but it shall be done much more often than when the body is in upright position.

When the man is in the kneeling position, the upper chakras start to work more intensively and spiritual energy comes up to reach the upper parts of the body, chakras and subtle bodies. Such position is considered a higher meditation when the man produces higher quality energy and at the same time this position contributes to development of high spiritual centres of the man.

Foot-washing is included into religious ritual. What does this procedure mean?

We know that on the footstep there are a lot of bioactive points or energy output channels going from every organ of human body. Every organ discharges polluted, waste energy via the channels brought out to the footsteps. If while walking the man feels pain in his feet it means that the channels are clogged and the dirty energy is getting accumulated in the feet and cannot be easily discharged into the ground which brings the feeling of pain.

Foot washing with cold water is deemed cleansing of channels which are brought out to the foot. Therefore it is recommended to wash feet with cold water every day.

The body shall be washed with water once a week. It is also recommended by the religion and not only in view of physiological hygiene but also of the spiritual one. Water, especially cold water, cleans the subtle bodies of the man removing energy vampires and other inferior creatures stuck to them; and on the body the energy channels brought out to the skin – i.e. acupuncture points – also get unclogged.

Anointing is also aimed at cleansing of chakras and at healthy influence of special chemicals on the subtle bodies.

Forehead and hands are anointed at certain points, namely at chakras, and through chakras this influence is transferred to the relevant bodies.

As for smells, odours, burning candles introduced by the church rites, they also have their physical meaning. Pleasant smell of special herbs, olibanum and wax produces beneficial effect on nervous system, calms down, relaxes, removes energetic and mental strains which benefits the energetic system of the man and hence contributes to his health improvement.

The smell of some herbs also helps to purify the subtle bodies of people, to remedy minor defects of bodies, to remove tentacles of stuck energy parasites, it also has favourable effect upon the conditions of subtle structures.

What is a smell? Of course as we know from botany it is deemed special fragrances dispersed by flowers and herbs for long distances and having irritating effect upon nasal cavity of the man. But on the subtle plane it is deemed energies of certain frequencies produced by flowers, herbs and vegetable gums. When being emitted the above energies prove to be higher by their frequencies than the energies of churchgoers themselves (not any plants are meant here but only strictly defined ones) therefore they exercise a salutary influence over them. At the same time the plants and herbs generating the frequencies that are lower than or equal to those generated by the man do not contribute to cleansing of his subtle bodies.

Olibanum is the gum, which when burning emits the high frequency waves producing negative effect upon inferior essences. Anointing oil also possesses high frequency emission spectrum.

Redolent odours help people to get relaxed and be able to reach the state of spiritual contemplation easily, to scare inferior essences from prayer places because, if they were not scared away, they could easily gain possession of the consciousness of the worshiper (who is in the state of relaxation) and give law to him when he is in such conditions. Therefore praying places were protected also by such methods as using special odours for spreading of frequencies which are harmful for inferior essences.

Church candles (while burning) also emit the odour repelling inferior essences and besides, the wax, its molecules easily assimilate information about the worshipper and having burnt out they transmit this information to higher spheres. It is enough to hold a candle in hands for ten minutes to enable all the information about the man to get transmitted to wax. And if in doing so you convey your request as well, then after the candle burn-out this request will surely reach the Higher spheres in the form of mental energy and will be heard by Those who it is intended for.

The energy of burning candles imparts additional starting power to the human thought energy because not every churchgoer possesses strong mental energy. Many people have so low mental energy that it dissipates just after its generation. It is true of people of low reasoning and those who are not apt to mental activity. Therefore to make their thought be heard, to make it go up the channel and reach Heavenly Teachers some additional starting energy shall be added to it, which in its turn again involves complex physical processes.

Our thought is deemed the subtle energy therefore when we direct it to the candle or wax (which is apt to good imbibing of exactly this type of energy), then the molecules and atoms record the information received. After the candle is burnt out the fire energy imparts an additional pulse to the subtle energy of thought and enables it to reach the Higher Planes.

Besides, it must be borne in mind that if the man is in the common channel and if the church is appropriately built on the relevant place, this contributes to the upward movement of the thought. In other places in absence of the channel the addressed thought will not reach its destination even if the candle is used which means that the given ritual requires that several requirements are met.

As a result of persistent praying some churchmen possessing high spirituality manage to break through their own individual channels to Higher Spheres and their requests may be heard even if they are outside the church.

Now let us discuss the bells which decorated Russian bell-towers. Besides their ritual purpose they also have some other uses.

Bells announced the time of the day as well the secular events important for citizens (marriages, funerals ...). They informed about inrushes of enemies, about victories over them, about fires, about disasters. Such is the outer side of the rite but its inner side discloses something different.

Bells shall be cast from specific alloys which impart certain properties to them, namely: build up relevant wave characteristics. Some scientists, for example, academician F.Y.Shipunov, carried out adequate investigations of waves the bells operate at and made wonderful discoveries which confirm that religion withholds in it a lot of secrets and every secret manifests first of all marvelous fantasy of Higher Mind, its immense ability to combine multitude in one.

The bell is a musical instrument and its shape allows combining the useful with the pleasing. Due to its specific configuration the acoustic waves are not transmitted upwards (as is the energy in the cross structure) but they propagate horizontally and cover the lower atmosphere layers with wave propagation field. It is designed so in order to improve the environment. It is just the shape of the bell (with due account to the material it is made of) that allows to project to the environment the waves of such frequencies which kill many bacteria bringing about epidemies and some infectious diseases. The scientists confirmed that in the areas where the bell was tolled regularly no outbreaks of cholera, plague and typhoid had not been registered. Therefore bells have high health improving effect at the bell chime hearing distance.

Let us discuss one more component of the funeral rite. Let us ask ourselves the following question – why should the cross be put at the foot of the grave?

According to an ancient custom the man is buried with his face eastwards and the cross is placed at the foot of the grave. Why is it done like this?

The above Christian rite is related to the flow of energies on which this type of people (orthodox Christians) is based. The energies which are released as a result of disintegration of the physical body go away in the direction from east to west; they get unwound in the Earth ecliptic direction before reaching the relevant energy collectors which are gathered to form a special energy container. Those are minus energies.

The cross is an aerial. It shall be placed at the foot because through the feet the spent minus energy of the body gets away. And as a result physical body disintegration only minus energy is released and it gets released through the feet. This is the way the energetic frame of the man is constructed. And the aerial-cross is used for collection of all minus energy and its transfer to the relevant container. The minus energy flows are picked up from the feet by the cross (which has different materials and consequently - the properties) and transmitted to special energy collectors intended for the low range energies. Everything is thought over. Even the custom to join the hands of the deceased on his breast is also related to the physical processes taking place in the body during the period of disintegration. The hands are good energy conductors (they can easily receive energies and give them away), and they are closed to form a circle so as to isolate them from other fluxes; through this the top energy rotation circle gets closed, as a result the decaying organism gets concentrated on its own energies and they have no other path of release except via the feet and then via the cross.

Since the process of body disintegration is a long-term one, then the aerial operates for several years. Therefore the cross shall be put to the grave by all means. It can be combined with a monument.

When people fail to place crosses on the graves they contribute to the disturbance of the energy balance between minus and plus energies of the Earth's organics. The minus energy gets accumulated above the graves, then it starts to spread over the towns and villages involving unfavourable exposures of living people. Hence the customs sent from the Above shall be executed in every particular.

Of course, the man introduced also a lot of his own customs into rites and rituals but the basis, the framework remains unchanged. Therefore even if relatives want to fix up a monument on the grave, they should combine its monumental frames with the structure of the cross: at least some small one fixed somewhere near but by all means at the foot of the grave. Naturally as for this the human fantasy is unlimited and it is important just to guide it properly.

So in religion many things have the deepest physical meaning and are addressed to generation of energies and their management. However a lot is added by the people themselves on their own grounds but such additions have nothing to do with any energy considerations, but still the key customs are preserved and fulfilled.

For the people of the fifth race religion will always be the school of education, school of improvement of their soils and upward progress along the evolution stages.

Other religions have other rites and rituals because other peoples (nations) generate energies of different range and they have their own energy collectors.

This or that people were given this or that religion: Islam, Buddhism, Christianity etc. because every people have its individual energetic architecture and is designed for generation of frequency range inherent in them. And for control and management of other energies another mechanism of operation and control is required. Besides, over the centuries the process of energy generation by people have been amended which has been done through introduction of new rites and rituals. Therefore religions differed from each other, rites and customs had their individualized characteristics, moral and ethic standards were also in line with generation of energies having the frequencies inherent in those peoples. And messengers of God (who were sent down to those people) brought new rules of behaviour, new moral standards and introduced relevant changes in the process of energy control. And in such a way they corrected the cosmic processes.

A Few Words about Psychics

Currently Mr. Kashpirovsky is one of the most well-known psychics. He always used energy in his miraculous and healing operations. Wherefrom did he take it?

For us the psychic practice is deemed the miracle which we got accustomed to already. And nobody even thinks about the basis on which psychics build their work. Any miracle is a process which is well-designed and engineered in the Higher Spheres.

Miracles of Mr. Kashpirovsky consumed a lot of energy. This energy was sent down from the Heavenly containers in which it had been accumulated before by the Hierarchical Systems. He received energy as an advance. Later that energy was renewed at the expense of the process of energy exchange with human populace. And this can be said about any energy possessed by any psychic.

A psychic is not a magician, a wizard or a superpersonality of any sort. It is just an ordinary energy conductor who is able to conduct a little more energy than an ordinary man. But they have special subtle plane structure and it is just their own energy structure that makes them different from other people. However they built themselves on their own during their previous reincarnations at the expense of hard spiritual work therefore in the present life the psychic practice ability is granted to them as an encouragement for their previous work.

The structure of the psychic is able to pass through it powerful energy flows, but we shall always remember that the psychic does not consume his own energy: he uses the energy stored in the containers and accumulated by more Higher reasonable beings, and the psychic himself is just a simple doer of someone else's will. And the psychic shall mandatory return the energy which he has consumed. So psychics do not only give energy during their work but also withdraw energy, draw it off.

Of course not all of them operate based on one and the same principle. Energy technology of their work varies. But compensation of energy consumed is mandatory. Moreover – every one of them shall not only make up for energy consumption but also secure profit: they shall give more than it has been consumed otherwise such expenses will make no sense for the Hierarchical Systems.

Currently there is a net of psychics introduced into mankind. What is it aimed at? Christ carried a new religion and moral principles. And what do the modern psychics of a smaller scale suggest? Can it be true that the wish to heal all people at once has suddenly crept on the Hierarchical Systems?

No, that is not the case of physical healing of masses – here the aim is to send down new energy to the Earth, to enable internal energetic reconstruction of the man, his adaptation to the new cosmic operations.

Since currently great changes take place: change of epoch, of the time potential and of the quality of the matter, the man (who is the key Operational Unit of the Earth) also needs to be reconstructed. Therefore there is no point in complaining that there are too many psychics and that too many of them practise deception. They themselves are not quite aware of what they are engaged in, namely: they participate in operations on changing mankind over to the new basis, they modify the internal energetic structure of people.

*   *   *

Now let us recall such interesting references met in literature as the references to seven beams send to the Earth. What kind of beams are they and who sends them? People often speak about them without understanding their inward meaning.

The seven beams are deemed the flows of strong energy which are sent down to the Earth by the Hierarchical Systems i.e. by our "Soyuz". This is aimed at implementation of transfer of our planet to the qualitatively new state. This is nothing else but transition of the Earth to the new orbital.

To be brought to the higher state, the planet needs some extra energy volume. Similarly for example, the electron inside the atom becomes able to reach the other orbit only after it has been imparted with additional energy pulse.

But as for the Earth, of course it is not the rotation orbit that is changed but its internal conditions. Currently our planet (2000) for the sixth time is changed over to the new orbital, for the sixth time it is about to reach the qualitatively new state. For this purpose the sixth beam is sent to it. The beam is deemed the flow of energy of certain magnitude and quality. This is not a one-time process: it is spread over several years. (By the way, the phenomenon of temperature increase on the planet is partially resultant from this energy supplied down to the Earth by the Higher but not from the greenhouse effect.)

Moreover the magnitude of the flows (beams) increases in the process of evolution. The first beam was the weakest. The second one was stronger and so on in ascending order. For instance, the flow sent down two thousand years ago was a thousand times weaker than the flow being sent just now. That is the fifth beam was a thousand times weaker than the sixth one. We quote this kind of proportion in order to give a general idea of their relative magnitudes. And the increase of the transferred energy is related to development of the planet itself: it keeps on growing, progressing but large scope needs more energy for transfer to the new state. And in the other two thousand years even more powerful flow named the seventh beam will be sent. Herein the evolution of the planet and mankind lies because everybody's energy potential gets increased.

How is the energy flow introduced to the Earth? It is not a one-time act, it takes several years. It is spread directly via the energy channels of the planet and through people who are deemed transmitting elements of the given physical process. But not everybody is involved in transformation of the sixth beam but only those whose subtle bodies are specially designed i.e. people who have got over quite a long evolutionary path and who have managed to organize themselves in a relevant way. These people include some representatives of bygone civilizations and also of our civilization, whose spiritual development progressed in the right direction.

Their souls were just implanted into the bodies of modern psychics, who are able to transform powerful energy flows. It is they as well as channelers and messengers who take upon themselves the main energy potential of the flow, transform it bringing it down to the required magnitude which is no longer dangerous for those people who did not manage to properly arrange their subtle structures. Basically these are young souls in terms of evolution. So ordinary people operate the potential, which has been reduced already.

Channelers and psychics assemble audience of listeners and patients around them and transmit the new energy i.e. they introduce the sixth beam. The energy transformed by the human organism is transferred to the planet through the feet and partially via subtle bodies it is distributed over its subtle structures.

The sixth beam or the new energy is sent for the sixth race which at a later stage will operate this type of energy, contributing to achievement of the new qualitative state of the Earth corresponding to its more higher status. After their joint fruitful activity the Earth will accumulate in its subtle structure new energy types, having increased its overall power which will help it to change over to the seventh orbital and this will be associated with coming of the seventh beam to the Earth. And again this energy circulation process will involve people of special subtle constitution who are able to withstand the energy potential which is more powerful than that withstood by the modern channelers and psychics. Everything develops in ascending order. And this is the objective law.

So psychics and channelers carry out a huge job in the cosmic plane because they participate in energy exchange. And such a factor as healing is deemed the advertising aspect used for the purpose of involvement into the given process of the certain category of people, i.e. they will be trusted only by those souls who have already reached a sufficient development level themselves and are able to adequately convert the energy transformed for them by the psychics.

And of course one cannot say that the job of psychics consists only in translation of energy. Undoubtedly the healing effect is mandatory in their work. And again the Higher Teachers improve the health of the man and in doing so they encourage him for his belief in their work and for participation in these immense processes. Everything is interdependent.

Prior to supply of the energy flows a great number of future psychic souls are sent down to the Earth. For the most part - the same as with Christ - their main energy translation channel is closed during the ordinary life although their strong field may be felt by the sick people and those having weak energy field.

Still generally their main channel opens prior to the time when the Hierarchical Systems start to send down energy. How has it been done over the present period? Who has opened the channels for the psychics?

Sessions carried out by Kashpirovsky and Chumak were wonderful and unrivalled in terms of their efficiency. They broadcasted their performances over television attracting millions of people. For what purposes were the healing sessions of such scale carried out?

Actually the purpose consisted in identification of people having extrasensory perception and opening their channels designed for receipt of high energy flows.

Why did it become necessary to identify psychics? In their present life many of them failed to form their subtle structures in such a way as to enable them to operate in the right manner. Therefore the above sessions helped to identify such people and to open their channels for translation of cosmic energy.

At the same time the sessions were aimed at determination of the average health indicator of people and at their intellectual testing.

So appearance of such a great number of psychics and channelers was not accidental. It was the pre-planned action of the Hierarchical Systems which was related to the global processes of transformation of the Earth and mankind on the whole.

Replacement of the Old for the New

By the end of the twentieth century Christianity became split into a number of trends, sects and sub-sects. The common stem of religion had branched to form Catholicism and Orthodoxy and then – smaller and smaller persuasions and sects.

And if we turn our mind to the past history, we can see that even two thousand years ago all kinds of orders and societies were formed and got separated from Christianity creating their own religion and customs. And such divisions always took place and there were always a lot of them. We can say that "dark forces" (by which we mean the Systems trying to delay development of mankind staking on depravity of man, on his vain passions, on his desire to stand out of the pack, to get separated, to enhance his reputation) managed to cut the one whole, the entire, which had been once given to us two thousand years ago. Human meanness, selfishness, misinterpretation of scriptures resulted in split of religion into a number of isolated groups, with internecine wars between them continuing up to this date.

Time moves on, and a new idea related to interpretation of this or that text of the Bible may cross the mind of some intellectual believer and he may announce it to be an absolute i.e. the basis of religion ideology on which some new world outlook, rites and customs shall be established. Then it is followed by struggle for dissemination of the new idea among people, for its popularization.

In this case if such a believer is a channeler, then through him and through appearance of the new branch of religion the Hierarchical System introduces changes into energy production by mankind and at the same time checks consciousness of the people themselves.

In the event that the believer is a vicious person in himself, then the Systems, contrary to mankind, try to split the Faith and reduce its power. In the latter case new ideas spring up on the basis of selfishness, wishes to aggrandize oneself, ambitions, lust for power and for master of the main masses of people, wish to get honours and privileges.

From what is said above we may deduce three basic courses of religion splitting in the social plane. They are as follows:

1) Different interpretation of one and the same text by different people (opinions differ).

2) Selfishness and depravity of people.

3) Struggle for power inside the religion, struggle for masses; i.e. here people try to take God himself into their service and to provide themselves with all creature comforts with the help of His name.

Now having identified causes of splitting let us understand the consequences of Christianity split into small sects and sub-sects which is induced by inferior systems with the purpose to reduce Faith and introduce disharmony into the spiritual domain of mankind.

Why does split into sects result in reduction of Christianity, for instance?

The Bible instructs that one day in a week i.e. Saturday shall be dedicated to God. On this day everybody shall say prayers and give the energy to God. First of all it is the rhythm (six day and one day) of operations of the Hierarchical System, guiding us. This System is in charge of supply of energy needed by the man and extraction of energy generated as a result of prayers said by the believers. The Hierarchical Systems have their own rhythm of work and they set it as one day in a week i.e. Sunday.

Dissociation of the religion results in disturbance of rites and violation of the common cosmic rhythm established by the Above.

Various sects assign for prayers their own days: Adventists, Sabbatarians observe such a day on Saturday, other sects – on Friday, still others – on Wednesday etc. As a result people are praying on different days. So the common energy flow gets split and weakened by two, three time and so on dependent on the number of sects.

That is why God commanded that one day of the week shall be dedicated to Him so that a strong ascendant energy flow can be created. Such a flow shall rise up to reach the Highest planes of the Earth due to the power generated by a great number of people operating in a common breathing rhythm. The fact is that churches were not always built at the relevant places due to the loss of ancient knowledge and practices. And to make the energy reach the relevant planes some additional stimulants are needed.

But if mankind is divided, for example, into two groups, that say prayers on different days the power of the ascendant energy flow becomes twice as less and this causes difficulties in energy collection. Hence separation of Christianity results in weakening of the common energy flow.

The requirement that all Christians shall pray on the same day of the week and dedicate this day to God did not only help to maintain the certain cosmic rhythm based on the figure seven but also allowed to unite people in their spiritual drive and in the energy output action. The fundamental principle of this process is the unity in action. Here it is a purely energetical principle. The energy generated by every praying worshiper is added to the energy of the general masses producing a strong flow which is able to reach their relevant energy collectors.

On Sunday the man should not work – this rule was one of the conditions of meditation. The work brings about tension and strains, recreation contributes to relaxation of the organism and better circulation of subtle energies.

Everything changes with time. The program of mankind which was launched two thousand years ago is completed. And a new powerful program is taken as a basis for the Earth's development. This is the program of the Aquarius epoch which brings about a drastic breakage of the old and establishment of the new.

Everything will change on our planet: its landscape, its climate, its continents: firm land will become smaller, the quantity of water will increase. The man will also change inside and outside. Our race will be replaced by the new sixth race. And as a result of those global reconstructions in the structure of entire mankind the need for existence of different religions will fall away. There will be only one nation on Earth called the golden race. In their spiritual research and advancement the people of this race will not relay on religion but on the knowledge of laws of existence of Higher worlds. And this new knowledge is laid down in the book "Laws of Macrocosm or Bases of the Heavenly Hierarchy Subsistence".

People will know about the existence of Higher Entities and Single God guiding our Earth and all Higher worlds and they themselves will try to be like their older Brothers. Faith will become absolutely different and it will be based on High consciousness of the people, on their true understanding of the meaning of the processes developing around them.

Already in remote antiquity Vivikananda, divining what the current future will be like, spoke about formation of certain universal religion which shall be rigorously scientific. He said, "It will be based on the laws of Spiritual world" and such laws are just the "Laws of Macrocosm or Bases of the Heavenly Hierarchy Subsistence" since they were given by God and they served a foundation for improvement of His Spiritual worlds which are deemed the Levels of the Heavenly Hierarchy.

Articles of faith of Vivikananda and his adherers included scientific theories because they believed that only the scientific theory in conjunction with the knowledge of Higher Laws would allow to establish the true framework of spiritual improvement of people. And their clairvoyance proved to be so exact since the new laws which God sends to people are able to unite science and religion in the deep knowledge of the physical fundamentals of construction and development of Spiritual worlds; they are able to unite the whole mankind in the uniform knowledge of the bases of Higher existence.

As for the current disputes between people and religions we can say that everything is transient. Time irons out differences, removes nations, states, and modifies the face of Earth itself. Let us recall the past.

On Earth one civilization followed another, and at the same time the historical landmarks which were associated with their development vanished into thin air. The first, the second and the third civilizations vanished completely; and the forth one left only some vague ideas about itself. Everything used to vanish without any trace left so that the forth civilization did not have a slightest idea of whether the third civilization had or had not any religion, and the third one did not know whether the second civilization had any. Therefore it is quite possible that people may forget about the causes of disputes which arose between them and reach the wishful spiritual unanimity.

As soon as the traces of the previous civilization are lost in the dust of past ages, for the new incipient civilization a new program of its development is sent down. According to such program the new race will generate for the Cosmos the energy of prescribed range which is more compacted but at the same time much more pure. And to control the produced flows a new process will be provided. The new race will be intended for production of one spectrum of spiritual energies. And their work will be focused on application of new natural knowledge of those overall and unitary processes which guide the development of the entire Hierarchy of God; and every member of society will comply with those processes by virtue of high individual consciousness and sense of duty to his All-father.

Hence such Core-religion, law knowledge, universal for the entire planet, and single God will depend on the physical processes taking place in the new sixth race. The very replacement of the fifth race for the sixth one results from the evolution of the Cosmos.

The purpose of any civilization consists in delivery to the Higher Hierarchical Systems of the relevant energy types – i.e. products of certain quality and quantity. But with time the types of the required products vary because requirements of God and Cosmos keep on changing.

Currently the Hierarchical Systems are changing over to the new stage of development and so they need another type of energy. Therefore a new type of man is being designed. This new man will produce energy of the required type and consciously participate in the immense energy exchange processes, he will learn how to control the relevant processes by himself so that after a lapse of certain development stages to be able to occupy a well-deserved position within the Hierarchy of God.

The man of the sixth race will cover several programs of the fifth race man – that is he will work for three-four of his ancestors. His freedom of choice will be reduced which will enable him to implement his individual program in more accurate and efficient manner and produce the designed energy in the right quantities. Hence the inward structure of the man and his cell itself will be modified; its energetic power will increase. The programs will become more rigid, the freedom of choice will be reduced because people lag considerably behind the program scheduled from the Above.

The man will deliver products of new quality to the Hierarchical Systems. But since a new type of energy is planned to be produced, a new method of its management and supply to the Hierarchical Systems is needed. And such mechanism has been already designed by the

Higher and is now at the stage of implementation and deployment. As soon as the new race comes, the new mechanism will be initiated.

Divine knowledge will be assumed as a basis of human development. Spiritual advancement will progress through comprehension of the macrocosm laws as well as higher level information. The more advanced will be the human mind, the more new information will be disclosed to people from the Above. But for this purpose the soul shall also reach the adequate qualitative level in its development because only a highly spiritual person is able to properly manage the Higher knowledge acquired and to let it work in the interest of people but not against them. Unity of spiritual and intellectual development will enable adequate management of new knowledge which will drive the further progress of mankind and will allow it to avoid the dead end development.

*   *   *

Glossary

The Absolute	1) God, Higher Mind; 2) spatial volume, which impersonates a living organism of Higher Creature embodying in itself all things in existence and which is deemed the apex of relevant cycle of development.
Absolute (*adj*)	- reached the highest state of development, containing complete set of relevant energy constituents.
The Higher	- personalities with the level of development above earthly plane who manage the Earth and mankind.
Soul	- matrix containing a certain amount of energy that gets modified in the process of evolution. Matrix is connected with permanent and temporary structures designed for the earthly world.
Unit	- designation of soul given by the computational minus System.
Nature	- spatial volume belonging to a huge cosmic organism in which all other things exist and develop .
Hierarchy	- a framed structure of "subtle" plane which includes in it a certain arrangement of God's worlds populated by individuals of appropriate level of development. Worlds (or planes of existence) are deemed Levels. Degree of their development gets increased in the direction from the base of the Hierarchy pyramid to its vertex from where God manages everything which is below. The Hierarchy houses in it a definite number of personalities.

Quality of energy	- homogeneous type of energy.
Composite	- a set of different types of energies (accumulated in matrix) forming the matrix texture, qualitative composition , determining expressiveness and individuality of personality.
Karma	- retribution to the man for plus and minus actions performed during previous lives (good or evil fate built into the program of the man's life).
Matrix	- framework of soul designed for fill-up and storage of different energies constituting the basis of character of personality. It has cellular design and is apt to add to itself new cells as the existing ones get filled up. Matrix is a self-growing spiritualized structure. It is filled up with energy in compliance with regular procedure prescribed by God.
Mightiness of soul (power)	1) it is its power consisting of potentials of accumulated energies; 2) ability of soul to perform any actions or processes (including mental ones), ability to do work per a unit of time.
Inferiors	- individuals belonging to earthly world. Material man is always lower in his development than those who are in Hierarchy because "subtle" energy is deemed the higher level of organized matter.
Common volume	- specific spatial over-all dimensions of global organism of Nature.
Orbital	- new energetic state of the Earth, which level of development is higher that the level of its previous state.

Plane (of objective reality)	- world, plane of existence is deemed the spatial-temporal continuum of relevant design, the living environment of specific forms of creatures. Planes of existence are either separated by spatial and time borders or arranged in continuums having different frequency- energetic characteristics of the matter.
Sublevel	- a part of Heavenly Hierarchy Level corresponding to a certain range of energies. Level consists of sublevels, which are arranged from bottom upwards starting with the first one.
Progress of soul	- accumulation of energies in its matrix in compliance with the preset program.
Soul potential	- power indicator of soul. It consists of potential of energies filling up its matrix and permanent sutle bodies.
Decoding	- disposal of soul in the "subtle" plane; withdrawal of awareness of the "ego" from the individual as from personality; disassembly of subtle energetical structures of soul accompanied by complete clean-up of matrix cells from energies accumulated by the individual during all previous lives of his.
Subject matter	- intrinsic meaning of something.
Entity	- personality developing in the Hierarchy of God (or Devil). Entities existing in Hierarchy are broken down into different development levels.
Essence (creature)	- reasonable individual belonging to other world and having the form, which is not similar to the human form, but possessing time structures adapting him to the world he exists in.
Subtle (world, construction structure etc.),	1) everything existing beyond the human apprehension; 2) everything produced from energy of the order, higher than physical matter.

Level	- level of development of something or somebody.
Level of Hierarchy	- world or plane of existence in Hierarchy. Levels are arranged in compliance with their orderness, i.e. in compliance with the regular logic of energy development from the level of inferiors, closest to Earth to the level of the Higher closest to God.
Energetics	1) new designation of the word "energy" containing in it (by its architecture) more powerful type of energies currently (2000) designed for delivery to the Earth from the Cosmos 2) total potential contained in limited volume.
Energy	1) any type of the matter both of physical and "subtle" planes. Is characterized by the level-wise orderness of development; 2) is the common measure of different modes of motions (classical definition).

Terms united by their meaning

Determinant	- (obsolete –Heavenly teacher) Higher Personality guiding the man or other creature through the life via computer. Monitors how the man carries out the program
Originator	- Entity standing next-higher order than Determinant. Prepares the plot of the future life of the man.
Manager	- Entity who is higher than Originators and Determinants and who is in charge of them.
Spiritual worlds	- reasonable communities of Higher Entities existing in God's Hierarchy i.e. belonging to the "subtle" world.

Material System	- community of reasonable creatures existing in material bodies and having the development level, which is many times as high as the level of people.
System	1) community of reasonable Entities united by the same development Level and existing in the Hierarchy. Systems maybe at the same Level or at different ones, with their development degree complying with the given Level. 2) the System belonging to the Hierarchy.
Cosmic System	- community of reasonable creatures existing beyond the limits of God's Hierarchy.
Medical System (or med. system)	- neutral detached Heavenly Hierarchy engaged in treatment of any creatures in God's and Devil's worlds as well as involved in pilot medical projects.

TABLE OF CONTENTS

The books of "Beyond the Bounds of Unknown" series
Writers: Larisa Seklitova, Ludmila Strelnikova

. «The Soul and Secrets of its Structure»
. «Secrets of Higher Worlds»
. «Unordinary Life of Heavenly Teachers»
. «Energy Structure of the Man and the Matter»
. «The Higher Mind Reveals the Secrets»
. «Rendezvous with the Invisibles»
. «Creation of Forms or Experiments of Higher Mind»
. «Life in Someone Else's Body»
. «The Man of Aquarius Epoch»
. «Gems of Higher Truths»
. «Glossary of the Cosmos Philosophy»
. «Philosophy of Eternity»
. «Philisophy of the Absolute»
. «Personality and Eternity»
. «Development of the Soul or Paradoxical Philosophy»
        volumes 1,2.
. «Laws of Macrocosm or Basis of Heavenly Hierarchy Subsistence»,
        volumes 1, 2.
. «Matrix as the Basis of the Soul».
. «The Finger of Fate»
. «New Model of Macrocosm or the Secret of Universe Disclosed»
. «The Worldly and the Eternity» (answers to the questions)
. «Prometheus's Fire or Mysticism in Our Life»

Writers: Aleksander Strelnikov, Ludmila Strelnikova
. «Revelations of the Cosmos»
. «Talks about the Unknown»

«Magic of Perfection» series
. «Freedom and Destiny»
. «Karmic Lessons of Fate»
. «Phenomenon of the Soul or Ways to Attain Perfection»
. «Great Transition or Versions of the Apocalypse»